CACTUS OF
MYSTERY

"An amiable, intelligent, and passionate introduction to the sacred medicine of the Andes. Ross Heaven's Cactus of Mystery is valuable not only as an orientation toward the ancient Huachuma tradition but also as an exploration of the experiences of healing and creativity common to all sacred medicine traditions."

ROBERT TINDALL, AUTHOR OF *THE JAGUAR THAT ROAMS THE MIND* AND *THE SHAMANIC ODYSSEY*

CACTUS OF MYSTERY

The Shamanic Powers of the Peruvian San Pedro Cactus

ROSS HEAVEN

with contributions by Eve Bruce, M.D.,
David Luke, Morgan Maher, and others

Park Street Press
Rochester, Vermont • Toronto, Canada

Park Street Press
One Park Street
Rochester, Vermont 05767
www.ParkStPress.com

Text stock is SFI certified

Park Street Press is a division of Inner Traditions International

Note to the Reader: The information provided in this book is for educational, historical, and cultural interest only and should not be construed as advocacy for the use of San Pedro and other hallucinogens. Neither the author nor the publisher assume any responsibility for physical, psychological, legal, or other consequences arising from these substances.

Library of Congress Cataloging-in-Publication Data

Heaven, Ross.

   Cactus of mystery : the shamanic powers of the Peruvian San Pedro cactus / Ross Heaven ; with contributions by Eve Bruce, David Luke, Morgan Maher, and others.

     p. cm.

   Includes bibliographical references and index.

   ISBN 978-1-59477-491-1 (pbk.) — ISBN 978-1-59477-513-0 (e-book)

   1. Shamanism—Peru. 2. Hallucinogenic plants—Peru. 3. Cactus—Religious aspects—Peru. 4. Hallucinogenic drugs and religious experience—Peru. I. Bruce, Eve, 1954– II. Luke, David (David P.) III. Maher, Morgan. IV. Title.

   BF1623.P5H425 2013

   204'.2—dc23

                      2012022320

Printed and bound in the United States by Lake Book Manufacturing, Inc. The text stock is SFI certified. The Sustainable Forestry Initiative® program promotes sustainable forest management.

10 9 8 7 6 5 4 3 2 1

Text design and layout by Priscilla Baker
This book was typeset in Garamond Premier Pro with Opti Luther and Myriad Pro used as display typefaces
All photographs by Ross Heaven unless otherwise noted

To send correspondence to the author of this book, mail a first-class letter to the author c/o Inner Traditions • Bear & Company, One Park Street, Rochester, VT 05767, and we will forward the communication or visit the author's website at **www.thefourgates.org**.

For the Sarah I knew then: *Echo en falta que la mayoría de todos skank-ho. Fuma y agua; amor para siempre. ¿Y el Sarah ahora? No le conozca.*

For those who contributed.
For Darryl, Bobby, Suzie, Emily, and Jeannie ~ who kept the faith and fire alight during darker nights.
For Teertha, Tania, Sue, and Emily ~ for new adventures.
For my children.

Contents

INTRODUCTION
The Mystery of San Pedro

~~~~~~

Ross Heaven

If you are reading this book you are in a privileged minority, for almost nothing has been written about San Pedro or its use in shamanism and healing. Before my 2009 book *The Hummingbird's Journey to God,* there was little information available on it at all apart from scattered references in a few other works. *Trout's Notes on San Pedro* (Mydriatic Productions, 2005), for example, is a study of the botany, chemistry, and history of the plant, but does not address its shamanic uses. One of the more useful books in the latter regard is Douglas Sharon's *Wizard of the Four Winds: A Shaman's Story* (Free Press, 1978), but this has its limitations also because it is more or less the story of a single individual (the book's subtitle suggests as much), Eduardo Calderon, an Andean healer whom Sharon worked with for a few seasons some decades ago. As such it focuses on one healer operating within the traditions of one part of Peru (the north) and is a study of *curanderismo* (Andean healing) in general rather than San Pedro, per se. A further limitation is that the book has been out of print for many years and is hard to come by, with copies on the web often selling for a hundred dollars or more.

1

A Google search will not help much either, yielding next to nothing useful for students of shamanism or San Pedro, apart from a few articles and interviews mostly stemming from me.

Frankly, I am amazed that so little research has been done on San Pedro, its effects, or its applications for healing, especially since the latter are, in my experience, real and profound.

I have worked with the plant since the late 1990s and increasingly so in the past decade, during which time I have also taken groups of people to Peru so they can drink it themselves. I have witnessed firsthand what some of the shamans in this book refer to as "healing miracles" during the course of these journeys, and seen people cured of cancer, depression, grief, childhood traumas, alcoholism, diabetes, and other debilitating and sometimes life-threatening diseases. And yet there is still almost nothing published about this plant.

WHY?

At least in part this lack of information is a reflection of the fact that the most ancient healing traditions of Peru, like those of other pre-Christian cultures, are transmitted orally. Not much is ever written down by shamans so where records do exist they have tended to be made by European explorers, invaders, or missionaries who have brought their religious beliefs with them and denigrated indigenous practices that did not sit well with their own notions of God.

As professor of cultural anthropology Irene Silverblatt put it, "History making (which includes history denying) is a cultural invention. . . . History tends to be 'made' by those who dominate . . . to celebrate their heroes and silence dissent."[1] Thus, one early Spanish missionary quoted by the ethnobotanist Richard Evans Schultes, for example, described San Pedro as "a plant with whose aid the devil is able to strengthen the Indians in their idolatry; those who drink its juice lose their senses and are as if dead; they are almost carried away by the drink and dream a thousand unusual things and believe that they are true."[2]

Another, Father Olivia, part of a seventeenth-century-church-sponsored scheme to "extirpate idolatries," wrote in 1631 that "after they drink it they [participants in San Pedro ceremonies] remain without judgment and deprived of their senses and they see visions that the Devil represents to them and consistent with them they judge their suspicions and the intentions of others."[3]

Fundamentalism like this never results in any pure or useful critique and, as Jim DeKorne remarks in *Psychedelic Shamanism* (Breakout Productions, 1994), rather than trying to understand native customs:

> The Spanish Inquisition reacted with characteristic savagery to anyone who dared to break their laws by eating [*sic*] [San Pedro] . . . a great many Indians were flogged and sometimes killed when they persisted in [doing so]. . . . [One man's] eyeballs were said to be gouged out after three days of torture; then the Spaniards cut a crucifix pattern in his belly and turned ravenous dogs loose on his innards. . . . This level of response to the ingestion of . . . San Pedro in Peru effectively drove the use of [the cactus] underground for hundreds of years.[4]

Even the name of the plant owes more to Catholicism than the shamanic traditions of the Andes, for the cactus (originally known as *huachuma*) was, as DeKorne relates, renamed after Saint Peter, "guardian of the threshold for the Catholic Paradise . . . an apparent strategy of the Indians to placate the Inquisition."

Juan Navarro, with whom I drank San Pedro in the 1990s, may be suggesting something along these lines as well when, in my book *Plant Spirit Shamanism* (Destiny Books, 2006), he remarks that San Pedro retains "a certain mystery to it."

Navarro's ceremonies are performed at night from a *mesa* (altar), which contains many Catholic symbols, crosses, staffs, rosaries, icons, and lithographs of the Christian saints. This may be a form of syncretism but most likely is also a sort of mask that draws attention away from the way that things were originally done within the San Pedro tradition. When Navarro performs a ceremony, for example, he prays to God, the saints, the Virgin, and to Jesus and he holds a cross aloft, but I have no doubt that these emblems have a different meaning to him than to us. Some anthropologists suggest that the Virgin of Guadalupe, whose image is ubiquitous in Andean healing rituals, is in fact a Christianized version of the Aztec lunar goddess Tonantzin, so whomever Navarro is praying to is most likely not the same Holy Virgin we know.

These historic considerations have been pushed aside in recent times, however, certainly by the shamans I know and work with in the Andes, who seem keen to lift the veils of secrecy surrounding San Pedro. The feeling among these shamans (some of whom have written for this book or been interviewed in its pages) is that the time for greater openness about this medicine is *now,* because we are entering a period of great change and its healing is needed more than ever before.

The feeling seems mutual among the scientific profession as well, and a number of academics are also beginning to look again (or for the first time) at San Pedro and the role it may play in healing, ESP, precognition, and other extrapersonal and transpersonal states. David Luke, Ph.D., is one such academic—in this book he examines the potential of San Pedro in this regard and reports on an intriguing experiment of his own.

But let's start with the basics. What exactly is San Pedro and what do we know of its usage?

THE CACTUS AND THE CEREMONY

Trichocereus pachanoi is a tall cactus that can reach heights of seven meters or more. Its cylindrical branches produce a funnel-shaped flower of green-tinged white that itself can grow to ten inches or so. It enjoys a tough, desert-like environment and grows readily in the highest parts of Peru, such as the Yunga and Quechua regions (2,300 meters and 3,500 meters above sea level, respectively) between Piura, Lambayeque, and La Libertad, and in the Huancabamba Valley.

It has many names among shamans and healers, including *cardo, chuma, gigantón, hermoso, huando, pene de Dios* (literally, "penis of God"), *wachuma,* and El Remedio, "the Remedy," the latter referring to its healing powers. Another Quechua name, *punku,* also suggests this quality. The word means "doorway" since the cactus is considered able to open a portal into a new world so that healing and visions can flow from the spiritual to the physical dimensions.

Even the Christianized name "San Pedro" has similar connotations. It refers to Saint Peter, who holds the keys to heaven, and is suggestive of the plant's power to open the gates between the visible and invisible worlds (the "doors of perception" as the novelist Aldous Huxley called them after taking mescaline himself), and between the sacred and profane, so those who drink it enter a realm where they can heal, know their true natures, and find purpose for their lives. "Just as the saint called San Pedro is 'keeper of the keys . . . and guardian of the doors of Heaven' so the San Pedro plant is called 'guardian of the doors of remedy,'" as one Peruvian curandera, Olinda, put it.[5]

Some of the shamans I have spoken with, informed by their country's colonial past, go further and relate that Saint Peter was so appalled at the behavior of the gold-greedy Spanish that he hid the keys to paradise from them in the one place he knew they would never look: within the cactus that contains the true spirit of God.

The curandero Eduardo Calderon defined this spirit in the following way:

> Many think of God the way the Christians depict him: as a bearded man with the world in his hands. . . . But God is the cosmic energy within ourselves. Yes, we are part of God because we have that energy and this energy is an elemental force.[6]

What Saint Peter required from the Catholics was not religious devotion but Earthly respect—where love and healing replaced the destructive lust for gold that seemed to dictate the Spaniards' actions.

Among healers, San Pedro is also known as huachuma, and the shamans who work with it are called *huachumeros* if male and *huachumeras* if female, sometimes also spelled *wachumeros* or *wachumeras*. Its use as a sacrament and in healing rituals is ancient. The earliest archaeological evidence so far discovered for this is a stone carving of a huachumero found at the Jaguar Temple of Chavín de Huantar in northern Peru, which is almost 3,500 years old, predating by more than a thousand years the religion that the Spanish brought with them to South America.

Textiles from the same region and period of history depict the cactus with jaguars and hummingbirds, its guardian spirits, and with stylized spirals representing the visionary experiences brought by the plant.

A decorated ceramic pot from the Chimú culture of Peru, dating to 1200 CE, has also been unearthed that shows an owl-faced woman holding a cactus. In the Andes the owl is the tutelary spirit and guardian of herbalists and shamans, and the woman depicted is, therefore, most likely a curandera and huachumera.

Some of the reasons that San Pedro ceremonies were (and continue to be) held are:

- To cure illnesses of a spiritual, emotional, mental, or physical nature
- To know the future through the prophetic and divinatory qualities of the plant
- To overcome sorcery or *saladera* (an inexplicable run of bad luck)
- To ensure success in one's ventures
- To rekindle love and enthusiasm for life
- To restore one's faith or find new meaning in life by experiencing the world as divine

San Pedro can perform healings like these because, in the words of Eduardo Calderon, it is "in tune with the powers of animals and beings that have supernatural powers. . . . Participants [in ceremonies] are set free from matter and engage in flight through cosmic regions . . . transported across time and distance in a rapid and safe fashion."[7]

Calderon also describes the effects of the plant as this healing takes place: "First, a dreamy state . . . then great visions, a clearing of all the faculties . . . and then detachment, a type of visual force inclusive of the sixth sense, the telepathic state of transmitting oneself across time and matter, like a removal of thoughts to a distant dimension."[8]

Like ayahuasca, the other great teacher plant of Peru, San Pedro is always taken as part of a shamanic ceremony with the intention of healing—never lightly and never as a "recreational drug." Healing in a ceremony like this is defined more widely than a Western doctor might understand the term, and means an ultimately beneficial or positive change in the mental, emotional, or spiritual aspects of one's life as well, often, as a physical cure or change.

The anthropologist Wade Davis described a ceremony performed in 1981, for example, where the people present included a girl who had been paralyzed and was suffering from back and stomach pains, members of a family whose cattle had become diseased, a person seeking healing for a relative who had gone mad, a man who had become unstable after seeing his wife with her lover, and a businessman wanting to know who had stolen money from his company.

To us, the last reason for attending may appear to have nothing in common with the first, but in the Andean view of healing the ability to bring order to one's financial and business affairs is just as valid in terms of restoring balance to the soul and peace to the mind as relieving the pains of a paralyzed girl. Both are healing.

Many San Pedro ceremonies involve their participants in lengthy and challenging procedures: the snorting of tobacco macerated in alcohol for example, the drinking of an emetic to purge evil spirits, beatings with sticks, and dousings in cold water. But others are less demanding so that the spirit of the plant is given the freedom to work directly with participants in the way it sees fit. In the latter case, the shaman defers to San Pedro, which he regards as the real healing force, rather than conducting a stylized ritual that in effect puts the shaman center stage. Whatever the inclination of the shaman, however, the mesa is always involved.

THE SAN PEDRO MESA

According to Eduardo Calderon, "The mesa is the important part of a curing session for the simple reason that it is the panel where all the elemental forces are computed." [9]

The mesa (the word literally means "table") is an altar that may be elaborate or simple, again depending on the shaman. Most are woven fabrics laid directly on the Earth, which contain objects (or *artes*: "arts") that hold spiritual energy in the form of artifacts from archaeological or ritual sites to represent the power of the ancestors, herbs and perfumes in ornate or antique bottles that bring good luck and healing, and swords and statues or stones from cemeteries and sacred sites that stand as emblems for the powers conferred on the shaman by his guides and allies in the Land of the Dead.

Other objects, in Davis's experience, include hardwood staffs, bones, quartz crystals, knives, toy soldiers (for the powers of opposition or victory), deer antlers and boar tusks (for strength in the face of challenges), shells, and photographs or paintings of saints. I have also seen torches (for spiritual illumination), mirrors (for self-reflection or the return of evil forces), and carvings of various animals that are symbolic of particular qualities. Participants may also place offerings of their own on the altar.

There are three fields to the mesa and where artes are placed in relation to these may also be significant. The left is the negative or "extraction" field ("the Field of Evil," in Calderon's words) while the right is positive and life-giving ("the Field of Justice") and "the Mediating Center" is the neutral, transformative space in the middle.

It is important to qualify our terms, however, because negative and positive have different connotations for us in the West and may suggest a quality or intent that is not present in Andean healing. Most shamans do not consider the two sides of the mesa to be "good" or "bad," and in a sense they are not even "sides" but parts of a continuum where every field is harmonious, and through their relationship to each other ensure that the world remains in balance.

In fact, even though Calderon uses terms like *justice* and *evil,* to him the Field of Justice is really "the primordial axis that moves everything in accord with my criteria, with my feeling, with my religion, most of all with my faith" while the Field of Evil is "where one looks for the cause of a problem."*[10] Rather than a repository for, or representation of, negative and positive forces, then, the fields on the left and right complement more than oppose each other. Thus for example, "good" and "bad" luck go hand in hand because without each we could not recognize the other.

In this sense then the mesa can be regarded as a representation of the divine (rather than human) scales of justice, where the goal is equilibrium and order, not a weighted outcome in favor of "light" or "dark," or, as Calderon puts it, it is "a control panel by which one is able to calibrate the infinity of accesses into each person."

Still another way of understanding the mesa, despite the linearity of its layout, is as a cosmic circle that brings everything back to its rightful place and represents the circularity of human experience. To signify this, the neutral field in the center of the mesa is the point of balance on which the world turns. "Everything is stabilized by the Mediating Center which computes the other two zones," says Calderon. "It is the balance of the other fields, the stability of the mesa."

It is also the place of transformation where illnesses can be cured by finding a point of equilibrium between negative and positive forces. Herbs that bring strength and energy may be placed by the shaman in this zone along with images of the sun (for light, brilliance, and regeneration) or reflective materials and lodestones to draw in appropriate energies and dismiss others so that balance is restored.

---

*This more neutral perspective, beyond "good" and "evil," is supported by the shamans whom Bonnie Glass-Coffin worked with. In their view, simply, "The right side of the mesa is frequently called *banco curandero* (curing bench or bank), while the left side of the mesa is frequently called the *banco ganadero*." *Ganadero* has several meanings in Spanish, including the occupational name given to those who herd livestock (ganado) and the nominative reference given to "one who wins or dominates" (from the verb *ganar*). —R.H.

Once the mesa is assembled the ritual can begin, with the altar as the point of focus: a portal through which all energies flow and a visual reminder to participants that the purpose of the ceremony is to heal imbalances so that order prevails and the will of God is done.

SOME CONTROVERSIES

I have heard shamans say that San Pedro ceremonies should only be performed at night (or on certain nights—Tuesdays and Fridays most notably, when supernatural energies are said to be most potent and able to flow more freely), while others say that in their original precolonial form these ceremonies were more typically performed in daylight. I have attended both and clearly, therefore, neither of these statements is wholly true in Andean healing today.

There is even some debate about who should take the medicine. For La Gringa, who is interviewed in these pages, the patient must always drink, because it is the spirit of the plant and not the shaman that performs the healing. For "old school" shamans like Juan Navarro,* however, San Pedro is a diagnostic tool for the *shaman* to use; it is there to help him do his work and not to heal the patient directly. "The maestro has a special relationship with its spirit," he says. "When it is taken by a patient it circulates in his body and where it finds abnormality it enables the shaman to detect it. It lets him know the pain the patient feels and where in his body it is. So it is the link between patient and maestro."[11]

Regarding the spiritual and revelatory powers of San Pedro, Navarro feels that "it won't work for everybody" (La Gringa disagrees), but as a healing plant or herbal remedy it is always effective: "It purifies the blood of the person who drinks it and balances the nervous system so people lose their fears and are charged with positive energy."

---

*Navarro belongs to what I have come to call the "old school" of shamans who employ far more ritual and have a much more rigid structure to their ceremonies than the "new wave" of modern practitioners—like La Gringa and Michael Simonato—who are generally more content to play a secondary role to the healing of the plant and who are the main focus of this book. —R.H.

Thus San Pedro, for shamans like Navarro, is a medicine more than a sacrament, an herbal cure more than a divine healer, and if it has any impact on a spiritual level it is for the benefit of the shaman more than the patient, because of the "special relationship" between the healer and the brew. Once in the patient's body, if San Pedro finds an illness or abnormality it enables the shaman to detect it so that he, rather than San Pedro, can do the healing.

Again, not all shamans feel the same, and the "new wave" of healers working in Cusco have a rather different relationship to the plant, preferring to get themselves out of the way so that the spirit of San Pedro can perform its healings directly. For Navarro though, just as a Catholic priest stands as an intermediary to God for the members of his congregation, so the shaman stands between the participants in his ceremony and their experience of the divine.

Peter Furst, in *Flesh of the Gods,* relates San Pedro ceremonies that are in many ways similar to Navarro's.[12] At the beginning the participant stands before the left side of the altar to drink the medicine as the shaman chants his name and looks for the form that the illness in his body has taken or the problems that have arisen consequentially in his life. Often these have the shape of threatening or frightening animals, an idea consistent generally with the shamanic vision of illness as an intrusive spiritual force that reveals itself in a primal and nonhuman (sometimes also insect) form so that the healer cannot miss or mistake it.

Having seen the intrusion, Furst reports that the shaman would sometimes massage or suck on the parts of the patient's body where it was located or use some other means to remove the spiritual affliction. In serious cases, he might take a sword from his mesa and charge out beyond the circle of participants to conduct a battle with the invisible forces he saw as attacking his patient. In one spectacular ceremony, the shaman performed seven somersaults in the form of a cross while grasping the sword in both hands with the sharp edge held forward. This was intended to drive off invading spirits and shock the sorcerer who was sending them to release his hold on the patient. In cases such as these, once again, it is the shaman and not San Pedro who performs the healing, while for the curanderos who appear in this book it is exactly the reverse.

MESCALINE, SAN PEDRO, AND SCIENCE

Researchers of a more scientific than shamanic persuasion have found that San Pedro contains mescaline at around the 1 percent level, about a third of the mescaline content of peyote, although some San Pedro cactuses can match the peyote concentration.

In my experience, however, it is usually of limited value and does not aid our understanding to equate a plant in its totality with a summary of its constituent parts, and then extrapolate from these in an attempt to explain its effects. Something gets lost when we do so, which shamans know as the spirit or "personality" of the plant. By the same token, the life of a man cannot be wholly described or explained by simply performing a blood test and listing the values found there.

Nonetheless, scientific studies into the effects of peyote and San Pedro (such as they are—for there are few enough of them) have tended to do just that, concentrating on mescaline and not the plant as a whole.

Mescaline was first isolated from peyote cactus by German scientists in the 1890s. However, as Rick Strassman points out in his book *DMT: The Spirit Molecule,* "Medical and psychiatric interest in mescaline was surprisingly restrained and researchers had published only a limited number of papers by the end of the 1930s."[13] A little while later "LSD made its revolutionary appearance" and mescaline was all but forgotten.

Early research into mescaline tended to be rather mechanical in nature. It suggested, for example, that mescaline stimulated the visual areas of the cortex and that this alone caused the brain to experience an altered state of consciousness and perception, producing "visual phenomena" that tended on the whole to take the form of geometric patterns, grids, lattices, tunnels, and spirals.

Those who have taken mescaline themselves would surely disagree that the experience is wholly about "visual phenomena" rather than meaningful visions, or that these "phenomena" can be easily compartmentalized as grids or spirals—but those at least are the conclusions of this early research.

Heinrich Klüver was one of the first to study the effects of mescaline, and in his *Mescal and Mechanisms of Hallucinations* (1928 and 1966), attempted to account for the (supposed) similarity of visual phenomena by reference to the structure of the brain and eye. He organized the images reported by mescaline users into four groups he called "form constants":

1. Tunnels and funnels
2. Spirals
3. Lattices, including honeycombs and triangles
4. Cobwebs

From this he concluded in effect that mescaline "hallucinations" are the result of seeing patterns on the retina under the influence of the "drug," with the images interpreted by the brain.

As the title of Klüver's book suggests, he was looking for a mechanism—something mechanical, physical, and nothing much to do with spirit—and this inevitably is what he found. At the time, his research was pioneering, but these days we might say that the Observer Effect also played a part in his conclusions—the process by which an experimenter changes the nature of the experiment, its outcome, or its findings by virtue of being part of the process himself. Or put more simply, whatever we look for we find.

A related problem, even for today's scientists, is what has come to be known as the Research Effect. Rick Strassman, who experienced the problem himself during his administration of DMT to volunteers in laboratories, explains it like this:

In the research setting there is the expectation of getting data from your subjects. This affects the relationship between those who administer and those who receive psychedelics. Volunteers know they need to give something to the project, and scientists want something from them. For the person under the influence, just having his or her trip is not enough. For the investigator, helping that person have the best possible outcome isn't fully adequate either. This sets up expectations, with the inevitable possibility of disappointments, resentment and miscommunication. The interpersonal setting is fundamentally altered.[14]

Then there is the "problem" of Klüver himself. Heinrich Klüver was born in 1897 and took his doctorate in physiological psychology—a discipline that also has a more mechanistic approach to human behavior than, say, the humanistic or psychoanalytic fields. He went on to make his mark in the study of animal behavior, a field where animals (and human beings) are, in the main, considered more or less automata, devoid of spirit or personality and reduced to components capable of analysis or conditioning based on physical processes, as demonstrated by the leading lights of behaviorism: Skinner and Pavlov. With this sort of background perhaps Klüver was in a way conditioned himself to find a physical (rather than a spiritual or emotional) basis for mescaline effects.

I am not dismissing his work, simply pointing to the limitations of its time and the belief that visions can be reduced to a series of lines and spirals. In fairness too, Klüver's work did extend beyond a purely mechanistic agenda. He coined the term *presque vu* for example (literally, "almost seen") to describe the sensation that accompanies mescaline visions that one is receiving a great insight or revelation that is beyond the ability of the rational mind to fully grasp or comprehend.

Some of the people who reported their experiences to Klüver demonstrated this. One said that he saw fretwork for example, but then that his arms and hands and finally his entire body *became* fretwork so there was no difference between him and it: "The fretwork is I," he wrote. As with many revelations by teacher plants, there is no doubt more philosophically to this statement than is captured by the words. The experience of *being* fretwork and realizing that there is no difference between I and That, for example, implies a sense of the numinous and of the connection between us and all things, which is beyond the simple reporting of an image.

In *Miserable Miracle,* the Belgian artist and poet Henri Michaux (1899–1984) described a similar experience with mescaline, where he realized that "one is nothing but oneself."[15]

"Hundreds of lines of force combed my being," he continued. "Enormous Z's are passing through me (stripes-vibrations-zig-zags?). Then either broken S's or what may be their halves, incomplete Os, a little like giant eggshells. . . . I have once more become a passage, a passage in time."

The last line is, I believe, key to Michaux's experience. It is not the shapes or patterns that are important in themselves, but the information they carry and the realizations they bring. For as plants like San Pedro teach us, we are all just a passage in time, a breath on the wind, vital to the world and at the same time a whisper or insignificant thought, of no more—or less—value or substance than a cloud or a blade of grass.

The sensation of being bathed in or bombarded by intense colors is also common to San Pedro, as the reports of Klüver's other mescaline explorers confirm. Once again, however, it is not the colors in themselves that are important but the conduits they provide for new revelations about the beauty around and within us, which is present in even the most mundane of worldly forms, and the realization that our gift of life is special.

As I gazed, every projecting angle, cornice and even the face of the stones at their joinings were by degrees covered or hung with clusters of what seemed to be huge precious stones . . . green, purple, red and orange. . . . All seemed to possess interior light and to give the faintest idea of the perfectly satisfying intensity and purity of these gorgeous colors is quite beyond my power . . . everywhere the vast pendant masses of emerald green, ruby red, and orange began to drip a slow rain of colors. Here were miles of rippled purple, half transparent, and of ineffable beauty. Now and then soft golden clouds floated from these folds . . . such singular brilliancy that I cannot even imagine them now.

As beautiful as these descriptions are, there is still a problem with the scientific method in trying to explain the impact and effects of teacher plants as simply visual. Klüver was interested in what people *saw* and explained their visions by reference to physical processes and biological or chemical mechanisms. The *experience* of mescaline was not really sought and so is never fully captured, although some of his accounts come close. He asked his subjects to recount what they had seen, and because seeing was regarded as a physical action, the temptation was to reduce and thereby "explain" their visions by reference to the architecture of the eye or the powers of the brain, without ever asking what these experiences *meant* to the subject himself.

Another problem is that of Klüver's inherent, though perhaps not deliberate, bias. He begins from the premise that mescaline experiences are first and foremost hallucinations; it is there in the title of his book. The word suggests that these visions contain no information or have little value in themselves. This in turn implies that our "normal" and everyday way of looking at the world is more important, significant, or "real" than anything mescaline or San Pedro might show us. But is this really the case?

The psychedelic explorer, Terence McKenna, writes in one of his books that there may well be "true hallucinations" where what we receive from visions is more real and operates at a deeper level than the things seen (or often not seen) in our habitual way of perceiving and processing information from the world.

One example of such a true hallucination was the discovery of the structure of DNA with its double helix by the Nobel Prize winner Francis Crick.

Crick wrote that he was struggling to understand how DNA worked one day and entered what he called a "dreaming state"* while he had the problem on his mind. He dreamed of snakes writhing together and winding themselves like the serpents of the caduceus. It was "a not insignificant thought" as he later, rather self-effacingly, put it—and from that true hallucination the problem of DNA was solved.

To regard one state (normal consciousness) as real and our "hallucinatory" world as unreal and without value may, therefore, be quite wrong. Such a distinction presupposes that there is actually a separation between the two states, that one exists in reality while the other is in some way false or abnormal. Shamans see no such division.

The curanderos of the Andes believe instead that the information given to us by San Pedro (or in dreams, meditations, and visions) is as valid, or more so, as that received from ordinary perception and thought. Furthermore, such information is given to us precisely so it *can* be used in daily life: not ignored, denied, or regarded as lacking in merit or purpose. To deny our dreams, after all, is to dismiss a third of our human and spiritual experience.

For San Pedro shamans the visions and insights gained from the plant are there to inform our everyday behavior in the real world so we can make changes, heal, or do whatever else is necessary to improve and enhance our lives. The changes we make as a consequence of our visions mean that we become new people and closer, in one of those shaman's words, to our real essence as "true human beings." In turn, these life changes mean that we start from a new perspective the next time we drink San Pedro, and so the process of spiritual and worldly advancement continues.

Archaeological and anthropological evidence points to the same unified view of life and healing on the part of ancient curanderos just as much as their modern-day counterparts, and to their perception of

---

*This "dreaming state" was also aided by a plant, LSD, a synthetic produced from ergot, a fungus that grows on wheat and has been suggested as the basis for the "flying ointments" of European witches. —R.H.

reality as a combination of the material and immaterial so that one informs the other.

Peter Furst writes that the shamanic worldview does not include the notion of duality or opposing forces that split the world into two, the sacred and the profane.[16] Instead, there is no purely physical world and no absolute and self-contained otherworld that is wholly of the spirit. On the contrary, the curandero, in his healing rituals, seeks to find unity and balance in the interactions between all the forces of the world through a vision that can inform—and transform—his patient's life, leading to an improvement in his existence.

This view of the world is flexible enough to incorporate even seemingly competing or contradictory elements; a person might find as a result of his visions that he is right *and* wrong, good *and* bad, blessed *and* cursed all at the same time. A new, more creative and open understanding of reality can then arise and the behavior of that person (and the outcomes that stem from it) can change as a result of the information San Pedro has given him. There is a very real sense then in which our visions *are* our reality, even if science cannot explain to us why or how.

THE BIRTH OF ENTHEOGENS

To differentiate plants like San Pedro (which provide the user with a visionary experience that may also include important real-life outcomes) from hallucinogens like LSD that had become so popular for recreational use in the 1960s and 1970s, the term *entheogen* was coined by a group of ethnobotanists including Richard Evans Schultes and R. Gordon Wasson. Both men were plant pioneers themselves who are particularly known for their work with ayahuasca and "magic" mushrooms.

Schultes and his colleagues felt that *hallucinogen* was an inappropriate term, partly due to its use by psychiatrists and medical doctors to describe states of delirium and insanity. The word *psychedelic,* in more popular use at the time, did not seem a better alternative because of its similarity to words like psychosis, which again implied that visionary or mystical states were a form of madness.

"In a strict sense," they wrote, "only those vision-producing drugs that can be shown to have figured in shamanic or religious rites would be designated entheogens."

The use of the word *drugs* in their definition is unfortunate because it has connotations of its own of course: "to be drugged" and, therefore, out of control, and so forth. Perhaps *substances* would have been a better choice. But still, the description as a whole is useful as it moves us out of the arena of recreational drug use and attaches a sacred value to a discrete and particular group of mind- and state-altering substances.

The literal meaning of the word *entheogen* is "that which causes God to be within an individual," or "which creates the divine within us." Perhaps "that which stimulates or reveals the divine or causes us to remember our own divinity" would, again, have been better still and certainly truer to the experience of San Pedro. These nuances, however, are less important than the fact that a definition was now available that set sacred plants apart from mainstream drugs.

Their emphasis on ritual and religious use (or what we might call sacred purpose) also made a distinction between shamanism and science: the former focusing on the divine and potentially life-changing aspects of such plants, the latter concentrating on reductionist logic and procedures that often missed—both physically and spiritually—the ways in which sacred plants actually worked.

Physically, as well as its mescaline content, San Pedro contains a range of compounds that have effects of their own.* By concentrating only on mescaline scientists may tend to miss or devalue their contribution to the experience as a whole.

Some of these compounds are *sympathomimetics,* or substances that mimic the effects of adrenalin and noradrenaline, the so-called fight or

---

*Including tyramine, hordenine, 3-methoxytyramine, anhalaninine, anhalonidine, 3,4-dimethoxyphen-ethylamine, 3,4-dimethoxy-4-hydroxy-B-phenethylamine, and 3,5-dimethoxy-4-hydroxy-B-phenethylamine. —R.H.

flight chemicals that are released naturally by our bodies to prepare us for action when reality shifts and we feel uncertain or anxious. Perhaps it is these, more than mescaline, that give rise to our sense of awe and the awareness that we are in the presence of something mysterious and more powerful than ourselves, which are common feelings under the influence of San Pedro?

A further consideration is that other plants—or, indeed, other substances—might be added to the San Pedro that is drunk in ceremonies, such as when healings are conducted for participants who have suffered a magical attack from a sorcerer. In these circumstances additives might include purgatives like tobacco, psychoactives like misha and datura (used by shamans, according to Furst, as "a drastic form of shock therapy"), or powdered bones, cemetery dust, and traces of soil from sacred sites and archaeological ruins.*[17]

In other ceremonies, while the San Pedro remains pure, other plants and medicines may be administered separately during the same ritual, such as the *singado* (tobacco and alcohol) and *contrachisa* (an emetic made from other cactus parts that do not contain mescaline). It is reasonable to suppose that these may also have an effect, however slight, on the San Pedro experience even though they are not mixed with the brew itself, because they are ingested during the same time frame. Their effects, however, have not been studied.

Working with a single extract and concluding that the part is equal to the whole may be one of the biggest errors made by scientists—although it is all too common in plant medicine research.

Scientific research—with measurement as its operating principle and goal—must also, by definition, discount the spiritual (as well as the emotional, individual, and psychological) experience of anyone who has ever taken San Pedro, mescaline, or peyote, because spirit (and personal

---

*Other plants that might be added to San Pedro include *perejil* (*Petroselinum crispum*) for overcoming *dano* (sorcery) and *susto* (fright, or for "forgetting love or trauma") and *apio cimarron* (*Apium graveolens*) for curing nervous disorders, insomnia, and anxiety as well as physical problems such as bronchitis and colic. —R.H.

experience) cannot be effectively measured but is subjective and anecdotal only. What scientists really measure in their laboratories, consequently, is a notion they have of "what is really going on" at a structural or chemical level. And so the reality of millions of people who have used plants for spiritual, emotional, or physical healing for thousands of years must be more or less ignored.

The philosopher Karl Popper wrote that the first principle of scientific method should be "falsifiability." To qualify as science, that is, every experiment and every law that scientists arrive at must be capable of being disproved and hold up to scrutiny so that consistent results are always produced despite this. Not many of science's discoveries truly fall into this category, and, therefore, come closer to scientific opinion than scientific fact. It is highly unlikely that an injection of mescaline sulphate in a lab will produce the same quality of personal experience as a San Pedro ceremony in the Andes (and, in fact, research within the latter environment has not yet even been conducted) but science presumes it so, continuing to discount the spirit and the validity of spiritual experience in a way that sometimes smacks of arrogance.

The scientist's position in this is not unlike that of Peru's famous son and mescaline explorer, Carlos Castaneda, when he first met his shamanic teacher, don Juan Matus. "I told him that I was interested in obtaining information about medicinal plants," Castaneda writes in *The Teachings of Don Juan*. "Although in truth I was almost totally ignorant about peyote I found myself pretending that I knew a great deal and even suggesting that it might be to his advantage to talk with me."[18] Once he had met Mescalito, the spirit of the plant, under the tutelage of don Juan, however, Castaneda quickly realized how little he actually knew about anything.

It seems to me, therefore, that the experiences of individuals who have taken part in genuine, real-life, not lab-based healing events and opened themselves to San Pedro are preferable on every level to the conclusions of scientific observers about the supposed workings of our brains or the rods and cones in our eyes. For that reason, this book contains several firsthand accounts of healings, written by participants themselves, so you can make up your own mind about how San Pedro works and what it may be capable of.

OTHER EARLY WORK WITH MESCALINE

Another early account of mescaline exploration comes from the British medical doctor and author, Havelock Ellis, and appeared in *The Contemporary Review* of January 1898 under the heading "Mescal: A New Artificial Paradise." Although it is presented as scientific enquiry, it hints once again at a deeper truth to be found beneath and beyond the scientist's fascination with "visual phenomena" for, just as Castaneda discovered with don Juan, what begins as an objective exercise can become a subjective and emotional experience.

Ellis writes, "The first symptom [sic] observed [upon taking mescaline] . . . was a certain consciousness of energy and intellectual power," which suggests an actual change in body and spirit and in thought patterns and thinking, not something that can be dismissed as a "hallucination" at all. This was followed by "kaleidoscopic, symmetrical images . . . a vast field of golden jewels, studded with red and green stones, ever changing. At the same time the air around me seemed to be flushed with vague perfume—producing with the visions a delicious effect— *and all discomfort had vanished*" (my italics).

If the sentence above suggests a healing element to the visionary experience, Ellis's next observation hints at an emerging spiritual relationship to the world at large, where some other aspect or quality is apparent in objects that are otherwise familiar and ordinary: "[My] visions . . . were extremely definite, but yet always novel; *they were constantly approaching, and yet constantly eluding, the semblance of known things*" (my italics).

This is the presque vu experience described by Klüver. It is a sensation well-known to those who have drunk San Pedro: that there is a unique personality, an almost Platonic quality or essence that exists beneath the forms that things take, or more prosaically, that there is more to reality than we know. It is as if the spirit or energy within things and between people is revealed to us and we understand that their identity—and our own—is more fluid than we have been led to believe while their spiritual essence is constant. "Who are you?" (or rather, "Who am I?") becomes one of the most important questions we can ask of ourselves and others and of all other forms around us.

One of my participants during a 2008 San Pedro ceremony said something similar in the account she later wrote of her experience:

> I was able to perceive a more subtle web of energy. . . . When I rejoined my fellow travelers I could observe how our energies interact and how connected we are to each other and to the physical world. We are constantly sharing portions of our energy fields. With every encounter, we exchange information and energy and we come away changed just a little bit. This realization made me aware of my influence on others and theirs on me and I became careful with my interactions. I became conscious of speaking only the truth and of keeping my intentions pure. I was also aware of the energy [of] other people and how it affected everyone. One friend came in enthused by the mountains and his enthusiasm sent ripples of excitement through the group.

Ellis gave mescaline to an artist friend who, it might be assumed from his account, also underwent a healing on a physical and spiritual level. "The first paroxysms . . . would come on with tinglings in the lower limbs, and with the sensation of a nauseous and suffocating gas mounting up into my head. Two or three times this was accompanied by a color vision of the gas bursting into flame as it passed up my throat."

These "paroxysms" and "tingling" are consistent with the physical sensations I have often experienced in ceremony, and I have concluded at these times that San Pedro is "checking me out" and scanning my body for weakness. They feel like mild cramps or jolts of electricity as the cactus spirit courses through the body. In the example Ellis gives, these illnesses and imperfections are then released through a vision of gas and flame. This would certainly be interpreted by a shaman as a form of healing—a spirit extraction where negative energies are removed—and not just an idle fantasy. Some of the healing accounts related by participants in my ceremonies (reported in this book and its predecessor, *The Hummingbird's Journey to God*) are of a similar nature.

The outcome of the example above is recorded in another passage from Ellis: "My body lost all substantiality. With the suddenness of a neuralgic pang, the back of my head seemed to open and emit streams of bright color; this was immediately followed by the feeling as of a draft blowing like a gale through the hair in the same region."

This sensation of "breaking open the head," to use the words of Daniel Pinchbeck,[19] is consistent with the visionary plant experience and with the shamanic extraction of illness; it too is a true hallucination where healing takes place through the removal of pain, experienced as streams of colors and the entrance into the body of a new energy, like a wind that blows away the cobwebs of our self-limiting beliefs and leaves us with healthier and more empowering ideas about who we are and our place in the world. "Henceforth," says Ellis's participant, "I should be more or less conscious of the interdependence of body and brain."

Ellis concludes that:

Mescal intoxication differs from the other artificial paradises which drugs procure. Under the influence of alcohol, for instance, as in normal dreaming, the intellect is impaired, although there may be a consciousness of unusual brilliance; hasheesh, again, produces an uncontrollable tendency to movement and bathes its victim in a sea of emotion.

The mescal drinker [meanwhile] remains calm and collected amid the sensory turmoil around him; his judgment is as clear as in the normal state; he falls into no oriental condition of vague and voluptuous reverie. . . . Further, unlike the other chief substances to which it may be compared, mescal does not wholly carry us away from the actual world, or plunge us into oblivion; a large part of its charm lies in the halo of beauty which it casts around the simplest and commonest things.

This latter statement is, to me, central to the San Pedro experience. Whereas ayahuasca sweeps us away from ordinary reality and into the spirit world, San Pedro brings us closer to *this* world and exposes its beauty to us. As may become apparent in the chapters that follow, it is this experience of beauty (in the world and in ourselves) that may in fact be the most profoundly healing and life-changing gift that San Pedro offers.

A NEW SCIENTIFIC PARADIGM FOR EXPLORING THE SAN PEDRO EXPERIENCE

When the English novelist Aldous Huxley was first given mescaline by Dr. Humphry Osmond in 1953, he concluded that it allowed man access to mystical states by overriding the brain's "reducing valve."

Huxley was quoting the ideas of the nineteenth-century French philosopher Henri Bergson, who hypothesized that the brain acts as a filter for memory and sensory experience so that our conscious awareness does not become overwhelmed by a mass of largely useless information that is mostly irrelevant to our survival.

Bergson developed the concept of "multiplicity" to explain his theory. This suggests that our moment-to-moment experience of the world is built (or invented) by us through our selection of specific information from "*les données immédiates de la conscience*" ("the immediate data of consciousness"). These data are both internal and external and include the memory of every experience we have ever had along with the perception of everything that is happening anywhere and everywhere in the universe.

Most of these data are unimportant to us, however, and some of them are even contradictory, so it would simply overburden and confuse us if we had to try to make sense of it all. It may even be detrimental to our survival if every split-second, life-or-death decision had to be made consciously while pondering the millions of options available to us.

Bergson believed, therefore, that the primary role of the brain, in the face of this multiplicity, is to act as a filter or gate for memory and sensory experience so we select what is useful from the range of data available according to the situations in which we find ourselves. In this way we construct the world by rejecting some of its information and embracing that which remains.

In a nutshell, what Bergson was saying is that the mind is capable of knowing everything—so clairvoyance, psychic abilities, self-healing, and encyclopedic knowledge (amongst other things) are all perfectly natural and available to us. Knowing what Julius Caesar was thinking at the moment of his death, however, or what is happening now on the farthest star in our solar system is of no use to us if our objective is simply to safely cross a road. To protect us, the mind "gates" this information so we are left with what is useful to us now.

Literally, therefore, we are self-limiting beings and there are things, forces, and energies around us at this very moment that we cannot under normal circumstances perceive, because our brains do not allow it. If these filters were bypassed, we would be capable of remembering and experiencing everything from a richer, fuller, and more "cosmic" perspective.

Huxley applied Bergson's theory to mescaline, suggesting that it does in fact override the reducing valve of the brain, bypassing the filters that limit us. He paraphrased this notion by quoting the English poet and mystic William Blake: "If the doors of perception were cleansed everything would appear to man as it is, infinite."

Recently Bergson's ideas have come back into prominence in modern psychology. David Luke, Ph.D., lecturer in psychology at the University of Greenwich London, is currently undertaking research with mescaline to explore Bergson's theories, and has provisionally concluded that the mescaline experience does indeed give us access to areas of our brains that we do not ordinarily use but which, when activated, allow us to perceive the cosmic order and know our place within it.

Luke writes:

> Recent research into the neurochemistry of psychedelics lends some support to [Bergson's] simple notion. For instance [the researchers] Vollenweider and Geyer propose that information processing in cortico-striato-thalamo-cortical (CSTC) feedback loops [in the brain] is disrupted by psychedelics via 5-HT (serotonin) receptor agonism (specifically 5-HT2A receptors), thereby inhibiting the "gating" of extraneous sensory stimuli and subsequently inhibiting the ability to attend selectively to salient environmental features.[20]

In other words, plants like San Pedro do indeed expand our normal brain processes and widen our perception and experience of the world.

"Furthermore," he continues:

> psychedelics are also thought to induce presynaptic release of glutamate from thalamic afferents, leading to a simultaneous overload of internal information in the cortex. It is thought that these combined information overload effects are at least partly responsible for the "hallucinogenic" experience with these drugs, which are known to induce greatly altered or amplified incoming sensory information. This disruption of the sensory gating function by psychedelics could also underpin the neurochemistry of ESP . . . elicited with any number of psychedelics such as mescaline.[21]

That entheogens like San Pedro have a central role to play in "psi experiences" is also supported, in Luke's words, by

> a wealth of collectively compelling anecdotal, anthropological, clinical and survey reports, along with a body of preliminary experimental research. . . . Mescaline is one substance in particular that,

according to the historical, anthropological, and anecdotal evidence, is known to induce psi experiences. Ever since the use of peyote was first documented in the mid-sixteenth century by the personal physician of King Philip II of Spain, Dr. Francisco Hernández, it has been reputed to have prophetic qualities.[22]

It causes those devouring it to be able to foresee and to predict things.

San Pedro has been used traditionally by the indigenous people of Peru, Bolivia, Chile and Ecuador for the same type of magico-religious practices, such as divination . . . a sixteenth century Spanish officer stationed in Cusco, Peru, described how the natives take the form they want and go through the air in a short time; and they see what is happening.[23]

This literature is backed up by experiential reports from non-indigenous mescaline users, like that of the French researchers who gave mescaline to six subjects, one of whom temporarily developed very detailed and accurate clairvoyant abilities. After his mescaline experiences in 1951, Humphry Osmond also claimed to have successfully transmitted telepathic information to a fellow researcher, Duncan Blewett, who was also under the influence of mescaline, "leading an independent observer to panic at the uncanny event."

Luke concludes from the research so far that "mescaline did indeed give rise to reports of telepathy and precognition among those using it," along with "the perception of auras, the experience of encountering the plant's spirit, and a sense of unity."[24]

He also refers to research he has conducted with his colleague Marios Kittenis, which found that there are typical "transpersonal" experiences of a mystical or paranormal type that most commonly occur with mescaline-containing cacti such as peyote and San Pedro. The most frequent of these is the experience of perceiving an aura around living things, followed by a sense of the intelligence or spirit of the cactus and a feeling of connection with the universal consciousness of all things. Other experiences include dissolving into energy, powerful and long-lasting religious awakenings, out-of-body experiences, clairvoyance, death and rebirth experiences and/or past life memories, psychokinesis (influencing objects or people with one's mind), encountering a divine being or a (nonanimal) intelligent entity, and a greater understanding of the interconnections and interrelationships between circumstances and things expressed as a sense of the loss of causality (i.e., that A must always cause B).

"For scientists, whether or not these experiences are 'real' is a matter of on-going debate between those who believe that these phenomena may be possible and those who reject them out of hand because they do not fit within their confined 'physicalistic' worldview," writes Luke. "For the people who experience these phenomena, however, they are often considered 'more real than real,' and although they challenge what we think we know about the world, those experiencing these extraordinary events often find it very difficult to reject them as mere hallucinations."

On the evidence of this, another gift of San Pedro may be the expansion in awareness it gives us. Through it we may come to understand the bigger picture of the universe, the flows of energy within it, and how we connect to them so we can learn to become the true human; that is, to know what it really means to be alive, to approach our lives accordingly, and to find the balance and healing we need.

THE SPIRIT OF THIS BOOK

Bergson's ideas provide a useful framework for us in understanding how San Pedro may work, and they are certainly compatible with the views of the shamans and participants quoted in this book. They are echoed in the words of the huachumera La Gringa when she tells us that "San Pedro opens our eyes to what is already there"; that is, to a world of miracles that is right before us all the time, but rarely seen because we are simply not looking for it. Her story of "hallucinating" a vision of a stairway of light while drinking San Pedro—which she was able to capture on film—appears in chapter 3 to illustrate the point she is making.

Bergson's theories may also be borne out to some extent in Alexia Gidding's account in part 3, "San Pedro Healing" (chapter 10), of a San Pedro experience where she was shown the truth of her repressed and presumed-dealt-with memories of early abuse. In this example, those memories were still fully present but gated by her mind in order to protect her from them. What she needed was to relive them—at an emotional rather than a rational level—in order to finally be free of her pain. San Pedro enabled this by opening the doors to her personal perception.

In part 4, "San Pedro and Creativity," the fine artist David Hewson speaks of the visions he has received from San Pedro and other plants, which have enabled him to win international commissions and express the infinite in his art (chapter 15). This too brings us back to Bergson's theory that everything is within us—all creativity—and needs only to be released.

And there will be many other examples, too, that suggest that the infinite is indeed within us. Perhaps this is also what the curandera Isabel meant when she told the author Bonnie Glass-Coffin that "God won't lie to you . . . He exists. He is a spirit in your heart and in your thoughts. . . . [He is] in your subconscience."[25]

That is for you to decide. In this book I present accounts from San Pedro shamans, from those who have been cured by San Pedro, and those who have been inspired by it. It is my aim to bring this remarkable plant teacher and healer to greater prominence and to make you aware of its benefits. What you choose to do with this information is up to you, although I hope that you will be inspired to try it and receive its blessings as many others have.

NOTES

1. Irene Silverblatt, *Moon, Sun, and Witches: Gender Ideologies and Class in Inca and Colonial Peru* (Princeton: Princeton University Press, 1987). Quoted in Bonnie Glass-Coffin, *The Gift of Life: Female Spirituality and*

Healing in Northern Peru (Albuquerque: University of New Mexico Press, 1998).

2. Richard Evans Schultes, Albert Hofmann, and Christian Ratsch, *Plants of the Gods: Their Sacred, Healing, and Hallucinogenic Powers* (Rochester, Vt.: Healing Arts Press, 2001).

3. Douglas Sharon, *Wizard of the Four Winds* (New York: Free Press, 1978).

4. Jim DeKorne, *Psychedelic Shamanism* (Port Townsend, Wash.: Breakout Productions, 1994).

5. Bonnie Glass-Coffin, *Gift of Life*.

6. Eduardo Calderon, Richard Cowan, Douglas Sharon, and F. Kaye Sharon, *Eduardo El Curandero: The Words of a Peruvian Healer* (Berkeley: North Atlantic Books, 2000).

7. Schultes, Hofmann, and Ratsch, *Plants of the Gods*.

8. Ibid.

9. Calderon, Cowan, Sharon, and Sharon, *Eduardo El Curandero*.

10. Glass-Coffin, *Gift of Life*.

11. Ross Heaven and Howard G. Charing, *Plant Spirit Shamanism: Traditional Techniques for Healing the Soul* (Rochester, Vt.: Destiny Books, 2006).

12. Peter T. Furst, *Flesh of the Gods: The Ritual Use of Hallucinogens* (Lake Zurich, Ill.: Waveland Press Inc., reprint edition, 1990).

13. Rick Strassman, *DMT: The Spirit Molecule* (Rochester, Vt.: Park Street Press, 2000).

14. Ibid.

15. Henri Michaux, *Miserable Miracle: La Mescaline* (Schoenhofs Foreign Books, 1991).

16. Furst, *Flesh of the Gods*.

17. See Rainer W. Bussmann and Douglas Sharon, *Plantas de los Cuatrovientos* (*Plants of the Four Winds: The Magic and Medicinal Flora of Peru*) (Peru, 2007).

18. Carlos Castaneda, *The Teachings of Don Juan* (Berkeley: University of California Press, 1998).

19. Daniel Pinchbeck, *Breaking Open the Head: A Psychedelic Journey into the Heart of Contemporary Shamanism* (Broadway, 2003).

20. In his summary of the literature as part of a research proposal he shared with me for his study of the psychic potentials of San Pedro. Personal communication.

21. Ibid.
22. Ibid.
23. Ibid.
24. Ibid.
25. In Bonnie Glass-Coffin, *Gift of Life*. "Subconscience" does not exist as a word of course but it is appropriate to the spirit of this quotation. It implies a combination of "subconscious," that God is within us and part of our deeper selves, and "sub-conscience"; that is, that our sense of God exists at a fundamental level beneath human conscience, as a sort of moral barometer or innate guide to right and wrong to which good and bad health may also be connected.

PART ONE

San Pedro Shamans and Shamanism

The most representative mystical experience of the archaic societies, that of shamanism, betrays the Nostalgia for Paradise, the desire to recover the state of freedom and beatitude before "the Fall."

MIRCEA ELIADE

IT IS ONLY RIGHT that we start with the shamans. They are the ones who are doing the work with San Pedro, who have devoted their lives to it, and who have committed themselves to the healing of others. They are the ones who know.

In this section we hear from three of the Andes' most celebrated shamans. Curiously perhaps, two of them are not Peruvian by birth, but in a way that makes them even more dedicated to the work and the medicine. It is a commitment and a true act of faith to leave your home-land and all that is familiar to you because you have been called by the spirit of a plant. Peruvian people recognize this too, and the reputations of these shamans are well-known and respected.

Rubén Orellana, Ph.D., is an archaeologist and anthropologist trained at the University of Cusco, Peru. Now an external consultant to the National Institute of Culture in Cusco, he was for many years the head of archaeology at Machu Picchu, discovering forty-four new sites of archaeological and historical interest. Alongside his scholarship he is also a shaman who has worked with San Pedro and the healing tradi-tions of the Andes for most of his life, as well as researching the history and methods of these practices and how they influence aspects of life and well-being for Andean people. As a shaman he is also the founding director of the Kamaquen ("source of energy") Healing Center in the Sacred Valley.

La Gringa is Rubén Orellana's most famous apprentice. Her work with San Pedro has featured in several articles and books—including my own—and since 2007 I have drunk her medicine extensively. South African by birth, she first visited Peru in the 1990s and has now lived in Cusco for almost twenty years, working as a healer and huachumera.

In 2008, during one of my visits to Peru to work with her, I interviewed La Gringa about her life and experiences with the cactus of vision. Her answers then showed not only the healing potential of this plant, but cast further light on the traditions that surround it and their evolution in the modern world. In 2011, I conducted a second interview with her, delving more deeply into the answers she had given. For those who wish to work with San Pedro, what La Gringa has to say is of great interest, because it shows the nature of shamanic healing with this medicine in the modern world, as well as illustrating the traditions from which it stems. For those who work as healers themselves, what La Gringa has learned from huachuma is also important, because it suggests where illness may come from and how it may be cured, even by those who do not administer San Pedro or drink it themselves.

Michael Simonato is part of the new wave of San Pedro healers now working in Peru. After a spiritual crisis and awakening of his own, he began a healing quest that eventually landed him in South America—initially, like many others, to drink ayahuasca in search of answers. This in turn led him to San Pedro, a plant he now works with extensively, leading ceremonies of his own in Pisaq after studying and drinking the plant medicine with many different shamans. In his article he relates his own healing story and offers practical advice for preparing and working with San Pedro, its admixtures, and complementary plants and practices.

To give you a context for understanding the work of these individuals, I first offer an overview of shamanism and curanderismo in Andean Peru that looks at the nature of shamanic beliefs and healing and at the cosmology of the shaman and the spirits he works with. Of course, a study of this kind is "overcomplicated" because the truth of San Pedro is very simple. Ask any of these shamans and they will tell you that it is about love. Just that. Love and compassion. But I hope that what I have to say is useful to you anyway.

1
Shamanism and *Curanderismo*
The Approach to Healing in Peru

Ross Heaven

Shamanism is a not a discrete activity like, say dentistry or aromatherapy, but a body of practices that have the effect of connecting the material and immaterial worlds, the worlds of man and God, matter and energy. These practices are performed by shamans who, by various means and methods (such as the use of San Pedro and ayahuasca in Peru, or a trance state arrived at by drumming in cultures like Mongolia and Siberia) are able to travel between these worlds to obtain solutions from their spirit guides and helpers, and in this way address the problems that are afflicting their patients or the community in general. These solutions may take the form of guidance, counsel, or direct and spirit-driven healing to ameliorate the sicknesses of the soul and restore balance and equilibrium.

The word *shaman* is not Peruvian in origin, but comes from the Tungus people of Siberia and arises from the word *saman,* which has a specific usage there. It literally means "priest of the Ural-Altaic people," although it is often interpreted more generally as "one who sees" or "one who knows." It has now come to be used generically for anyone who carries out healing, counseling, or divinatory work in partnership with spirit guides, allies, and helpers, and which normally involves ritual or ceremonial procedures to make these spirits manifest and elicit their help to create beneficial change.

This way of working is the oldest psychospiritual tradition known to humankind. Shamanic artifacts discovered in the African Rift Valley date back four hundred thousand years, and cave paintings depicting shamanic scenes of shape-shifting (where the shaman takes on nonhuman powers and shifts into animal or plant forms), such as those at Lascaux and Tassili, though not as old as this, certainly date back thousands of years.[1]

Compartmentalizing spiritual and healing approaches into various camps and specialties (such as aromatherapy, reiki, massage, herbalism, crystal healing, and so on) is a modern fascination—traditional shamans worked with all of these and more, doing whatever was necessary to provide the right medicine for his or her people. This is still the case in Peru, where San Pedro shamans may also use sound healing during ceremonies, for example, or reiki-like techniques to change the energies of their patients into a new and more positive alignment, or offer herbal preparations and teas to help with particular ailments.

Many of the theories or working concepts that we now accept as the inventions or discoveries of modern science and psychology are also to be found in much more ancient shamanic belief systems, and are embedded in healing traditions from thousands of years ago. For example, quantum physics now tells us that we live in a "holographic universe" where all things are part of and mirror the whole, where all is composed of energy, and where this energy can be made to change its shape and form (e.g., from a particle to a wave) depending on our interactions with it.[2]

Shamans have been saying the same thing for thousands of years. Black Elk, the Sioux medicine man written about by John Niehardt in his book *Black Elk Speaks,* was quoted two hundred years before quantum physics, remarking that "we are all one" and that all things are part of the whole, the "sacred hoop" of life.[3] It is a point that La Gringa and other shamans in this book continue to make: we are all connected and we can shape the world we live in to create any reality we want. The Shuar people of the Columbian Amazon have an expression, "The world is as you dream It," which means much the same thing.

THE CRISIS OF SHAMANISM

How do people become shamans? It begins with a calling—not always in the sense of a "spiritual vocation," which implies a desire on the part of the shaman-elect to become a healer, like someone who wishes to become a priest might have, but a calling from the spirits themselves who have recognized the natural gifts and skills of that person and have chosen him to become their ambassador on Earth and a partner in their work, sometimes irrespective of his own wishes.

Often the call begins as a whisper—with an awareness on the part of the shaman-to-be that the world is not quite as he has been taught to view it, that there are signs, subtleties, and shades of meaning out there, not black-and-white scientific or mathematical certainties. He may have "special knowledge"—the ability to see, hear, and know things that others do not—for example, a future-seeing awareness of things yet to happen or an "active imagination" that sees spirits where others just see common reality.

If the shaman ignores these signs and does not explore what they might mean, then the whispers of spirit may get louder until they become a roar. If he still ignores them, then typically the shaman-to-be will enter what it known as an initiatory crisis.

A mysterious illness of a mental, emotional, physical, or spiritual nature—or even all four at once—may suddenly afflict him, for which there is no known cause and often no orthodox cure. Such is the story of Black Elk, who was close to death as a child and could not be saved by medical or shamanic healing, but only by the spirits themselves.

The classical literature, such as Mircea Eliade's work *Shamanism,*[4] also describes people being near fatally wounded by wild animals or hit by a mysterious shower of rocks that falls from the sky. Being struck by lightning is also a sure sign of a calling to shamanize, and in fact the highest level of shaman in the Andes of Peru (the *altomisayoq*) must be struck three times in order to be recognized as a true healer. Puma, one of the shamans I work with in Peru and who features later in this book, has been struck once but comes from a lineage of shamans that included his grandfather who was one of the "lucky" ones to be struck three times. "The first time, you die," says Puma, "the second time you are taken to the spirit world. To those around you, you just vanish into the air. The third time you are reborn as something new: a healer."

All of these events may be literal descriptions of actual occurrences, but they have a symbolic or mythical quality as well. To be struck by lightning means literally to become en-lightened; to be hit by a mysterious shower of rocks means to fall beneath a heavy load, to realize that the everyday world can no longer fully sustain you. Whatever its nature, it is an event that takes the shaman-elect out of ordinary reality, sometimes physically as well as psychologically. He may have to lay in the relative isolation of a hospital bed or a healing room to recover from his injuries, giving him time to ponder the mysteries of his life and circumstances, or he may need to enter the landscape of his mind and personal myths in the case of a mental or emotional crisis. He begins in this way to see beneath the veneer of the "normal" world and more deeply into himself and the nature of its underlying reality.

What saves the shaman-to-be in all of these cases is the spirits themselves. It is they who intervene, bringing him out of decline by magical means against the odds and often in impossible circumstances. This is the "roar" of the spirits—their proof and evidence for the shaman that there is more to the world than consensus reality and that by working with them he will be healthy and empowered. Once he accepts this and agrees to work as the earthly agent of spirit his illness will mysteriously vanish as quickly as it arose, and he will be reborn with new powers of healing and new allies with which to heal.

Because the shaman has survived his encounter with death he is not only stronger but knows the "theory of disease" as Eliade puts it—the idea that all illness is merely a suggestion or a potential and that if we do not meet it or agree to its presence in our lives then we cannot be touched by it—and is also able to cure illness in others since he has had firsthand experience of it.

It is for this reason that shamans are also called "wounded healers"— they are not just dealing in concepts but in real experience as they have been hurt or ill themselves. Through this they learn about disease and how to negotiate with its spirit to make others well.

BECOMING A SHAMAN

There are many culture-specific variations of shamanism but they are united by a set of common beliefs identified by Eliade as the "shamanic archetype":

- The belief that spirits exist and play an important role in our individual lives and in the life and health of the community.
- That these spirits can be good (i.e., useful to human beings) or evil (i.e., a dangerous or disturbing force).
- That the shaman can communicate with these spirits and enter their world to take guidance from them, to locate gifts of power and healing, or to do battle with malevolent energies for the good of the human soul.
- That the shaman can treat the sicknesses caused by spirits.
- That to do so the shaman must enter a state of trance at will or with the aid of a plant such as San Pedro. When fully in a state of visionary ecstasy or *ekstasis* (being outside of the self) he is able to go on "journeys" or "vision quests" where his spirit leaves his physical body to find the answers he needs in the Otherworlds.
- That to assist in his work the shaman is able to evoke beneficent spirits, guides, and helpers, known as allies.

- And that with the aid of these allies the shaman can perform other extraordinary acts (such as divining the future) that those who have not undergone his spiritual initiation cannot.

The core belief of all shamans operating within this archetype is that the cause of disease is to be found in the spiritual realm. Early anthropologists took a rather simplistic view of this and assumed that shamans were talking solely about possessions by malicious spirits or witchcraft and *brujeria* (sorcery), but in fact things are more complex than that. To a shaman, anything that is not seen is a spiritual force; this includes beliefs, ideas, and the processes of socialization, all of them intangibles that nevertheless have an impact on the way we approach our lives. Psychoanalysts deal in the same "spiritual realm" and are experts on the ways in which our thoughts and ways of thinking can lead to unhealthy choices and illnesses in the "real" world.

Sometimes too it is the circumstances of our lives and the moods they evoke in us (again unseen and intangible) that can lead to problems. Stress is a modern example. There is no such thing as "a Stress" of course, in the sense that we can touch one or hold it up for examination, and yet it is the cause of many physical problems that have real and detrimental consequences, such as cancer, hypertension, heart attacks, and strokes. In the shaman's definition, stress is a spirit (a mood or an atmosphere), and it is this rather than the symptoms of stress that needs to be dealt with during a healing.

In this way, as La Gringa puts it, all illness is psychosomatic: it is of the body *and* the mind or soul, never one without the other. This is a notion long recognized by healers and philosophers—including Socrates who even in his day was chiding the reluctance of some physicians to accept this fact: "The cure of the part should not be attempted without treatment of the whole" he wrote. "No attempt should be made to cure the body without the Soul. Let no one persuade you to cure the mind until he has first given you his Spirit. For the great error of our day is that physicians separate the heart from the mind and the mind from the body."

SHAMANISM IN PERU

In the Andes, shamanism is more properly known as *curanderismo* (from the Spanish *curar:* to heal). It is a form of folk healing that includes various techniques such as prayer, herbal medicine, healing rituals, spiritualism, and psychic healing.

As with other forms of shamanism, the curanderos' knowledge of healing may be passed down from relatives (as is the case with Puma whose grandfather was the highest form of shaman) or learned through apprenticeships (as is the case for La Gringa and Michael Simonato, two of the shamans we will hear from in this section). In other cases healing powers may simply arise spontaneously in a curandero or curandera and be described by the healer as a *don,* or divine gift. Such was the case with Julia Calderon, the daughter of Eduardo, one of Peru's most famous healers. While her father was alive Julia never paid much attention to his healing work. On his passing, however, she spontaneously received the don of healing and knew how to cure. She feels that in some way the knowledge or spirit of her father passed into her at his death and she, in turn, has become a well-known healer in Las Delicias and northern Peru.[5] However they have learned the arts of healing, all curanderos believe that their ability arises from divine energy being channeled through their bodies.

In addition to curanderos, the shamans who often (though not always) work with San Pedro to affect their cures, there are various specialist healers within this field. *Yerberos* are herbalists, *parteras* are midwives, and *sobadors* or *sobadoras* use massage, bone manipulation, and acupressure to treat physical ailments.

Curanderismo in Peru is usually the first point of call for anyone suffering from an illness or problem. It has proven effective for thousands of years and there is still some suspicion of orthodox medicine, precisely because its physicians refuse to treat the whole person or to acknowledge the existence of God and the soul.

Curanderismo, by contrast, can be used to treat a wide range of social, spiritual, psychological, and physical problems—everything from headaches, gastrointestinal problems, back pain and fever to anxiety, irritability, fatigue, depression, "bad luck" (*mal suerte*), marital discord, and illnesses caused by *susto* (fright or soul loss). In contrast again to orthodox medicine, treatments typically involve spiritual, emotional, and mental approaches as well as more physical means.

Some of the more common causes of illness in the Andes in fact are almost entirely spiritual in nature, such as *mal de ojo* (the evil eye), susto, and *empacho* (a blockage of the digestive tract caused by *envidia*: "jealousy") and since medical science cannot treat these it is another reason why a healer rather than a doctor might be sought.

In all of the cases above the curandero may perform *limpias* or *barridas* (ritual cleansings) to rebalance the body and soul of the sick person, or else recommend them to a San Pedro ceremony where the spirit of the plant will perform the healing for them.

THE ANDEAN COSMOLOGY

If all things, including ill health and well-being, stem ultimately from the world of spirit, what then is the Andean view of the spiritual universe? What does this realm look like and where are the spirits to be found?

As a way of depicting the Andean spiritual belief system it is helpful to imagine the universe as like a series of eggs nested one inside the other (the egg in Andean healing also stands as a metaphor for the soul).

The first of these "eggs"—and the purest form of reality—is Jatun: "the great force of life." It is a dimension so mysterious and unmanifest that it can only really be known by God, and it is here that all of his plans for—and the true reality of—everything resides.

In this dimension everything that happens (or does not happen) to us—whether "good" or "bad" in our terms and whether embraced and accepted by us or wholly and completely rejected—has a healing and evolutionary purpose. This purpose may elude us completely because it is so beyond our understanding, but it nevertheless flows through all things as an energy that stands for what is ultimately right, even if it manifests as unwelcome fates that befall us as individuals.

If we are wise, therefore, we accept our lives for what they are, expressions of the divine, and renounce our need to comprehend and control everything around us. By letting go we find peace. If we are not so wise (and, therefore, more or less like every other being on the planet!) we may rail against God for our "misfortunes" or against the world in general and refuse to accept anything but our own position or point of view. Such actions are futile because human beings are not God, and we are bound to fail if we try to do battle with a force so powerful that we cannot even comprehend it and that in the whole scheme of things has our best interests at heart in any case.

As La Gringa puts it:

Every "bad" thing that happens to us is a gift from God because it is an opportunity for learning and growth. If we accept it as that we transmute it and it becomes a force for good; it is only if we cling to what we have lost or what can never be that we begin to engage with misfortune. The answer is often a case of simple gratitude. In situations of loss for example be thankful for what you had, be thankful for what was lost and be thankful for what remains. In this way we do not stand in God's way and His work for us can be done.

To be healthy, that is, we must abandon our fears and let go so that the plan of the universe can unfold and carry us with it. San Pedro is our ally in this because it allows us—even if it is fleeting and ever so distant—to understand the will of God and remove ourselves from the fight.

Within the egg of Jatun is another called Wirococha, which is described by some as a lake of memory and wisdom, similar to the collective unconscious imagined by Jung. It contains the spirit-essence or soul of every being on Earth and it is to this place most commonly that San Pedro takes us to draw from the knowledge and experiences of those who have walked our path before us: the ancestors, the "soul of the world," and the spirit allies to be found there.

More subtly, within the Wirococha is another egg: Pachamama, the world as we perceive it. Pachamama is the most tangible of energies because it is the one we belong to, the one we recognize, and the one most manifest. It is soul in its bluntest form: physical reality and its spiritual or energetic shadow. This reality is the point at which we enter San Pedro ceremonies so we can be blasted free of form and enter the next level of being: the realms where our healing takes place.

Andean healing practices are addressed first to Pachamama in the hope that they will make their way through the power of prayer and vision to the ultimate realms of the intangible, where true blessings are found.

In fact, since Andean healing does not really embrace the concepts of duality and separation, its philosophy of healing is even simpler than this because a change at the individual level of Pachamama also changes, in some small way, the nature of Wirococha and Jatun. As our energies become clearer and more pure, God is better able to recognize us, or perhaps we become more "God-like" ourselves, in a way similar to that proposed by the religious philosopher Teilhard de Chardin, where we evolve through our actions until we merge once again with "the Godhead."

Within Pachamama there are three levels that broadly correspond to the shamanic cosmology of the "three worlds" (upper, middle, and lower) that provide a means of understanding the universe for many traditional cultures.

In the Andes they are known as Ukupacha (lower world), Hanaqpacha (upper or divine world), and Kaypacha (the middle world). The latter includes physical reality as we know it and its spiritual counterpart so that every material thing has its energetic parallel or, as science now tells us, is made up of energy and has very little that is actually solid about it.

In Andean psychology these three realms are also planes or states of consciousness, in some ways similar to Freud's notion of the makeup of the psyche. The first, Ukupacha, in Freudian terms, would correspond to the id, the place of primal experience and the shadow self where our instincts, intuitions, and fears hold sway. The second, Hanaqpacha, is the superego, the moral or divine self that drives us to act in an ethical and compassionate way toward ourselves and the world we live in. The last, Kaypacha, is the ego, the moderator between the two that enables us to make choices so we can operate effectively in the world.

During San Pedro ceremonies, within this model of understanding, the shaman and/or the spirit of the plant leads the patient from Kaypacha (ego)—a situation that is not working for him because of his unbalanced interactions with the spiritual and material forces in his life—to Hanaqpacha (superego), the transcendent plane where the human spirit meets the more universal forces and subtle energies that surround him. These energies can then be experienced, directed, and integrated so they play a more central role in his life, and he can move from denser ego-led concerns to a lighter and more expansive way of being.

In order to reach this state, however, it is often necessary for the patient to descend into the more shadowy world of Ukupacha (the id), because it is here that he can unveil and best explore the hidden forces of his unconscious and see the beliefs, patterns, and complexes that are driving his behavior and leading to unhealthy outcomes.

You will see this journey described in most of the accounts in this book by those people who have been healed by San Pedro. In one way or another all of them were led by the spirit of the cactus out of the mundane world to a deeper understanding of their thoughts, beliefs, life stories, causes, and effects until they arrived in a new world, which was touched by God. At the end of it they felt healed and at peace.

A similar journey taken by a more conventional Western route might have meant years of psychotherapy or spiritual study to arrive at the same place: the knowledge that pain, fear, anger, and sadness all stem from a feeling of being alone and that our salvation comes from opening our hearts and reaching out to the people and the spirit around us, because they are we; I am That.

This understanding of the human condition is fundamental to Andean shamanism, which is sometimes called "the path of the heart" and is guided by the desire to find beauty in life moment by moment. The principles on which it is based are as follows:

Munay: "Doing the little things" with compassionate and loving intent so that every day is infused with a sense of beauty and when we close our eyes at night we can rest in the knowledge that as far as we were able and aware we hurt no one by our actions, including ourselves.

Yachay: An informed wisdom that is greater and deeper than simple "knowledge." The former is provided by spirit while the latter is a function of the more limited rational mind that is led by ego, habit, and shadow. Yachay is one of the gifts of San Pedro that helps us to understand the truths of our lives at a more soulful level and—if we choose—to live in beauty.

Llankay: Taking appropriate, wise, and compassionate actions so we build a soul that is powerful and light. In this way we also become good ancestors and helpful spirits when we move on from this world, and the energy we leave behind is healing in itself—a "good wind"—even if it is only a beautiful memory for our lovers and the knowledge that they were loved. In this way the world becomes less fearful and more loving for us all.

Kawsay: Respect for all life in the awareness that we are connected, one, and part of the whole or, in the words of Henri Michaux, that we are all just "a passage in time." Knowing this, we understand the fragility of our condition and the need for love and forgiveness because whatever we do in the world or to others we also do to ourselves.

Ayni: Perhaps the best-known and most important of Andean principles, ayni is the way of reciprocity, a form of giving without the desire to receive in return but in the awareness that we *will* be rewarded for our actions as the energy they create continues to circulate. Again, in the words of Michaux, it is the realization that "one is nothing but oneself" and at the same time, everything: part of a shared fate.

THE ORIGIN OF DISEASE IS SPIRITUAL

In this way, according to curanderismo, disease is not just caused by physical processes but by social, psychological, emotional, and spiritual factors too. Thus, "there is a natural form of diabetes and a form caused by a supernatural agent, such as a *brujo* (witch or sorcerer). The same is true for alcoholism, cancer, and so on." Curanderos therefore "manipulate the supernatural world as well as the physical world" to effect their cures and "on the spiritual level, illness can be caused, diagnosed, and cured by spiritual forces called *corrientes espirituales* (spiritual currents)."[6]

Bilis (rage) is one example of a disease that is both physical and spiritual in nature. It arises from emotional causes and is common in people who feel themselves wronged by another and so excluded from justice that they carry their anger like an energy within them, which is strong enough to lead to stomach upsets or ulcers unless it is released. Their burning desire is for the wrongs they have suffered to be recompensed and while they are not, a churning acidity is felt in their guts—an impotent or repressed anger at wrongs that go unavenged.

Empacho and *pulsario* are similar conditions that also result from emotional causes. Both are blockages of energy at the top of the stomach that prevent its normal function and cause digestive disorders. Shamans describe such conditions as a form of crystallized pain, sorrow, or anger. They are more frequently diagnosed in women and may be related to hormonal imbalances, but men can experience them, too. Symptoms include restlessness, anxiety, and irritability.

Illnesses in both sexes and especially in children can also arise from *mal aire*. This is literally "bad air" although it refers more to a "bad atmosphere" surrounding an individual or family. Children are particularly susceptible as they are more sensitive to moods and environments. It can result in colds, shaking, and earaches, all of which may have a symbolic meaning as well as a physical presence (earache for example might result from a desire not to hear what is being said to, or around, the child).

Problems arising from social factors include *envidia,* "envy or jealousy," such as when a neighbor desires what is yours or resents you for your success. Instead of seeing you as an inspiration and working to achieve the same things themselves, they direct an unhealthy energy toward you and this becomes a form of spirit intrusion, which works away at your soul. *Mal puesto* (hexing or cursing) and mal d'ojo (the evil eye: staring intently with the desire to harm) are related to envidia and can result in vomiting, diarrhea, fever, insomnia, and depression in the person who receives the attack.

A more spiritual problem can also arise, known as mal suerte or saladera, "bad luck," where the sufferer's energy becomes so low or they become so disheartened that they cannot achieve anything positive. A related condition more common in the Amazon is *daño* (harm), a magical illness that is often sent by a sorcerer working on behalf of a client and is, therefore, a serious attack. Its symptoms include pain, fatigue, problems with breathing, and, over time, the appearance of tumors or other diseases that take physical forms in the body. Daño must be treated magically to remove the spiritual poison or *virote*—the "evil thorn" or dart—that has been sent to the sufferer and return it to its source.

Susto is soul loss: a condition where we lose part of our spirit or our energy becomes so blocked and depleted that we no longer have access to our full power or to aspects of ourselves that we need for our well-being and to get on with our lives. It may arise from shock, trauma, abuse, or injustice, and its symptoms can include nervous disorders, feelings of fear and panic, loss of appetite and energy, lack of trust in or engagement with the world, or a general malaise and decline as if from a broken heart.

Jean-Pierre Chaumeil makes an interesting observation about illnesses like these in his work, "Varieties of Amazonian Shamanism."[7] In the jungle traditions of the ayahuasca shaman, he says, diseases are more often diagnosed as having been sent to the sufferer by a neighbor or sorcerer (as in cases of daño). The cure normally involves removing the problem and returning its energy with full force to whoever has sent it. In the modern urban setting and in the Andes where San Pedro is the medicine of choice, such approaches have become softened—or in Chaumeil's word, "moralized"—so that the healer is more inclined to locate the source of suffering not wholly in the spirit world or with an external enemy but within the patient himself.

This is congruent with the teachings of San Pedro: we must not blame others for what they have done, but face ourselves and our responsibilities so we find our salvation within—because that is where true healing lies. By doing so we understand the connections between us and the imbalances that have led to our illnesses, and we find that these often relate to some moral or social transgression on our parts as well, which has caused our problems or at least contributed to them through a chain of events that gave rise to a negative energy, which caused our disease. Thus, even if the illness has been deliberately wished on us by a rival, we as sufferers must ask ourselves honestly what we have done to provoke this attack; we are not absolved of all accountability just because we are victims, but are part of the web of interactions that led to it.

Mal aire is an example of this. It is commonly diagnosed as arising from a bad atmosphere in a home, so it is not an entirely spiritual problem but also relates to the social and psychological makeup of the people who live in that household. If they were happy and powerful they would not attract such an intrusive force. So the questions arise: What is the true nature of the problem? Why is there discord in the home? And what, practically, can be done to resolve this? The onus is also on the patient to identify and correct whatever he has been doing to weaken his spirit and put himself at risk. By taking responsibility for his illness he also gives himself the power to heal it.

It could be argued in view of this that Andean curanderismo is more sophisticated than jungle medicine. It does not involve just one cause and effect or one action and counteraction, but necessitates a deeper examination of our psychology, including our morals and motivations, behavior and underlying beliefs. In this way we come to understand the wider pattern of our interactions and the subtle flows of energy that influence our lives. The San Pedro shaman, then, as well as being a plant alchemist and spiritual expert often becomes a sort of psychologist, priest, confessor, or therapist who can help us see our behavior and how it fits into the wider universe.

THE PROCESS OF HEALING

The spiritual cosmology of the Andean healer is one where invisible forces are born from unseen worlds that exist both within and without us. These forces, although immaterial, can affect us not only emotionally but physically and bring us good fortune or ill health depending on our alignment to and relationship with them. The work of the curandero is to restore the patient to balance so he is in harmonious standing to these powers and not acting against them or allowing them to overwhelm him.

To create this necessary balance three things are important:

1. Faith. Convincing the patient that a cure is possible and enlisting his help to find it in the diagnosis and treatment that follows. This may require a confessional or psychotherapeutic approach on the part of the healer to discover what the patient has done to contribute to his own ill health, a process that in curanderismo is known as *placitas,* "a heart-to-heart, soul-to-soul discussion" in the words of curandera Elena Avila.[8] Once the patient's role is understood, part of the cure may then be for him to make amends in a practical way to those he has offended—even if they have also done him harm. In this way balance is at least restored between the patient and the cosmic forces that act upon him,

and he can also let go of the event itself and the energy of it within him. He can know that he has "done his part" and is not resisting or holding on to things from the past but allowing the energy of God to flow more freely into the present.

2. Hope. Persuading the patient that his mind, spirit, and other resources are powerful and, with the help of the curandero, his greatest assets for dealing effectively with his problems, that "one frightens oneself" or "the mind makes one fly," as Eduardo Calderon put it.[9] Knowing this, the patient is empowered and has a new and vital hope that things can change for the better, and, as psychotherapists like Viktor Frankl have found, hope is the most powerful medicine of all.[10]

3. Love. Enabling the patient to become more aware of the forces around him, his relationship and responsibility toward them, to others, and to himself so that continuing good health is assured. And through it all, to understand that he is loved by God and never beyond redemption or well-being.

San Pedro is of help in all of these areas but it has special significance in the latter for, as David Luke says in chapter 6, there is research to suggest that the mescaline cactus gives us access to areas of our brains that we do not ordinarily use, but that when activated allow us to perceive the entire cosmic order and experience ourselves within it.

More than this, however, as La Gringa continually makes clear, San Pedro is "the medicine of love," so what better means could there be for us to realize how loved we are and, no matter what we have done or what has been done to us, how precious we remain in the eyes of God?

In this section we hear from three San Pedro shamans about their healing work and see how some of these principles are enacted in the real world of ceremony and curanderismo.

NOTES

1. Ross Heaven, *The Journey to You* (New York: Bantam, 2001), for more on the archaic nature of shamanism and the artifacts and cave art that prove its long-standing historical roots.

2. Ibid., for a full discussion of the holographic universe concept and how it relates to shamanism.

3. John G. Neihardt, *Black Elk Speaks: Being the Life Story of a Holy Man of the Oglala Sioux,* annotated edition (New York: State University of New York Press, 2008).

4. Mircea Eliade, *Shamanism: Archaic Techniques of Ecstasy* (Princeton: Princeton University Press, 2004).

5. For an interesting independent documentary on curanderismo in northwest Peru, which features Julia Calderon, visit http://mesaworks.com/resources/ youtubevideos.html (Munay Productions). Current as of July 21, 2011.

6. Robert T. Trotter and Juan Antonio Chavira, *Curanderismo: Mexican American Folk Healing* (Athens, Ga.: University of Georgia Press, 1997).

7. Jean-Pierre Chaumeil, "Varieties of Amazonian Shamanism. Shamans and Shamanisms: On the Threshold of the Next Millennium," *Diogenes* (Summer 1992, no. 158).

8. Elena Avila, *Woman Who Glows in the Dark: A Curandera Reveals Traditional Aztec Secrets of Physical and Spiritual Health* (New York: Tarcher, 2000).

9. Eduardo Calderon, Richard Cowan, Douglas Sharon, and F. Kaye Sharon, *Eduardo El Curandero: The Words of a Peruvian Healer* (Berkeley: North Atlantic Books, 1982).

10. Viktor Frankl, *Man's Search for Meaning* (Boston: Beacon Press, 2006).

2

Traditions of San Pedro Healing: Ancient and Modern

An Interview with Rubén Orellana

Ross Heaven and La Gringa

Rubén Orellana, Ph.D., is an expert on the historical and contemporary aspects of San Pedro shamanism and healing in Peru. As well as his academic credentials as a historian, he was for many years curator of the Machu Picchu sacred site and is a practicing shaman himself.

In this interview Orellana discusses the role of San Pedro in the ancient and modern world, the role of the healer, and the nature of healing itself. He also touches on contemporary trends and practices such as the "globalization" or standardization of ceremonial healing and the impact of these movements for Peruvian and Western healing and culture.

Thank you for talking to us, Rubén. First, can you tell us a little about yourself? You are a shaman—a healer who works with San Pedro—but you are also a successful academic. How did these two worlds meet?

Orellana: I studied in the 1970s at the University of Cusco, majoring in chemistry and then in social sciences, anthropology, psychology, philosophy, and archaeology.

After I graduated I began work in 1976 with a team of archaeologists and anthropologists at the national park of Machu Picchu. My first job there was to find the original name of the place, a mission in which we succeeded. I was also employed to discover new archaeological sites in this area. In 1986 we found forty-four new sites at the sanctuary and in 1989 we produced the seminal report on its history. After thirty years of working here I now know exactly what Machu Picchu is and what its purpose was. It is very different from what people think.

The sanctuary is a very special place, and I had beautiful spiritual experiences during my time there. The first gift I was given by Pachamama was when I was able to connect with the sanctuary and as a result I was told about the forty-four new sites that I discovered. I was working in ceremony there and images of these sacred places appeared in my visions and called to me. They gave me clear directions for finding them.

I have had many other experiences there, too, but they are personal and I must keep them to myself in case others should read about them and try to emulate my findings and endanger the place.

Alongside my work as an archaeologist and historian I am a healer. I was trained in these arts since I was a young boy but I do not call myself a shaman as this is not a Quechua word but one that comes from the Tungus people of Russia. I studied with the healers of the Andes who have their own tradition from Incan and pre-Incan times. In Quechua *paqo* is the name of the healer.

This work is a spiritual path, which I chose to follow, so I could be of service to others. Nobody pushed me into it. I work with local people but also with those from other countries. I make no distinction between them because my job is to work with human beings—people who need help and who give me responsibility for their healing.

When these people come to me I first spend time with them to find out what they want and need. There is a big difference between the two! I give people what they *need* because what they want may be irrelevant to their healing or may even be harmful to them. It might in fact be the cause of their problems—like *envidia,* jealousy of others and what they have, a desire that can cause problems of its own.*

When we talk about my career at Machu Picchu and my calling as a healer we are speaking of two different things. To be a healer is a vocation of the heart. To be an academic is a way that I play my part in society. What I have discovered through archaeology and anthropology though has supported what I know as a healer and both paths have led me into what you call shamanism. My university training also helps me to translate the Andean traditions so they can be understood by Western society and in this way to preserve the wisdom of my land.

Who did you train with as a healer, and what did it involve?

Orellana: I started with my mentor when I had seven years of age, forty-nine years ago. But even now I am still at the beginning because there is so much to know.

Every day I learn something new about San Pedro and about spirit and healing and I connect with my intuition a little more. In this way a healer can never really finish his training because every client is unique. There is no standard approach and no textbook to consult because we are dealing with individual emotions and thoughts, so every person is different.

I have worked in ceremonies for many years and it is difficult to

---

Envidia—or envy—is regarded in Peru as one of the most common causes of disease. Those affected by it may become so overwhelmed by jealousy of another person's looks, good fortune, or belongings that they lose their mental or emotional balance and become ill. The disease may express itself as rage, which, if repressed, can give rise to a blockage in the digestive system and to excess bile and acidity in the stomach. If expressed it may manifest instead as *mal d'ojo*—the evil eye—where the person affected by envidia directs negative energy with such force toward someone they resent that this can lead to suffering and illness for the one who receives it. Many homes in Peru have marigolds outside their doors as these flowers are said to absorb and diffuse the harmful energies of the evil eye. —R.H.

know how many I have done—many hundreds I know—but healing with San Pedro is not about numbers in any case. It is not about linear time; it is about cycles.

Do you now have apprentices of your own?

Orellana: *Apprentice* is not a word I use but I have many brothers and sisters who I share this tradition with. Most are women because females are more connected to energy, to intuition, and have greater balance between the right and left hemispheres of their brains. There are also some exceptional men. But yes, I have brothers and sisters from Peru and many other countries.

A lot of people these days would like to become healers themselves—especially Westerners it seems. What would an apprenticeship with you involve? How long would it take?

Orellana: I cannot say that it will take so many weeks or months or years to become a healer. Linear time does not apply with San Pedro or with healing. After five decades as a healer I am still learning myself.

Today we want definitions and definite answers: How long will it take? What will it cost? What is our schedule? We love the instant—instant coffee, instant healing, instant visions . . . instant shaman! But that is not the way in our tradition.

If I take you as an apprentice I must first look deeply into your mind, your heart, and your soul because all I have is you. Then I start to work with you, and as your knowledge deepens there may also come a time when you feel that I have abandoned you because the answers do not come fast enough for you or because information is not passed to you exactly when you think you must have it. I have not abandoned you; it is simply that you need to go inside yourself for a while to understand your part in this world then come back to me when you are ready and we begin again.

And so receiving this knowledge is a cycle. It is not linear but requires that you do your own processing, however long that takes. For some it is a short while, for others it may take years, so there is no way for me to say, "Okay, I will train you for six months or two months or one year and after this you will be a shaman!" It depends on you. What is always true though is that the person who has chosen this path must believe in the cycles of times not in calendars and the illusions of linear time.

The student must also be clear about what apprenticeship means. A lot of people want "initiation" into Andean medicine but this is an ill-defined word. For Westerners it usually means an ending or an accomplishment: to be "an initiate." In my tradition the term *initiation* simply does not exist but even its true meaning in the West is "a beginning," and this beginning never really ends because every day you are alive you learn a little more.

Apprenticeship is not just about the accumulation of knowledge, however, but the achievement of wisdom. Knowledge may come easily to you so you may learn how to perform a particular ceremony in just a few days for example but wisdom—understanding what the rituals mean, the forces they invoke, and when to use these processes—might take you a lifetime.

It is important for people to know, as well, that becoming a shaman does not make you a god or a guru, only a healer, so the apprenticeship must be entered into with the right spirit and not from a place of ego.

In the Quechua tradition, as with many others, we have two types of shaman: those who practice black magic and those who practice white magic. These are just people who have chosen a particular path and who use the same forces but in different ways. Dark and light exist within all of us because we are human beings. Sometimes we are sober, sometimes we drink, sometimes we are lazy, sometimes we work, sometimes we are sad, sometimes we are happy, sometimes we are horny, sometimes we cry. Whatever. We are human. The intention of the healer is to do his best for people while acknowledging the light and the darkness—the humanity—within all of us, including himself, and denying nothing, for to repress it is to give it power.

In the study of healing there are also many practical things to learn—about the conditions of human beings, the reason for those conditions, and the healing provided by plants and other medicines.

Some plants must be treated with caution for example. Tóe is one such.* It is a plant that is not for everybody. Just like penicillin, which is one of the most powerful medicines of the Western world, some people may have a reaction to it according to their DNA.

For Western people my recommendation is not to ingest tóe because it contains atropine and many people are allergic to this. That is why some Westerners who drink ayahuasca, which contains tóe, do not have a nice journey but find themselves attacked by demons. It is because of the atropine in the tóe, which means they do not receive enough oxygen to their brains.

With Westerners I never work with tóe. Even with the people of Lima I will not use it because they have lost some of their native sense and natural reactions due to the effects of "civilization" and city living. With jungle people, however, I have no problems in using tóe.

We are all people, yes, and in some ways we are all the same but we have different information in our DNA.

In the same way we have seventy-nine varieties of San Pedro and I also know two hundred and fourteen ways to cook ayahuasca. Which is chosen and the methods I use vary according to the needs of the

---

*Tóe (*Brugmansia suaveolens*)—also known as *floripondio, maikoa* (Jivaro), *chuchupanda* (Amahuaca), *aiipa* (Amarakaeri), *kanachiari* (Shipibo-Conibo), and by many other names—is part of the *Solanaceae* family. Its principal biochemicals are the tropane alkaloids hyoscyamine, atropine, and scopolamine. The plant is used in magical practices for shamanic flight, visionary journeys, shape-shifting, and divination by *curanderos* (healers) and *brujos* (witches). In the Andes it is commonly taken as an infusion of pulverized seeds, while in the Amazon leaves and/or flowers are more usually added to ayahuasca (*Banisteriopsis caapi*) to fortify the visionary effects of the "vine of souls." Tóe intoxication is marked by frenzied initial effects followed by deep sleep in which visions occur that enable the shamans who drink it to diagnose the origin and nature of disease, to communicate with ancestral spirits, and to divine the future. —R.H.

patient and what I sense about the interactions between the plant and the condition of the client, so even this is not simple knowledge. It is very important for healers to know and appreciate these things and to understand the differences in people and the different uses of plants.

How do you prepare San Pedro and teach others to make it?

Orellana: How I cook San Pedro is on an esoteric level; it is not a formula that can just be passed on or written down on a page, nor is it a simple recipe that you might find on the Internet!

"Esoteric" means that you must be a serious student of San Pedro and form your own relationship with it because there is no standard way to prepare it. You need to be ready for it and want to know more; then the medicine will itself teach you all that you need to know. This is what I tell my students. It is not that I want to keep secrets from them; it is simply that the medicine speaks for itself.

There is a great mystery about San Pedro and its origins just as there is with ayahuasca. It seems strange after all that anyone in ancient history would cut down a cactus and brew it for its effects. How did they even know it would have effects or what those effects would be . . . or how to prepare it in the first place?

Because of this mystery we cannot say where our healing tradition began or who the first shaman was or even, in linear time, when San Pedro first spoke to us. But it is clear that San Pedro itself called that first healer and passed on its secrets and in the same way each person who drinks it must come to San Pedro alone and learn its language, develop a personal relationship with it, and find a way to befriend the plant. It will then teach them and gradually reveal its mysteries. Then when the healer finally connects with the wisdom of this beautiful medicine is the moment when they really know truth.

Can you give an example of how San Pedro might speak to a healer?

Orellana: Yes, one example is that when I cook San Pedro I often see images in the brew of the people who will come to drink it. I see in the liquid the parts of their bodies where healing is needed, like the heart or the kidneys. Or maybe the messages are more symbolic and concern a feeling or state of mind. In this way I receive premonitions of who will drink, and the particular conditions they have. This is normal and one of the ways that the plant might speak with us. As people develop their own connections with San Pedro and learn its secret language they will also see these things, and it helps them to prepare as healers.

For this reason whenever I cook any medicine—not only San Pedro—I carefully watch the brew. When you do this you also send energy to it so you empower the medicine with your intention and tell it what you want from it so it can learn from you too. I always cook fresh medicine for each patient—I do not have bottles on my shelves like a pharmacy—so the thoughts that I send are uniquely about that person and the healing they need and the plants can begin their work as soon as they receive my intentions. They tune in to the patient and begin the process of arranging their qualities and powers in accordance with that person's needs.

So a lot of information appears even in the cooking pot and this helps me as a healer. The energy of intent is a very powerful force, and all healers must master it because the plants respond to it in their own language.

How frequently do you hold ceremonies and what conditions might you treat?

Orellana: I provide ceremonies whenever they are needed so there is no rule to it. I know some healers say that ceremonies should only be held on certain days like Tuesday or Friday because those are when San Pedro works best and when the powers of the fates are strongest, but that is to forget the most fundamental teaching of San Pedro: that there is no such thing as time! Linear time does not exist so there is no calendar, no special days of the week—no weeks!

Instead we should follow natural cycles. If someone has a very grave problem and I need to work deeply with them for example then I will hold a ceremony at the full moon because the energy then is very high.

What conditions do I treat? Any may be possible. No matter what the problems of a particular client, however, most diseases are psychosomatic in origin because when people break the balance of their emotions their immunological systems are always affected and in this way they lose power so the body will accept any disease. The purpose of ceremony is to strengthen the emotions and bring the patient back to equilibrium as well as empowering the body with medicine plants.

To be a healer I must also put myself in the place of the patient, so I become in a sense the person who needs my help. One example is a man who comes to me to cure his alcoholism. The solution is not to say, "Well okay then, don't drink"; it is for that person to fully accept that they are alcoholic and acknowledge the problems it is causing in their life. The next step is to identify the true cause of this disease and find healing for that.

I know healers who will simply give a patient like this plants and herbs that make him sick if he should drink alcohol, assuming he will therefore avoid it. But this does not solve the problem. Instead he may just stop taking the herbs if the spirit of alcohol is stronger than his desire to be well.

I put myself in the position of the alcoholic to see what has caused his condition because such diseases are a response to circumstances. A healer must have empathy in this way and be clear about the responsibilities that are involved in healing.

You also use San Pedro to heal conditions that Western medicine finds difficult to cure, like cancer. If disease is a response to circumstances why do people get sick with conditions like cancer and how can they heal it?

Orellana: One of the big problems for modern society is stress. It has been there from the beginning of course but our ancestors had rituals to release it. In today's world nobody is doing that. You take a pill or you drink alcohol or take drugs and you think this solves the problem but it does not release the energy of stress; it merely suppresses it so it stays with you, hidden by the effects of the drugs or the alcohol you've consumed.

The pH levels of your body start to change because of the stress itself and the "cures" you have taken for it, and so you become more acid. As a result your body will automatically accept any disease.

When you use alkaline to restore the body's natural pH it makes a big difference because then it will start to heal itself. So the idea with San Pedro is not really to provide a "miracle cure" but to create balance in the body and emotions and in this way cancer and many other diseases will start to disappear.

Just to be clear, are you saying that San Pedro heals because it contains chemicals that change the pH of the body—or that it de-stresses and relaxes you so the body functions differently and releases its own chemicals, which will restore the natural pH balance?

Orellana: Both! First of all the medicine itself switches the body to alkaline. Secondly, San Pedro relaxes you and brings new understanding of your problems so you have a resolution in mind. For both of these reasons your body changes and becomes more alkaline.

San Pedro also teaches you why your problems exist. What I mean by this is that there is no "cancer" in itself—or "diabetes" or "heart attack." All of these conditions are messages from the body about the true origins of the problem and by-products of an underlying mood or state of mind that I am calling stress. Once you know what is really wrong the problem is more easily solved and the body can return to balance and health.

More importantly, San Pedro releases the stress itself so you don't really need to do anything but accept its healing and the information it gives you.

Medicine ceremonies are not like Western psychoanalysis because San Pedro does not show you how to control stress or find a way to cope with it. Instead it removes the stress so you don't have that problem anymore. The information it provides you with is about how to stay free of stress by bringing your life back into balance.

With San Pedro you can no longer lie to yourself. That is one of the great differences between medicine and psychoanalysis.

We've used the example of cancer but you also mentioned heart problems. Can you say something about conditions like these?

Orellana: When I see people with heart conditions I first explain to them about the nature of time: the fact that a journey begins for us on the day we are born and so starts our work to die well. That is the truth, and it is important for all of us to understand that we are not here for eternity. This is the first step toward healing and the appreciation of our lives.

According to the person I am working with and the true nature and origins of their disease I will then select the methods of healing and the plants most appropriate for them. Nowadays San Pedro and ayahuasca are very popular but we have more than seventy plants that can help with conditions like this.

Can you explain the elements of the *mesa* you use during healing ceremonies?*[1]

---

*The *mesa* is both the altar, or sacred space, of the shaman and his "work station" containing the healing tools of his profession. Many mesas have three defined areas or "fields"—the "dark" field where the origins of disease may be determined, the "light" where healing may be found and positive energy restored, and the center, which is the place of harmony and balance and symbolically the bridge, which must be crossed between ill health and well-being. These different fields also represent what Orellana calls "the three worlds," which compose the cosmological map used by shamans during their flight to other realms. —R.H.

Orellana: The first rule of shamanism, of Andean healing—and therefore of mesa work—is that there are no rules.

The mesa is the personal altar of the healer; the place where he stores his power. In our tradition there is not just one layout for the mesa or a standard series of objects or elements, which must always be used, since all healers work in different ways.

On my mesa I have a clear division between the left and the right sides—the female and the male—and between the three worlds: the upper world, this world, and the internal world.* I also work with the four elements of wind, water, earth, and fire. The objects or *artes*† on my mesa reflect these allies and the powers they contain. This is my personal choice, and other healers may take a different approach. That is allowable!

Along with San Pedro I also work with tobacco, which connects me to the element of fire, and I use a lot of perfumes and aromas because these start to change the way we are thinking so that bad ideas can be transformed

---

*This notion of the "three worlds: the upper world, this world, and the internal world" corresponds broadly to (but differs slightly from) the typical cosmology of the shaman, which provides the map of the spiritual otherworld traversed by healers of many traditions. The three realms of spirit are depicted by these shamans as forming a circle containing the World Tree or *axis mundi* (the center of all things) and divided into three levels: what the anthropologist Michael Harner has called the upper, middle, and lower worlds. The former is the source of angelic, philosophical, or "higher" powers, while the latter is the home of elemental and animal powers. The middle world, meanwhile, is the spiritual equivalent of mundane reality, the place of the ancestors and the realm of ideas and energies, which can be manifested through our thoughts and actions. —R.H.

†*Artes* (or arts) are the power objects or tools used by Andean healers. As Orellana explains, they may include swords (which are typically employed as weapons against negative forces and to cut through black magic); *chonta* staffs (which might be run over the body to absorb ill health or cause the flow of useful energy); and crystals, rocks, and herbs (for grounding or, in the case of crystals, "illuminating" a patient and to summon the forces of healing). Others may appear more bizarre, such as car headlights (for "light") or animal fetuses (for "new beginnings and growth"), but all have a symbolic and spiritual purpose as containers of power and representations of healing. Since the arrival of the Spanish in Peru it is also common to see Catholic symbols like crosses and rosaries used on mesas. —R.H.

and healing can follow.*[2] The intention of these perfumes and of healing in general is to play with the brain† because our first enemy and our first blockage to healing is usually our brains. Unhealthy thoughts or beliefs lead to disease since illness arises from the mind as much as the body.‡

---

*The olfactory is one of our most developed and ancient senses, and science has shown that aromas and scents can have a subtle but profound effect on our feelings and moods. In Peru specialist shamans called *perfumeros* use these qualities to change states of mind and create good health by blending flowers and herbs to make perfumes and potions, which are said to be so strong that they can control the fates as well as human behavior—such as the *pusanga* (the so-called "love medicine of the Amazon"), which can cause someone to fall madly in love with the person who wears it or attract financial success and good fortune when sprayed in business premises. —R.H.

†The idea of "playing" with the brain, with the health of a patient, and with universal forces is a common one in the Andes—as in this incantation about hummingbirds (an affectionate term for San Pedro and the shamans who use it to heal) by the Peruvian healer Eduardo Calderon:

> *Los chupaflores juntan*
> The hummingbirds gather
> *Todos los dolores malos y enfermedades*
> All the bad pains and sicknesses
> *Juegan con sus encantos*
> They play with their enchantments

The shamanic understanding behind the use of the word *play* is that good and bad health, luck, or ill fortune (and indeed the whole of human existence) are the result of an interplay of forces, some seen and some unseen, that determine our fates and that these forces can be controlled by the will of the shaman and the use of magical practices. It is also a reminder to both healer and patient that life and health, while serious, should not be solemn matters. —R.H.

‡"Illness begins in the mind." One of the common notions in the Andes is that of good and bad "ideas." The concept really refers to what we might call thoughtforms so that when someone says, for example, that you have "good ideas" they do not mean that you are a creative genius as we might use the term in the West, but that your thoughts (which in turn generate your actions and so manifest reality) are in alignment with the truth and goodness that is at the heart of existence. Conversely, if you are said to have "bad ideas" it means that you are in some way out of balance with the way things really are and may, therefore, be inviting disease into your life. Shamans also talk about good and bad "winds." These are an accumulation of thoughts and energies, which are attracted to each other because they share a common affinity. The energies of many people having positive and uplifting thoughts can create a good wind, for example, while negative ideas can also band together to form a bad wind, which becomes a sentient force that circulates in the world bringing misfortune and illness. The concept is not dissimilar to Jung's notion of the collective unconscious. —R.H.

The tools of the mesa are ways of summoning power in order to change the mind.

One of the reasons I asked about the mesa is because I have seen a lot of altars with swords and sticks[3] (chonta) and other "obviously powerful" symbols.* Do you use chonta and swords? Are they important?

Orellana: All of the elements we use in ceremony have a purpose and it is simply this: they are containers of energy. Some people have chosen to work with chonta. This is a wood of the jungle that is rich in silica crystals. Some also work with swords, tobacco, Florida water,† and other objects. We have a civilization and healing approach that is twenty thousand years old, and many different races like the Incas and the Spanish have been part of our evolution. Each added something of themselves to the way that healing is done and to the elements that might, therefore, appear on an altar.

Each of these elements holds a very different energy even if they appear the same, so every sword or stick or crystal on every altar is different, just as Titicaca Lake in Peru and Titicaca Lake in Bolivia are both composed of the same water but contain different powers because each part of the lake has its own unique qualities. What is most important, then, when working with the mesa is not the items on it or how many are there but the special connection you have to each one. Your mesa may feature the *singado,* the *seguro,* or

---

*Juan Navarro is another of the San Pedro shamans I have worked with. On his mesa Navarro has more than a hundred different *artes* including several staffs, chonta, swords, and metal bars, as well as Catholic artifacts and other items of power. —R.H.

†Florida water—or *agua florida*—is a cologne made from flowers and herbs with magical qualities to attract good fortune, dispel evil spirits, or protect against disease. Many different varieties can be found in Peru, such as *rosa* (rose), *ruda* (rue), and *clavelles* (carnations), each with its own spiritual purpose. In ceremonies these perfumes may be rubbed on the body or sprayed on participants to "flourish" them and balance the energies of the body. —R.H.

tobacco*⁴ . . . maybe a thousand different elements . . . but it is your relationship to each and the way you employ their energies not the objects that matter.

I know some people who say, "This—and only this—is the mesa of the Andes"—but what part of the Andes do they even mean? It is not the same throughout, just like the people of Titicaca Lake and the people of Cusco are different.

I use the elements of the jungle and the elements of the mountains and the coast but does this make my mesa more powerful? No. It is the way I use these things that is important. I know very good healers who use only three elements on their altars, and some people might look at this and say, "This guy only has three elements; he's not powerful," but they would be mistaken because those are the most powerful shamans.

So what I am saying is that it doesn't matter what you use or whether you have swords or chonta or little at all as long as you have a strong connection to each and it works with you as your ally. The element is only the bridge to the spirit, which we use to move energy.

The Huaringas, the lakes in the north of Peru in the highlands of Piura, are also seen by many as a special place, and they have their own mythology among those who want to include their waters on their mesas. But again it is not only the Huaringas that contain this power of healing. The Huaringas are important because they are sacred waters, which can be used in cleansing, but in Cusco we have many other beautiful places where there is powerful running water, which comes from the *apus* [mountain spirits] and has special qualities of healing so you don't need to visit the Huaringas or have the water from these lakes on your mesa.

In fact so many people now visit the Huaringas to take their waters

---

Singado is a tincture of alcohol, tobacco, and honey, which is snorted into the nostrils to cleanse the body and attract good luck. The *seguro* is a combination of plants with symbolic and magical qualities, which is used as a charm, and in some applications may also act as a "friend" or counsellor for the person who owns it (see my book, *Plant Spirit Shamanism*, for more details of this). Tobacco is one of the sacred plants of Peru and used as a healer and cleanser in its own right and also as a channel for spiritual energies. —R.H.

or bathe there that the lakes themselves are losing power so it is better to look for alternative sources of healing.

As well as adopting mesa practices Westerners who want to learn Andean healing increasingly talk about initiation into "*munay ki.*"*⁵ As far as I can tell this is similar to reiki with a transmission of symbols and realignment of energy and so forth. How do you understand it from an Andean perspective? Is it important, and do you work with it?

Orellana: I don't even know it! In our tradition we don't even have this word. The Q'ero healer Manuel invented the term *munay ki* but he is now dead so he cannot speak for himself and there is no way for us to confront him. All I can say is that his own grandchildren do not know what I mean when I put the term to them. But it is easy for anybody to be guilty when he is not here to defend himself.

Since its invention the idea of munay ki has unfortunately gathered momentum and it is now a creation on the part of many people, which is destroying our tradition. I do not agree with these people. Through their pretenses they have in the past twenty years begun to ruin a healing tradition that has survived for thousands of years.

I know the Q'ero and the Andean people well because I have spent many years of my life with them and they know nothing of munay ki.

---

*Wikipedia says of the *munay ki* that it is:

A series of nine rites brought to Western society by Dr. Alberto Villoldo, a medical anthropologist who has studied the shamanic healing practices of the Amazon and Inca shamans for more than twenty-five years. Dr. Villoldo assembled the munay ki as a series of fabricated rites [that he] states are derived . . . the great initiations from the Indus Valley that were brought to the Americas by the first medicine men and women who crossed the Bering Strait from Siberia during the glacial period some 30,000 years ago and who were known as the Laika, the Earthkeepers of old. . . . Some believe it is an evolution of traditional shamanic practice while others hold it represents a "fast food" version of high commercial appeal but little value. People who have received the munay ki rites generally report satisfaction with the results. —R.H.

Traditions do change over time though and those who support munay ki have defended it on the grounds that it is an "evolution" of Andean healing. In a similar way I've also heard people say that before the Spanish came to Peru San Pedro ceremonies were different—that they were held in daylight and there was less ritual involved. Do you agree or disagree with this?

Orellana: Yes, we have the influence of the Catholic tradition for more than five hundred years and behind this the Inquisition.

There is a lot of information preserved in the documents of the Inquisition and even now in the countryside of Peru we have the oral tradition, which goes back to the beginning of time, and which tells us how ceremonies were conducted before the Catholics.

What I know from these sources is that there were two forms of ceremony. Those for healing were held at night while those in the day had the purpose of growth so that the people could connect with the energy of the universe and ask the father sun to return to their lives. That is the difference between the two.

According to these records healing ceremonies were held at night because then you do not have cognition of time and space. In daylight you know whether it is morning, afternoon, or evening because of the sun in the sky and what you can see around you, so you are still connected to the mundane world. At night we work with the penumbra, which is neither light nor dark, but the threshold between both where the nature of reality changes. It is the penumbra that allows you to truly see.

The night, you may notice, is not really dark. We think it is because we live in the light of cities but really we can see clouds and trees and animals just as we do at other times. It is the *way* that we see that changes. The penumbra allows us to go into deep meditation and we may also move backward and forward in time because time and space both open up. This helps us go deeper into healing.

Our way of healing did change as a result of the Catholics of course.

Even the name of our medicine was altered to hide the true meaning of our ceremonies from them. We gave it the name San Pedro because in English this refers to Saint Peter who has keys to the heaven, which Catholics approve of. The real name of this plant, however, is *huachuma*, which simply means "dizzy" and refers to one of its effects on human beings, although not to its most important effect of healing, which would still remain hidden, even if the word was translated.

We have syncretism in our ceremonies too where healers have absorbed Catholic elements into their mesas, which now feature many religious symbols, like the cross and the Madonna. We accept these symbols because there is only one creator of the universe so all of these elements contain divine energy, which helps us connect with the universal creative force.

You have said that once a person drinks San Pedro it is always in them and they will feel it working on them even if they never drink it again. What do you mean by this?

Orellana: We are talking about two different things when we speak of San Pedro. Western society puts emphasis on the chemicals it contains but its other aspect is the special energy of this plant.

The chemicals and their effects—the dizziness and dilation of your pupils and so forth—will eventually leave your body, but the energy will always stay with you, as will the wisdom of the plant, which becomes a part of your brain. The medicine wakes up your memory so you remember who you are, and this knowledge is yours for the rest of your life so you can never forget the most important truths.

Your awareness will then connect with the other experiences you have so you see the world in a different way, and through San Pedro you continue to learn and grow. That is why when people ask me how many hours they will be affected by San Pedro after they drink it I tell them it will not be hours but the rest of their lives!

Does that also mean, for example, that if you drink San Pedro and at some point in the future you have a child the effects of San Pedro will be passed on to that child?

Orellana: Not the chemical effects of course but the unique vibration and teachings of the plant, yes. Then that child will begin life with a special advantage because within them there will be a divine connection that others do not have.

This connection is a potential but it must still be activated by the child itself so in this way free will is preserved.

What do you see as the future of San Pedro? There is a lot of interest in ayahuasca these days and perhaps less so in San Pedro. Why do you think that is and do you foresee any change in this?

Orellana: First I must say that I do not agree with the globalization of these medicines. I believe that every nation and every group must find the roots of its own spirituality and work with their own medicine plants because each tribe has its own wisdom. Globalization destroys individual traditions. Tribal wisdom, however, remains.

Peru calls to many because our traditions are still alive, and we can therefore offer those who come a shortcut so they can reconnect with their spiritual selves. But they must also rediscover their own traditions in order to be truly whole.

Fortunately it is possible because on this planet we have thousands of medicine plants that can help people to heal and feel better about themselves so they find peace and freedom within their own culture. This is wisdom that should not be lost or swallowed up by globalization and the modern desire for instant fixes.

People want shortcuts because they are thinking only in linear time. We need to teach them that they can step outside of this and return to their divine origin wherever they are.

NOTES

1. There is more information on the mesa and its layout in my book, Ross Heaven, *The Hummingbird's Journey to God: Perspectives on San Pedro, the Cactus of Vision* (New York: O Books, 2009).

2. There is more information on pusanga and an interview with an Amazonian perfumero in the book by Ross Heaven and Howard G. Charing, *Plant Spirit Shamanism: Techniques for Healing the Soul* (Rochester, Vt.: Destiny Books, 2006).

3. For those interested in seeing one of these "obviously powerful" mesas there is a photograph of Navarro standing before his altar with one of his swords held aloft in front of him in Heaven and Charing, *Plant Spirit Shamanism.*

4. Ibid.

5. (Retrieved from http://en.wikipedia.org/wiki/Munay-ki. March 11, 2010). I did write to Dr. Villoldo's office for a comment on the munay ki after reading Orellana's observations of them. At the time of going to press no reply has been received.

3

San Pedro, the "Miracle Healer"

An Interview with La Gringa, an Andean San Pedro Shaman

Ross Heaven

Since 2007 I have worked extensively with La Gringa and her San Pedro. They have guided some of my deepest insights and been present during some of the greatest and lowest moments of my life. I fell in love on La Gringa's San Pedro, I married my wife to it, and I when I lost her I was able to discover and heal a number of things in myself because of it.

In a sense our lives have become intertwined, La Gringa and I. She began as my shaman, has become a friend over the years, and I now regard her as both of these as well as a mentor. It is clear that she has really done the work with San Pedro and it permeates all that she is and does. Many people remark on her compassion, her empathy, her humility and kindness, and the love that radiates from her. The most frequent word I hear used about her by others is that she is an "angel." But through our friendship I know her as a woman too, and I know that she has concerns and cares like the rest of us, that she can lack confidence at times or worry that she is not good enough or doing enough for others. It is her honesty about these things that makes her human and an example to others of how we should face our concerns and frailties: with dignity and courage.

In doing this work (on herself and for others) La Gringa has never lost faith in San Pedro, even when it has shown her things about herself and her life that she would rather not have seen; all of them, as she says, are opportunities for learning, for growth, and for improvement.

I have spoken many times with her about shamanic and spiritual matters and her guidance has always been insightful—she is helping me to become a better person—but I have only formally interviewed her twice about her ideas and practices. The first time was in 2008 (a longer interview appears in my book *The Hummingbird's Journey to God*) and the second in 2011. This article includes both of those interviews and discusses, among other things, her life, her thoughts on ceremony and San Pedro, and her ideas and observations about how San Pedro heals. What she has to say reveals again the influence of this medicine and the impact it can have on our lives.

PART ONE: THE 2008 INTERVIEW

How did you come to be involved in shamanism?

La Gringa: I first drank San Pedro in the 1990s, an experience that overturned everything I thought I knew about reality. During my visions out in the mountains I saw a stairway of light on a nearby hill and I called my shaman over to explain it. "There is nothing to explain," he shrugged. "It is a stairway of light."

"You mean you see it too?" I asked.

"Of course," he said. "Take a photograph if you don't believe it is there." I thought he was crazy. How could I photograph a vision: something that was just in my head? But I didn't want to be disrespectful so I took the picture anyway.

Later I got it developed and there it was: a stairway of light just as

I'd seen it, although it had never been there in the mountains before and you may not see it there now. I called my shaman and he came over to look at the picture although he didn't seem surprised by it. "That's what I've been trying to tell you!" he said. "These things are not just in your mind. They exist. San Pedro opens your eyes to what is real!"

San Pedro had shown me reality as it actually is and it also changed what I thought of as real. I now understood the power that human beings have to manifest anything we choose; we just have to believe we can. San Pedro gives us that belief. It shows us that we are part of everything and that nature in its true form is beautiful. It wakes us up and teaches us to be conscious of the Earth. Before San Pedro I used to walk through life and not notice it. Now I notice everything and I have a new respect for the world.

That wasn't the only "miracle" I saw that day though. My shaman was a gentle man and I felt peaceful and protected as I lay in the sun. So when I opened my eyes and saw two children looking down at me, they were so beautiful I thought they were angels. I was in awe of them and it took me some moments to realize that they were real and that they were crying and asking for help. They said their father was sick at home and they had no mother so they didn't know what to do. They were frightened that he was dying.

I went to their house with my shaman and when I saw the man I thought he was dying too. But the shaman walked calmly over to him and started to blow on the top of his head through some coca leaves he had with him. He then used a feather, running it over the sick man's head and body while he said a prayer.

As soon as that was done the man sat up and started to vomit then he immediately looked better. The shaman said he'd be fine after that and when we left the house he was already out of bed and taking care of his children.

That was my first experience of a shamanic healing and all the shaman had used was a feather and some leaves and, of course, the knowledge given to him by San Pedro. After that I knew that I wanted to work with this plant.

You trained with other shamans too. Tell us about your present teacher.

La Gringa: His name is Rubén [see chapter 2]. I met him ten years ago in a church in the Sacred Valley, quite by chance. He is a famous anthropologist who for many years ran the Machu Picchu sacred site, but he is also a shaman so he knows why and how things work from a historical and a spiritual perspective.

This training was very hard. He was not like my first shamanic teachers who were much gentler. He made me drink San Pedro twice a week for several years. Sometimes I would beg him not to have to! I'd sob and say I was too sick to drink because I just couldn't face another session. But he would say, "Good! You're sick! That—and the fact that you can't face the healing you need—is exactly why you need to drink it! Get your coat and let's go!"

At the time it was agony but now I know he was right and that drinking all that San Pedro was the best thing that could have happened to me. I saw all the bad things in my life in a new light and was able to let them go. I cleared whole lifetimes of shit in those years and I learned a lot about San Pedro and healing too.

He is a more traditional shaman, isn't he, with lots of ritual as part of his ceremonies—the *singado* and *contrachisa,* et cetera. Did he teach you those things too?

La Gringa: Oh yes. But I never felt comfortable with those rituals and Rubén agreed that I should work differently, especially as I was now healing many Westerners who didn't understand those rituals anyway. San Pedro guided me and said I should keep things simple. So now I say a prayer to open the ceremony and then as much as possible allow San Pedro to do its work without getting in its way.

I do sometimes use tobacco in ceremonies, but not the singado,* just tobacco smoke. It is good to blow the smoke over people if they are going through a tough time or have stuck energy within them. The smoke frees it up. I also use *agua florida*† to balance people's energies. Mostly I ask them to sniff it from the bottle and it helps to ground them but sometimes I spray it over them.

And of course I also use a *mesa*‡ although mine is much simpler than many others. In Peru shamans work with many different layouts of mesa but when you have your own you learn to use it in a way that suits you. It is a living thing so you develop a relationship with it. San Pedro teaches you how to use it.

The objects at the center of my mesa are shells and stones that have meaning and power for me. I arrange them in a straight line, like a spinal column with the stones as the vertebrae. This follows the notion in Peru that spiritual energy is held in the small of the back and as we advance on our paths and the plants guide us it begins to rise up the spine to the head, where it resides when we become fully conscious.§

In the Andes we have three sacred animals: the serpent, puma, and condor. The serpent represents the divine energy we hold in our spine, the puma is the body, and the condor is the awakened self: the mind that soars above the world. So my mesa is also a representation of energy flowing through us and bringing us into new consciousness.

Some shamans use *chonta*¶ and swords on their mesas as well, as protections and to change the energies of patients and heal them. I don't

---

*Tobacco leaf macerated in honey and alcohol, which many shamans ask participants to snort into their nostrils to clear negative energies and bring good luck. —R.H.
†A plant-based perfume with healing properties. —R.H.
‡A cloth altar that is laid out in a specific ritual way. —R.H.
§A concept not dissimilar to that of kundalini energy, which is believed in the Hindu tradition to reside at the base of the spine and to rise as a result of spiritual awakening, leading eventually to enlightenment as it reaches the third eye. —R.H.
¶Wooden staffs sometimes used to beat participants and move their spiritual energies around. —R.H.

because I have always known that San Pedro protects me and my participants anyway and that there is no greater or more powerful healer than
the plant itself. So why would I need to hit participants with sticks—
and interrupt their healings by doing so?

Rubén is a historian and regards my approach as a form of evolution
that gives people the healing they need through the correct ceremonies
for our times. But it is also devolution because so many rituals and
objects have been artificially added to San Pedro mesas and ceremonies
through the influence of the Spanish Catholics.

Before the Spanish came to Peru, Andeans believed in Inti, the god
of the sun, and Pachamama, the Earth, so their rituals were simpler and
needed fewer symbols, appeasements to God, or ways to keep evil at bay.
The idea of guilt and of a God who needed appeasing arrived with the
Catholics and it was they who made our ancestors change their rituals.
Before this they were more natural and flowing. So what I do may be
an evolution as Rubén calls it, but it is also a return to what was always
done. It is as if we have evolved backward rather than forward in time.

**Is your decision to hold ceremonies in the day instead of at night
part of this "backward evolution" too?**

La Gringa: Rubén holds his ceremonies at night* and that is how he
taught me, but as I grew in my understanding of San Pedro, ceremonies at night—for practical as well as spiritual reasons—became another
thing that did not work for me.

Perhaps it is to do with the Spanish again and their Catholic notions
of guilt and "suffering for our sins" that many San Pedro ceremonies
are held at night. I always found it so cold and uncomfortable that I
could never really relax enough to receive the blessings of San Pedro. I

---

*In his interview in this book, Orellana makes a distinction between nighttime ceremonies
held for healing and daytime ceremonies that encourage spiritual growth and enhance the
fertility of the land. La Gringa does not recognize this distinction and holds ceremonies in
the day that have the dual function of healing and spiritual evolution. —R.H.

mentioned this to Rubén and he understood, so he began to hold ceremonies for me during the day. Then I really noticed the difference. In daylight is where all my breakthroughs have come.

For one thing, with San Pedro you can look around you and see the beauty of the world and notice how connected you are to everything: that you are beautiful and part of a beautiful creation. You can't do that in darkness.

What people need to understand is that San Pedro is not a hallucinogen like ayahuasca, so they will never see images and pictures, and there is no point, therefore, in lying in the dark waiting for something to happen. San Pedro's teaching is visionary instead, in the revelations it brings about the natural world, and in daylight you can see that more clearly. That is why we hold our ceremonies in sunlight: because San Pedro wants it that way and that is how it was first done.

How do you prepare your San Pedro?

La Gringa: Most shamans peel and cut the cactus then boil it for between four and eight hours. They may also add alcohol and sometimes other plants or ingredients such as tobacco. I cook mine for twenty hours, so it is much stronger and also means that people are less likely to vomit when they drink it. Other San Pedro brews feel weak to me now and rarely give the same visions.

Some shamans say you don't really need visions for a healing to take place with San Pedro, but I think they are important because as well as the healing people receive they also need to know they have been healed. When the visions come they can feel it, then they understand it is real and pay attention to what they are shown. Without the visions they can't know this.

There are other things to consider when preparing San Pedro too. I only work with cactuses that have seven or nine spines because they produce the most gentle and beautiful brews. Those with six or eight spines are not so strong, while elevens and thirteens can be very intense and dark. I never use either with patients. Those with four spines are only ever used for exorcisms and the patient and healer must both drink. You don't ever want to try a San Pedro like this though. It is horrible and the visions take you straight to hell.

While the cactus is cooking we sing to it or offer prayers that it will produce good healings. Every time we stir it we offer a new prayer so maybe twenty prayers go into each bottle.

Sometimes the spirit of San Pedro shows up while we are cooking it, in patterns on the surface of the water that tell us who will be coming to drink it and why. I have seen patterns in the form of ovaries, for example, complete in every detail, or hearts enclosed by circles. Then the next day a woman has arrived for help with a fertility problem and brought with her a man whose heart was closed to her dreams. In this way San Pedro can show us what people need before they even arrive.

What healings have you witnessed?

La Gringa: One that meant a lot to me was for a woman who had always said she would never drink San Pedro and did not believe in it, so her story shows in a way that you don't even need to have faith in the plant for it to heal you—although it is better if you do.

This woman's husband had died a few years ago. He was a strong man but his disease meant that he wasted away to nothing. It took him a year to die while the woman nursed him. Then just three months later her son was murdered. He was just twenty-six. The woman was shattered. She became like the walking dead. Soon afterward she had a stroke that paralyzed her arm and from the shock of all she had been through she got diabetes as well.

Finally, despite all her reservations, she asked me if she could drink San Pedro. I gave her the tiniest amount and she lay in my arms and cried her heart out for five hours. That is a good expression for what happened actually because I had drunk San Pedro too and through its eyes I saw strands of energy coming from her heart and circling her chest and arm like a tourniquet. I began pulling them out of her and throwing them away.

The next morning was like a miracle. Her arm, which had been totally paralyzed, had regained its movement. Then when she got home she saw a specialist who tested her diabetes and that had gone too.

I asked her later about her San Pedro experience and she said she had felt a lot of pain in her heart, which is where I had also seen the energy of grief that was binding her. So as well as curing her physical problems San Pedro showed her why she had them: because of the emotional distress she had been unable to let go of.

What I have learned from San Pedro is that illness is never a "thing" that is in us; it is not "diabetes" or "a stroke." It is a belief that we carry: that we must mourn for the ones we have lost, for example, or for ourselves through a pain or disability that makes our suffering visible and "real." So illness is a thoughtform: a negative pattern we hold on to and reproduce. San Pedro not only heals us but shows us this thoughtform. Then the next time it arises we know it and can make a conscious decision to think and act differently.

The woman you described sounds like she had a "psychosomatic" [mind-body] problem, a term that has lost much of its power in the West today, so that such illnesses are often dismissed as imaginary and not real. Can you elaborate?

La Gringa: Every illness we have is psychosomatic. It may affect the body but it arises from our minds and our souls. Another woman came to me after she was diagnosed with cancer and had been receiving chemotherapy. She looked so ill that I took her in and she spent the next seven days with me. She vomited constantly. At the end of the week she realized that her doctors were not helping her and she decided to work with the plants instead. Now, through San Pedro, she is healed.

The plant again showed her why she had cancer—which no Western medicine can do—and told her she had a choice: in blunt terms that she could die or change her mind and live the life she wanted. I know that sounds easy but it really can be as simple as that. She decided not to have cancer anymore because she realized through San Pedro that life was just too precious to lose.

That sounds like soul retrieval in a way, but instead of the shaman performing it the plant does it for them.

La Gringa: That's right. It is soul retrieval or, rather, *life retrieval*. We hold our negative beliefs about ourselves as tensions in our bodies. If we don't release them they become hardened there and manifest as physical or emotional problems. At the same time our good energies are blocked so that the fullness of our souls is not expressed and parts of us stay buried. San Pedro removes our negative beliefs so the positive ones can shine. So it is a form of soul retrieval, one where we return ourselves from ourselves.

Can you say more about how negative beliefs affect us?

La Gringa: In the Andes shamans talk about "good" and "bad ideas" and these are, in a way, what I mean by thoughtforms. Sometimes they talk about a "good" or "bad wind" as well. These "winds" are an accumulation of thoughts or energies that are attracted to each other and share a common affinity.

I recently took a horse ride with a friend, for example, to visit the Q'ero people of the high Andes and some way into our journey, miles from anywhere and from medical help, my friend swooned and fell from her horse then lay on the ground shaking.

Luckily we had a shaman with us who knew what had happened, and taking out his coca leaves he placed them on her and blew through them into her crown. She stopped shaking straightaway and then began to come round.

When I asked him what had happened he just shrugged and said "a bad wind." She had been hit by a thoughtform that had, in a way, possessed her. He had blown a different energy into her to remove it and fill her with light.

But imagine: if stray thoughts can do this much damage how much stronger are our own ideas? Our beliefs about ourselves, our sicknesses and our powers or weaknesses are not random after all; they are personal to us and may have been with us for many years. So it is literally true that our thoughts can kill or cure us and we must be careful about what we think. San Pedro heals us by showing us the origins of our beliefs and replacing those that don't serve us with better and more wholesome ideas.

There is a diet that goes with San Pedro, just as there is for ayahuasca. But with San Pedro it is easier. Can you say something about it?

La Gringa: All teacher plants require some ritual precautions prior to and during the ceremony. This is what we call the diet. It refers not just to restrictions around food and drink as the name might suggest, but to other behaviors as well so we approach the plant with a pure intent. So when we talk about the "diet" it is really more like the ancient Greek understanding of a *dieta,* a change in lifestyle not just in what we eat.

San Pedro does not ask for major changes but, nevertheless, the day before it is drunk food should be as bland as possible and contain no alcohol, meat, oils or fats, spices, citrus fruits, or juices and there should be no sex.

For about twelve hours before the ceremony there should be no food at all. This means a day of fasting if you are drinking San Pedro at night, or no food from about 8 p.m. on the night before if you are drinking it the next day. For a few hours before the ritual there should also be a period of quiet reflection so you can think about what you would like to heal or learn about yourself.

That is really all that the diet requires, although there are some specific conditions where a consultation with your shaman and medical doctor is recommended in advance of drinking San Pedro. These include problems with the colon, high blood pressure, heart conditions, diabetes, or mental illness. None of these will necessarily prevent you from drinking since the condition itself may be the very thing that you want San Pedro to cure, but your shaman and doctor must know.

I've heard it said that the "processes" involved in ceremonies can contribute to the effects, that the shaman acts as a sort of hypnotherapist, for example, and offers healing suggestions to the patient, while the ritual contains practices like meditation that are themselves relaxing and healing. What do you think of that idea?

La Gringa: I sometimes get asked things like that by people who want to know what the "makeup" of San Pedro is, what its "active ingredients" are, and "how it works." I tell them I don't know and don't care!

For me, it is not San Pedro's "mescaline content" or "properties" that are important; it is a healing spirit that produces miracles that I have seen with my own eyes. So I really don't know or care how it works because I can't explain a miracle any more than those who ask me about it can! But I know this: if you *needed* a miracle because your life was in that much pain and if—by the grace of God and San Pedro—you got one, you wouldn't care how or why it worked either!

Part of our disease, it seems to me, is to want to "understand" the world in terms of its "mechanisms" when its nuts and bolts really don't matter at all. It is the beauty of the world that should attract, engage, and inspire us! When we drink San Pedro that is one of the first things we learn—and then our questions become irrelevant anyway. So the real answer for those who want to know the hows and whys of San Pedro is simple: drink it and you will see!

PART TWO: THE 2011 INTERVIEW

You've described your early encounters with San Pedro as sometimes painful, and said that you didn't always want to drink it but Rubén made you. Can you say some more about these experiences—what San Pedro showed you, why it was painful, and what you learned from it? Also what was it about San Pedro and the experience that kept you coming back to it given that it was sometimes unpleasant for you?

La Gringa: Every encounter I have had with San Pedro has been profound. The early days of drinking were sometimes painful and emotional as it's difficult to face yourself, your fears, to confront issues that are hidden deep inside, to discover the truth. What kept me going back was that even in the pain, the emotions, the fear, I knew I was cleansing and healing, facing my past, this lifetime and past lifetimes, understanding the whys of everything that had happened and getting the lesson, releasing the past, and most of all because San Pedro taught me to love myself, something that I had never been able to do before.

The plant taught me how to really see, feel, and love this beautiful world and everything in it—which was another new experience for me. It taught me to trust, to trust myself and the universe too—that it would supply me with more than I need to believe in miracles, to believe in myself, to learn to let go of the past, stop worrying about the illusion of the future and live with gratitude for each moment. That's why I totally trust this medicine for myself, my family, my dogs, and for everyone that this plant calls.

San Pedro has changed you personally then?

La Gringa: *Wachuma* has changed me so much that I don't even recognize the girl I used to be! From the age of thirteen I suffered from severe depression, right up until I started drinking plant medicine at about the age of thirty-eight. That depression was like a deep, dark downward spiral that I couldn't get out of; there seemed like there was no light at the end of the tunnel. It was continuous. I still do get depressed at times, which is a pain, but at least now it only visits once or twice a year for a short period of time, maybe a day to a week. And now it's easy for me to get out of it again too because I know that I can. Then when I am free of it I can actually laugh at myself.

The plant has shown me how to love myself; to be grateful for the incredible people in my life, friends, family, and strangers; to experience gratitude for the gift of being part of this magnificent world; to see and feel energy; to love and receive love in so many ways each day. It has taught me to be softer, kinder and has shown me how creative I am, making me realize that I can manifest anything in my life as long as I am absolutely clear on what I want.

Of course there are things that I would still like to change about myself, and San Pedro shows and reminds me; it won't even let a nasty thought enter my head without drawing my attention to it. But as I said, it's all our choice in the end and sometimes I don't put the wisdom from wachuma into action. But it stays in us always and will always be there to teach us even if we don't want to know sometimes. But at least I am aware of my thoughts, feelings, and actions so much more than before.

Could you describe a particularly profound experience you've had with San Pedro ("good" or "bad")?

La Gringa: All San Pedro experiences are profound really. One that was a huge wake-up call for me though was in 2002. I had been having bad financial problems, my nerves were shot, I was on the verge of anorexia, in an awful relationship, and just nothing seemed to be going well for me. I was feeling desperate; I didn't know what to do.

A man [a patient] came from Chile to drink San Pedro with me. I knew I wasn't in good shape to run a ceremony, but I also realized that

San Pedro was calling me, as it was him, because I had not taken the medicine for a long time. So off we headed to the mountains, to the same sacred place that I had drunk my first time.

Named Chakan, it's also known as the Rainbow Rocks and it's quite far from anything. I felt that it would be a good place for me to reconnect to. We both drank, and I was sitting against a rock with my eyes closed, then behind my closed eyes I felt the presence of this man but somehow he had changed. I opened my eyes and he had kind of shape-shifted. He didn't look anything like the man I had arrived with and I was quite startled.

He then said in perfect English (which by the way, he didn't speak; he had very broken English), "Lesley [La Gringa's birth name], when are you going to follow the instructions?"

As he said this my first thought was, "Oh my God, that sounds like my father." And just as I thought this he said, "This is a message from your father."

I was shocked but knew that something very important was about to happen. He carried on, "I am going to give you several instructions and if you follow them you will be going home to South Africa for a visit and everything will change for you. You will no longer have these problems and you will be very happy and have all you need to support you. But you have to follow the instructions!"

My first reaction was to laugh and think someone was playing a trick on me. I said, "I can't even buy a local bus ticket so how am I going to go to South Africa?" He replied, "Someone in your family will buy you a ticket."

I laughed even louder. "My family isn't even talking to me right now and haven't for a long while as they don't understand my love for Peru or why I abandoned everything to be here." He replied that it will be as he said as long as I follow the instructions . . .

1. Get rid of your boyfriend tonight! (He even mentioned his name even though he didn't know him and had no connection to us).

Well that was clear to me, that I had to do that in order for me to regain my dignity and be at peace.

2. Never sleep with anyone that you are not in love with.

3. Give up smoking.

4. Eat three good meals a day, with something in between.

5. Drink a minimum of two liters of water every day because, he said, I am living in very high vibration and I needed water to reach both sides of my brain. Two liters would bring back stability and harmony. He said that was true for everybody.

6. When I got to South Africa I should act in the way that would bring peace and happiness to my family. I replied that no, I would not act because acting was a lie. He said that acting was acting and a lie was a lie. I should learn the difference.

7. Once I could act in a way so that my family could feel happy, harmony would be regained. At that point my life would change and good things would happen for me. Once I got to South Africa I would be given a fantastic holiday, many gifts, and would receive money. And while I was away my business would prosper and all my debts would be paid. I would have a really good amount of money to return to.

And all I had to do was follow the instructions!

So the first thing I did was throw my cigarette away and I actually stopped smoking from that moment for five years. (I am now an on-and-off smoker again and San Pedro is not pleased with that; nor am I).

On my arrival home that night, immediately as I entered my house, I said to my boyfriend, "I want you to leave right now please." He just looked at me and said, "Yes, I understand and I will leave right away." Not another word was spoken between us. He just left and I felt very relieved.

I followed the instructions, started to eat well again, put on some weight, drank my two liters a day and was feeling really happy and positive. Then a few months later, as I was in my garden enjoying the sun and the flowers, I received a phone call from my ex-husband whom I hadn't spoken to for about a year. I was surprised to hear his voice and asked him why he was calling. He replied that he had been thinking about me and that it was time for me to come home to visit my family and he would like to buy me a ticket! I was astounded of course but very happy to know that after many years of not seeing them I was about to meet my family again!

He bought my ticket and I arrived in Cape Town with about $20 in my pocket. I went first to see my daughter, my new grandson, and my ex-husband. I then went to visit my mom and sister and brother and everyone showered gifts and cash on me! I understood what the channeling with my father had meant, and I "acted" in the way that they could see another side of who I am, a "me" they could finally understand. I made them feel happy. (Before San Pedro I was known as "the Fighter" in the family, now my sister jokingly calls me "the Wimp"). Our relationships since then have been wonderfully loving, caring, and great fun.

I was gifted holidays: one with my friend Milly to a private game lodge with wild animals wandering near us, and another from my friend Uppy to Mozambique where I swam with dolphins every day at sunrise. What incredible gifts! Gifts that can never be forgotten, from beautiful friends and family. And in all this I realized how much I am loved and this is a gift that I am reminded of frequently. Family and good friends are great gifts for us in this beautiful universe!

After my fabulous vacation I returned back to my home in Cusco to find that the hostel I own had been completely full every day and that people didn't want to leave! My friend Valeria had run things incredibly well for me, paid all the outstanding bills, and handed me a huge wad of cash!

Another part of the play of my life had unfolded so beautifully and better than I could ever have envisioned. And all because I had followed the instructions!

My dad must have heaved a huge sigh of relief because I *never* followed instructions and now for the first time I listened! (Thank you dad!) My dad passed over in 1993 but every time I drink San Pedro he is nearby, whispering instructions in my ear and now I always listen!

Has San Pedro ever given you a more "cosmic" vision or understanding of life? For example, what has your training or experience taught you about God, reality, human purpose, et cetera? What are we doing here and why? How do human beings "fit" on the planet—what's our role?

La Gringa: The understanding I have received is firstly that life is simple! We should stop thinking that it is complicated or hard because thinking it so makes it so! Seek the truth of everything and learn to live in a simple and clear way. Learn to live from the heart not the mind, because the heart is all truth and love.

That is another thing: we are here to learn love—for ourselves first so that we can then *really* love our brothers and sisters (for that's what we are on this planet, all of us brothers and sisters). Within the term *love* fits compassion, understanding, caring, action in love, and learning to let go of the past in order to move forward.

I have had visions with San Pedro of upward spirals of pure light, with humans moving up these spirals and angelic beings helping us into this spiral. I have felt myself within it too. To me it doesn't matter if that represents a physical spiral of evolution with us really moving into another dimension or if it's symbolic of humans moving upward into enlightenment, they are basically the same. We are in the process of enormous change and we can choose to stay as we are or become light beings, become like God or stay human. Neither is wrong or right but we have a choice and I believe that billions of people now are choosing to become like God. Call it Christ Consciousness if you want.

The word *God* . . . Sometimes people ask me if I am religious or what I believe in. To me, God is supreme intelligence, high-voltage pure electrical energy, intense blinding light, unconditional love, all wrapped into One. Sometimes I think we humans are laughable for us to think that God has to be in human form. God is so much more . . .

Following from that, has San Pedro taught you anything about life and death and the soul? Is there an afterlife for example—and if so what is it like? Have you experienced "death" yourself through San Pedro? Ayahuasca is often about death—the "vine of the dead" and so forth—is San Pedro similar in any way? And if so what has it shown you about death?

La Gringa: I have been through a few intense death experiences with ayahuasca, but death in San Pedro is really more like rebirth. It's like a death of our programming and old habits, like a release more than the kind of physical death you experience in aya.

When I drink San Pedro I always have experiences with my loved ones who have died. These experiences are as real to me as if those people were physically with me. My father died in 1993 and he always comes to me in San Pedro. I can feel his arms holding me and he talks to me, gives me guidance and messages and they are always the right ones for me. I can see him as clearly as when he was alive although I see him as pure light too.

My nephew Leighton has visited me and told me that we should just practice to see them [our loved ones who have passed] because they are always around us, even though they are different now. He says they are very happy and also very busy. As he explained it to me, they are doing many things at the same time but different parts of them are doing different things simultaneously.

I was about to embark on my third journey to Peru in 1993 when my dad discovered he had cancer. The doctors gave him three weeks to three months to live. My dad did not fight this, he simply said take me home to die. I told my dad I was cancelling my trip to Peru to stay with him during this time. He said, "No Lesley, I want you to go, but this time for me." I argued and said, "Dad, you only have a short time and I want to be with you." He replied, "I promise I'll wait for you Les. I will not go before you return." I said that no one could say when they were going to die and he asked me if I hadn't learned anything from him. He always taught me that we could control anything, that we were in charge of our lives. He said I must go on my journey and that he would definitely be waiting for me. So off I went, nervously, and when I got back, true to his word, he was still there, very weak, but the first thing he said was, "I told you so. I hope you have learned something!"

A few days later I was sitting outside at the pool and my mom came running out to say that my father was calling for me. She looked scared and when I went in he was sitting up in bed with his arms outstretched and with huge eyes. He said, "Lesley, help me. There is a gate here and I need to go through it but I don't know how, but I know that *you* know how! Help me."

I was very panicky and had no idea how to get him through the gate so I prayed and asked that God speak for me and I thanked him in advance for it being so.

I said, "Dad, do you see people on the other side of the gate?" He looked and said, "Yes! I see my mother, my father, and all my brothers! Please get me to them."

I then said, "Do you see Michael on this side of the gate?" (My thoughts were, "Oh no! Who is Michael? I have no idea. Please don't ask me Dad!") He said, "Oh of course, you mean the Archangel . . . Yes, he is there."

I heaved a sigh of relief and then said, "Dad, all you have to do is put your hand in Michael's hand and he will take you through." I was terrified actually, I had no idea what would happen.

My dad took one last look at me and asked, "Are you sure Lesley?" I replied firmly, "Yes!" But the fear in me was huge, not knowing what if anything would happen. He stretched out his arm, put his hand out, breathed a huge sigh and went into an instant coma, with a smile on his face.

That night, sleeping on the floor next to his bed I heard his breathing change. I woke my mother and sister and told them that Dad was about to leave. We held him in our arms as he took his last breath and we saw a beautiful white light leave his heart. We held him with tears streaming down our faces but with smiles too because as my mom said, he didn't die, he was reborn into something way beyond, something of such beauty.

On my next journey to Peru I had my first ayahuasca experience. Aya told me that "They" [the spirits] gave me my name as they give everyone their names even though our parents think they thought of it. Aya said it was important for me to know what my name means, as everyone should, because there is something in our names that will give a clue as to what our life service is. I eventually found a names book and it said that Lesley means "the Gatekeeper." I was shocked but so grateful to realize that I had accomplished one thing that had great meaning for my life.

Being with my father on his "rebirth" was one of the most incredibly beautiful experiences of my life, one that I will forever be grateful for, and one that fills me with awe at the magnificence of death. It is as miraculous as birth.

I believe that I would not have been able to assist my father if I had not drunk San Pedro first, as the message of this plant is one of being in harmony and peace with everything. San Pedro opened my heart and mind to all things miraculous, to the God inside each of us, and to the understanding that death as we know it is just an illusion. We are forever a part of everything.

Your San Pedro is very different from the others I have drunk. For one thing there seems more "love" in it. Where do you find it and how do you account for this difference?

La Gringa: I went through phases of trying San Pedro from different parts of Peru. For a while I thought cactus from the Lima area was stronger but then a friend brought me San Pedro that he had collected from Arequipa, northern Peru, and Ayacucho. I tried them all, cooking them in the same way, and to my surprise found that they were all equally strong. I drank all three, plus the medicine from Lima, over a period of a few months, asking which was the San Pedro for me, and of course the answer was that the spirit of San Pedro is always the same if treated with the same respect and love. San Pedro told me that no matter which cactus I cooked, if I did it with the same respect, all of it would be perfect and all of it would heal, the secret being the belief I had in this spirit. So bang went my old theory! Now I have San Pedro growing in my garden from many different parts of Peru and I treat them all as equals.

I was taught by Rubén about the different ribs and their uses [i.e., the different number of ridges around the cactus. See chapter 4 by Michael Simonato for a discussion of these and their different effects]. I prefer to use seven and nine ribs as they seem to be the ones that speak to each individual in the way they best understand, and always with love and healing. I also look for cactus that has a darkish green color just because they look perfect!

I cook my medicine for anything between twelve and twenty hours. I find that in this way there is less purging. Purging is not a bad thing but we don't physically *have* to purge either. If there is purging to be done as a cleansing it can be done energetically too, which is a smoother process. I prefer smooth. I don't like to suffer if I don't have to!

I don't normally add anything to my brew although on some occasions I do add little extras, like flowers usually, just because the plant tells me to. I sometimes add flower essences that my friend Star Ripparetti from Santa Barbara makes. Star is very connected to flowers, her essences are awesome, and every now and then, when one of her essences calls to be added, the San Pedro experience is always more special. But in the end San Pedro is all that is needed.

You asked about my secret cooking process . . . well if I told you, then it wouldn't be secret would it? [Laughing] But what I *can* tell you is that it takes a few years to get the "secret." It takes a lot of experience of actually drinking the medicine, for many years sometimes, before you receive your personal recipe from San Pedro. That's the secret I was telling you about.

For example, my teacher Rubén taught me the basics of cooking and it's the same that you could probably find on the Internet; it's a simple process and it works. But he never revealed his secret to me; he told me I would receive my own if I had patience and respect for this process. I waited many years before I received my gift from the plant and that's my secret, given to me personally by my teacher.

I don't add anything to wachuma, even if a patient has a particular problem and that's why they are drinking it, to be healed. I do, however, prepare special herbal teas for particular ailments such as diabetes, a heart condition, headache, or such. But these teas are not particularly for the healing (San Pedro does that); they are used to assist.

I'd like to know more about why you run ceremonies in the way you do. Rubén taught you the "old fashioned" way—so why did you change things to daytime ceremonies and less ritual, and so forth?

La Gringa: Most *wachumeros* [San Pedro shamans] hold their ceremonies at night and as you know, mine are held during the day. They both have their virtues but an important aspect for me is to feel safe, warm, and comfortable in order to receive the most benefits from the ceremony.

As you know, I come from South Africa where heat is abundant. I love heat and sunshine and nights in Cusco are always cold. There is no such thing as a warm night in Cusco! I have done many ceremonies at night and they can be intense, sometimes akin to an ayahuasca experience because there is no escape, it's all "inward." But I have also experienced ceremonies at night where I have not been able to have any breakthrough, feeling almost like I am not experiencing the medicine because I am so cold. As one's body temperature drops anyway with this medicine it becomes increasingly harder to journey.

This is frustrating and uncomfortable for me—and presuming I am the same as most people, I prefer to have the gift of sunshine on my face and to see, feel, and hear the wonders of daytime. It's so easy to connect to nature when you are outside, seeing the powerful energy in the clouds, hearing the winds talking to you, watching the Earth breathe, and knowing what each flower has to teach us. It's a happy reconnection to this beautiful universe and comfort and warmth is always a good way to go!

The night ceremonies are usually done inside, which can sometimes provide the warmth but then you are missing out on our beautiful Mother Earth dressed in all her many-colored garments and jewels. She is so magnificent. To experience her in this way is such an incredible gift and one that will, for sure, show the true beauty of existence and our perfect connection to this wondrous universe we are so privileged to be part of. Just to experience that is enough to change our view of everything forever.

I asked our friend Danny [a San Pedro assistant and local historian] what he knew of the past wachumero way and he explained to me some of the old ways. It makes perfect sense.

San Pedro (or wachuma) was the traditional shamanic way to treat people by Andean shamans. (Traditionally the word *shaman* does not exist here. Healers are called wachumeros if they work with San Pedro, *ayahuaskeros* for ayahuasca, *altomisayoc* in the Q'ero tradition, *paqos* in the Alturas, or *curanderos,* the healers). Danny said that in the past the techniques used were sometimes shocking, harsh, and difficult,*

---

*At Chavin de Huantar for example (said to be the birthplace of the San Pedro "cult") anthropologists believe that San Pedro ceremonies and initiations were conducted in underground chambers. Only rudimentary light would enter through small "windows" (actually thin channels dug out of the rock), and mirrors would be placed strategically to direct this light in particular ways so as to create a disorientating otherworldly feel. There are other channels dug into the caves so that running water could be directed to specific locations, its sound creating an odd, echoing eeriness. The initiate, led into this chamber in darkness, would not expect any of this, and having drunk San Pedro would be totally unprepared and unable to comprehend this other world he had been brought to. In this way the familiar landscape of "reality" would vanish and he would be face-to-face with the spirits. —R.H.

but these methods worked for that time because people also knew less about "finding themselves" and needed more tools to help them let go. In our time we have access to all sorts of information on self-knowledge, healing, et cetera, and have more understanding and knowledge. The myths of shamanism have also changed so there is less "awe" attached to us—people see that shamans are not dark legendary creatures but sacred keepers of lost spiritual knowledge that can aid our complex evolution into a new way of life.

Daytime ceremonies allow us to see and understand without fear all that we already know but have hidden from ourselves. Night represents what we don't know or understand clearly (we directly face our fears with no light to help us). Day allows us to see all that we have achieved already and how that can be used as a tool of spiritual realization and awareness. It opens the possibility of spreading the message further to all who ask and need.

The early shamans were very adaptive to social changes. They guarded important spiritual wisdom in hard times but they spread it again in its right moment—and now it feels like the right moment. Wachuma is spreading its magic now; this is the time.

We need to remember that we live in a world of day and night. Day was used to feel comfortable and enjoy the beauty of life, to work and play. Night had less action and was not as comfortable as the days; that's why we made shelters. Probably that's why shamans held ceremonies at night too, because darkness challenges one to naturally attempt to defeat fears. But something has changed in these last decades.

With the social changes we have seen, we have been bringing more light to our nighttime in the attempt to create a more balanced world. There are still many people, however, who are living unhealthy lifestyles because they can't see the differences between our "brain light" and natural light. That's why San Pedro during the day makes more sense. Then we start to understand about the natural light that is within us and about the light of the universe, and to understand balance within ourselves. Wachuma helps us to see this clearly. It teaches us about balance. Day and Night. Light and Darkness.

So yes, the traditional way of the wachumeros is during the night. But we are in a new time and I know that San Pedro supports me in every way and gives me blessings in what I do. It was San Pedro that told me to do my ceremonies during the day and also told me to do these ceremonies in a simple way, with prayer. Wachuma told me that this is a way for us to understand and relate to. So that's what I do.

Can you give some more examples of people who have been healed by San Pedro? How do you think San Pedro heals? Are there any conditions you are aware of that it won't heal? Any failures?

La Gringa: San Pedro teaches us to heal ourselves by showing us the truth and once you experience the truth there is no getting away from it.

It teaches us that no experience is bad if we learn from it, because when we get the truth we understand and we release the "old feelings," whether they are anger, betrayal, loss, fear, et cetera, therefore changing the energy in our bodies. This heals us of emotional and physical illnesses.

San Pedro is heart medicine in that it teaches us to use our hearts, knowing that all our answers are within us. It shows us our connection to everyone and everything, opens our hearts, teaching us how to think with the heart. (Rubén used to tell me to think with the heart and feel with the brain. Not easy!)

This medicine teaches us to really live in the moment, to understand how much time and energy we waste on "re-creating" the past, imagining that we are still in that moment of pain or fear or loss when in fact it is just a memory, we cannot really re-live the past. It teaches us to let go of the past, learn from it, and move on. It also shows us how much time we waste on the future when in fact no one knows what the next second will bring. That's one of Pedro's ways of teaching us to really live in the moment, to show and feel gratitude for everyone and everything around us. Once we start truly showing gratitude for this wondrous world we live in, that's when we start to receive the gifts from the universe in abundance and with ease.

San Pedro is known as "rebirthing medicine," enabling us to feel clean and healed and to get a new start. Some people even go through the motions of giving birth during their San Pedro journeys and it's a very real experience for them.

This medicine also helps us to restore pH balance, which is imperative to good health, therefore getting us back into balance. Many diseases today are because of this. We do not eat well anymore—too much meat, colas, and so forth, and not enough greens. San Pedro can balance this for us again but of course it's up to us to use the knowledge we receive from the plant and make healthy decisions every moment. Yes, San Pedro can heal us but in the end it's up to us to choose to help our bodies to be in balance.

Of course there are times when the medicine hasn't healed the body (or the mind for that matter). My thoughts on this vary. Sometimes, for example, a person with an addiction may come for healing and although he might believe he has been healed, he may then go back to his addiction. It is not that San Pedro has not done the healing, however; I would say that the person just changed his decision. We all do that mostly. We have free will and can decide whatever we want. But sometimes we just make bad decisions.

What of our angel friend Ross from South Africa who passed on last year? [Ross was a patient with cancer who drank ayahuasca at the healing center I then owned in Iquitos and San Pedro with La Gringa in a search for healing.] He was intent on healing and tried many different methods. They didn't work on a physical level but on a spiritual level those of us who knew Ross saw an angel before us. He was obviously prepared for something much higher, he was ready, and he left a great legacy to all of us. He taught us how to keep searching, to respect, love, and be in gratitude every moment. Ross was always peaceful, giving, and loving and he did not fear death. He knew there was something more and he taught us how to accept and never give up on love. So you asked me if there have been failures with this plant medicine. My answer is NO, but it all depends on our perspectives. Ross did not survive but he was able to live and die well and to teach us all something precious and important before he left us.

It's a pity that this medicine is not "available" in most countries as the cure list goes on and on. San Pedro can cure schizophrenia, for example, if the patient has not taken the usual drugs to supposedly heal this illness. Those drugs stay in the body for seven or eight years, making it impossible to use San Pedro to heal as this could be dangerous. But if no meds have been taken, San Pedro can heal this.

To illustrate some of the healing that San Pedro is capable of and the ways in which it works, La Gringa then handed me two recent accounts she had just received from people who had drunk the medicine with her. I am including them here as examples, but also see the reports of others in the appendix of this book who have drunk San Pedro to heal a range of conditions.

Regan's Story

My first experience with San Pedro was when La Gringa visited South Africa at the beginning of 2010. I was sceptical about plant medicine even though I had read so many miracles about it and the work it does. I live in a country where traditional medicine has been around for centuries but I felt that it never applied to me.

I was diagnosed with bipolar mood disorder and had been medicated for well over ten years. According to my GP I was one of the highest functioning patients he'd treated. I faithfully swallowed my plethora of drugs every morning, never skipping a day because I was terrified of what the implications would be for me and my family. I was "stable."

The San Pedro ceremony was conducted in the tranquillity of a garden under the warm African sun. La Gringa advised us all to *open our hearts and ask San Pedro our questions and know that the answers would be forthcoming.*

Swallowing the medicine was the hardest (physical) part. I'd heard it described as liquidized frog and willed myself to swallow it without tasting it. The process that day wasn't easy for me. I had to take two large doses before I managed to open myself enough for San Pedro to do his work.

Answers that had evaded me for years hit me like a bolt of lightning. The day was difficult, with me oscillating between joy and sadness. Sadness because the answers that I was desperately searching for were locked deeply inside me and I was holding on to the pain so tightly instead of just releasing it to the universe and trusting that I could be healed.

One of the realizations I had was that I needed to travel to Peru to complete the work that I started. Standing in the kitchen, I put my arms around La Gringa and promised to visit her at the end of the year. We could hardly believe that the decision was so easy for me to make.

Before I left South Africa La Gringa told me that I had to stop taking ALL of my medication for at least two weeks before I was due to arrive in Peru, as if I believed I was coming for healing then I had to trust in that process. For the first time in over a decade I would not have any pharmaceuticals in my system. A terrifying prospect!

Our first trip after my arrival was to an ayahuascero shaman, Javier, in the heart of the Peruvian jungle. La Gringa accompanied me to the lodge and was staying in a reed chalet for the night while the ceremony was being held. Based on what I'd read and the numerous discussions La Gringa and I had about what to expect I'd mentally prepared myself for the journey I was about to embark on and this adorable man (Javier) did everything in his power to put me at ease before we began.

That evening, I remember looking at the supplies that were laid out next to my mattress in the temple and saying, "One bucket [used during the purge] will NEVER be enough for all of MY issues!" much to the amusement of the other three participants. Each participant is supplied with their own mattress and pillow, a puke bucket, a plastic cup that held just enough water to wash your mouth out, and a roll of toilet paper. The ayahuasca journey is an intensely personal and lonely one and is conducted in the black of the Amazon night.

I swallowed the dark, tarlike liquid and silently begged Mother Ayahuasca to be gentle with me. Almost immediately, as it hit my stomach, I felt myself lurch forward and speed off into the darkness. At the end of the wooden pier that I saw in my mind was a large woman, dressed in psychedelic clothing, beckoning me to follow her. How bad was this going to be?

Almost instantaneously everything went dark and I began to purge. Long threads of thick black tar were being pulled out my body from a cellular level. For hours, years of imbibing psychotropic pharmaceuticals were being ripped out of my body and splashing into the plastic bucket that I gripped desperately in my lap. I was no longer physically part of the process. My body lay like a bunch of rags on the reed-thin mattress as Mother Ayahuasca violently clawed at me to cleanse my spirit.

A silent guardian continuously doused me with buckets of water while the ayahuascero chanted and walked beside me throughout the process. I knew that this was La Gringa who had come to offer me love and support, even though she was not really "allowed" into the ceremony since she was not drinking the brew.

After what seemed like an eternity my soul reentered my physical body just as the sun was rising. It had been a difficult night for me and I was exhausted and emotional. Javier had been witness to the difficult time I was having but even he had not been able to negotiate with Mother Ayahuasca to be gentle with me. It was a violent experience and even though it left me feeling bruised and battered I knew that my healing had truly begun.

That morning as we sat around a table in Javier's kitchen discussing our experiences I thanked La Gringa for breaking the rules of the ceremony and coming to me when I called out to her for help. Surprised, she looked at me with a huge smile on her face and told me that she'd been fast asleep through the whole process and had never physically been anywhere near me. In that moment I knew that the vision of her that I'd seen next to my mattress was in fact her beautiful spirit that had come to calm and reassure me and she had, in fact, never left her bed!

Next stop was Cusco. My first San Pedro experience in Peru with La Gringa in her blessed garden at the foot of the Temple of the Moon can only be described as warm and tender. I remember literally crying for hours that day. We're conditioned to believe that tears are because we're sad but that day I learned that tears are cleansing. I had years of abusive and harmful relationships that I had to work through under the guidance of San Pedro and La Gringa. My heart was in tatters and emotionally I was a cripple but I was in a safe place and finally able to let go of all the pain and hurt that I had been holding on to.

My second SP process was near to the end of my visit. This time my personal work was almost complete and I floated around the garden giving to others.

Other healing experiences that I had in Peru were a coca leaf reading with Puma and energy shifting with La Gringa's teacher, Rubén. Rubén explained what he saw to me as my heart existing out of my body. It was completely out of alignment due to my experiences and history.

Angels were put in my path every day to guide and assist me through the work that I had to do to become whole again. I feel very privileged to have met and worked with these amazing people and plant medicines.

I've been completely medicine free since returning to South Africa at the beginning of January 2011. All of the healers in Peru gave me wonderful tools to bring back home with me. I carry the plant within me and am able to connect with it on a subconscious level whenever I feel that I need it.

My experience taught me that we are a product of our influences. If we choose to allow negativity to become a part of our life then we will become physically ill and stifled. This is not how the universe intends us to live. Using the tools of meditation, music, and healing we can all become angels, beings of light.

Jane's Story

I am writing word-for-word from my journal, changing nothing.

Pre–San Pedro

So, my thoughts before the ceremony . . . I've just finished meditating although all I did was cry. I was letting myself feel all the hurt that Jim [name changed by the author to preserve anonymity] had ever caused and all the anger I've felt especially in the past few days. I just want to let it all go. I want to feel it, acknowledge it, and let it go so it isn't what I am thinking about tomorrow.

I know it's a powerful plant but I am nervous I won't get anything out of it or that I will only be thinking about Jim.

What I want to concentrate on is my digestive system. Since it is a healing plant I would love to have a normal digestive system. Also, my negativity and brattiness I want gone. Patience in its place. I know how I act when I either don't get what I want, something doesn't go my way, or someone tells me no or disagrees with me. I am a brat. I don't like the way I treat people when I let anger take control. I want all negativity out and positivity in. I want a better grasp on my anger and patience to control my thoughts and tongue.

I am kind of unsure what to expect. I can write all day about what I want or don't want to happen but I am just going to open my mind tomorrow to whatever does happen. I just want the most out of tomorrow. Whatever the universe wants to give I'll take.

Post–San Pedro

First off, no matter what I write it will never come close to how beautiful my experience was. Words are not enough. Music or painting could come a bit closer but just plain words, no matter how many adjectives are used, will never be enough.

My whole experience lasted a little over eleven hours. I woke up, stretched, and got ready. We met La Gringa, who was the one guiding us. She had been properly taught from a shaman and has over seventeen years experience. Also met another girl who was going to partake in the ceremony. She had a kind spirit and I liked her right away.

We got into a taxi and drove to the top of a mountain where La Gringa lives. She's got a nice house with a pretty garden and dogs. They became very special to me throughout the day.

We got called to sit on these cushions in the garden. She explained a bit about San Pedro. She said that it was a healing plant proven to be used in sacred ceremonies two thousand years before Christ. She said that San Pedro will talk to our hearts and will know what we need. Before we drank it we had to put our intentions in the cup. My intentions were negativity out, positivity in and some clarity in my life. She said that San Pedro goes into your subconscious and into your past, which will reveal the root of any illness or anything in your life. She said sickness is brought on by your own self.

I thought, "Well, I don't really have anything specifically in my past that San Pedro needs to reveal." But thought, "Whatever happens will happen." I had no idea what to expect.

We drank it. It didn't taste nearly as bad as I kept reading it did. It tasted bad just not as bad as I thought it would. It was very, very thick, thick liquid. They said it was better just to gulp it all down.

After we drank we had forty minutes until it would hit us. So we went around just talking about ourselves. Then she told us it was time to go and find a comfortable place and relax.

It began. Well, kind of. I was lying with my eyes closed trying to meditate or stay out of my mind like La Gringa told me to and listen to my heart. But all I could hear was noise. People talking, the water pump, workmen outside. I was restless and wasn't really sure what to do. So I got up and found La Gringa. I told her that I'm not really sure what I should be doing. She said to just relax that's all. Just relax. And this guy that I didn't even know said, "It's a beautiful day."

I got angry at him. I thought, "Okay, it's a beautiful day for you because you know what you're doing!" So I went away from all the talking but could still hear the workmen on the other side of the garden wall digging up the road. I was getting very, very frustrated. I thought, "This is crazy. What am I doing? This is supposed to be a relaxed atmosphere and it's not." Then I started hearing the girl, Othelia, vomiting. I thought, "Shhhh . . . will you. You are ruining my meditation." Aaahhhh.

So I moved to a hammock and plugged my ears with my fingers. It did block out all the noise but was super uncomfortable. So I went back to a chair. I heard Othelia keep coughing or sighing and all I could think was, "Shut up!" but then I thought, "Hmmm. That's pretty mean huh? Selfish even. Okay, San Pedro is that what you are showing me? That I am selfish?? Yeah, thanks but I already knew that!"

Then every angry thought made a tighter and tighter knot in my stomach. I thought sarcastically, "Okay, San Pedro, really profound— negative thoughts cause my stomach problem. Thanks again."

I just didn't feel anything but anger and frustration. Plus I kept thinking my mind was making all this up and not my heart. So I moved again to the original cushion and got comfy. I closed my eyes but nothing. Then I thought she must not have given me enough. She gave me three-quarters of a glass and everyone else a full glass or more. Basically blaming everything and everyone for my inability to quiet my mind and meditate. I'm lying there with my eyes closed trying hard when it was like my heart screamed at me, "Well if you can't look inside yourself then open your eyes and see yourself from outside yourself."

I opened my eyes and looked at the sky. There were all these clouds but they started moving and taking shapes. These shapes formed into every gross horrible depiction or image of what you would imagine evil or scary creatures to be. There were devils and gargoyles and witches if you will. Just anything you can create that is ugly and scary. The more I looked at them the more ridiculous they became so I started to smile. I almost laughed at how funny these ugly things were. Smiled at how utterly ridiculous they looked.

At that moment my heart told me they represented fear. My fear. So I thought, "Okay, so I will put a fear to each one of these faces and let it go." But in reality there is only one fear I had. So then I realized these monsters in the clouds represented my excuses for keeping my fear in place. My fear was that I didn't want to be forty and alone. As soon as my heart revealed that, I closed my eyes and it was like in a movie when they go back in time and there's these twisty tubey things that go way back into my past. And along the way I saw an old journal entry I wrote when I was maybe twelve years old. I wrote, "This boy likes me and this one and this one. . . ." Basically putting all my self worth on what other people thought of me.

Fear of not being good enough, fear of not being as good as I want to be. My main fear came from the lack of love for myself. I thought I was special only if other people did. For example, probably since I was twelve I have never been without a boyfriend. Sometimes two or three at a time and of course always a backup. Then my mind went through all these photos of cool places I've been. And all my traveling I've done was just for the pictures to show everyone how cool I was/am. I've been such a social chameleon, changing groups of friends, "taking bits of them" because I never had a sound sense of who I am. It was like in my heart I saw this huge rock with barbed wire around it with a little piece of paper with black writing that said FEAR.

I let the fear go. I closed my eyes and asked San Pedro, "Let my heart know, how do I love myself? How can I love me?" I heard the girl, Othelia, throwing up crazily so my heart said, "Show some compassion." I went over to her and rubbed her back and said, "Sorry you're so sick." It was more or less, "I'm sorry for being angry with you earlier." It was compassion and empathy I need to find in myself for other people.

I never got a clear answer about how I can love myself but I guess that's just what I need to work on. To build a relationship with myself so that other people can love the same me as I do. So I figured I got my big revelation and all would be well. Nope, there was so much to come.

I thought, "Where is everyone else? Maybe I should go outside too." But my heart said, "Stay. Be content with being with you. Be content with where you are. Be content with all that you have here."

I opened my eyes and just watched the clouds again to see what they would reveal. Again I saw faces. Scary ones but then they turned into good ones and I saw animals and every single animal or face I saw I noticed the eyes. They were all kind eyes. Then right in the midst of all the clouds I saw God. He had those same kind eyes that I saw in all those faces and animals. I realized then and there that God is in everything and is everywhere. It was so profound but simple at the same time. Then the sky went back to the scary faces but this time it was like I was coming face-to-face with my fears and conquering them. Realizing that God is in me and I have the power to control these inner demons of mine. Facing them wasn't so hard. It was so easy.

I started to get very hot in the sun so I moved to the shade. It was cold. Then I had a feeling that my heart was letting me feel what it is to be alone. Cold and lonely. I laid in the shade on the earth, cold and alone. I hugged myself for warmth and support. My heart kept telling me, "This is your worst fear realized. Now was that so bad? Now you know how it feels so there is no need to fear it. You fear the unknown but no longer have to because you know how it feels. If you have to go though it again it'll be okay because you've been there, done that, and got out ok."

I got back up and went to warm up a bit and lay in the hammock. I was just pondering all that I had experienced so far. I thought I'd give back the necklace that Jim gave me because I didn't need him to buy it for me. But I thought it's all so irrelevant! I thought about what I'd tell all my friends and family or how I'd act after, but again everything is irrelevant.

I went outside the gate (pants rolled up and no shoes or socks). Wow! I didn't remember this view when we first got there. There were sheep all over the place. I could hear their baaaaaaa's ringing in my ears. I could feel their energy. I just walked across a small field toward the Temple of the Moon.

I sat on a patch of grass just blown away at the sight of everything. The view was amazing. I saw and felt the energy of every blade of grass. I again felt God in everything.

I climbed a bit of the temple and sat on this rock that looked like the head of a condor. I sat in its brain and felt not like I was flying but like I could see the way the condor could see. I looked at the mountains. They were all moving like they were breathing but felt like they were unstable. So I steadied my eyes and willed them to stop. Representing me being in control to stabilize my own life. I then remembered one of my intentions was some clarity in my life but the mountains told me that if I trusted the person I love that I'd know what to do. The decisions I make I need to trust. Maybe that'll help with my indecisiveness. All my original intentions seemed so small and insignificant and easy to manage from here on out.

A group of tourists came to the Temple of the Moon and I thought, "Okay, I've been in the sun without water for hours. I need to take care of this me I love and get some water." I walked past the tourists but they didn't really seem to notice me. It was like I was of this world but not in it. It brought a whole new meaning to that saying, "Be of this world but not in it." But then I thought, "What if my body is back at La Gringa's and I'm dead. What if she brought us all up here to die."

But death wasn't scary and essentially a big part of me did die. I thought, "Well, I am in this beautiful place." So instead of going back to the garden I climbed to the top of the Temple of the Moon. I didn't feel the sharp rocks under my feet or the cold wind that blows at the top of the mountain. More tourists came and were basically looking at me like I was crazy. Dead and born again. One guy started playing the wind pipes and the wind was roaring in my ears. Just beautiful.

I decided I needed to go back so I chose my own path to walk down from the temple. I got back to the garden and drank lots of water. A lady brought me some tea. I went back to the cushions and lay there. My body moved with the music and I kept going through these cycles of coldness, alone, shaking, then back to normal. My logical mind told me that was dehydration but my spiritual mind told me that it was the circle of life that basically (what Peter says in the Bible) you die daily. But it is never as bad as you think and you do get over it.

I kind of came out of it a bit. Enough to share a bit of my experience with others.

We got in the cab and went back down to Cusco but I still wasn't out of it. Jim and I decided to go get something to eat. We went to a restaurant but everything seemed so intense that I just wanted out instead of being in there. Finally about 11:00 p.m., I felt back to normal.

Overall my experience of San Pedro was very profound yet simple, revealing, eye opening, and it awoke my mind. I had a very powerful journey. One time when I thought about healing my stomach it was like San Pedro said, "You don't have to heal your stomach. You have to heal your heart. Get rid of your fear and your sickness won't be a problem, especially since you are in control." What I put in my body, whether physical or thoughts that aren't good for it is what I'll get out.

What impact do you think the environment (set and setting) has on taking San Pedro?

La Gringa: Environment is very important while drinking this medicine. It's important to feel safe and cared for. Don't drink with someone that you don't trust or feel safe with. The setting should be outdoors, preferably in the country, or at least a beautiful garden and not noisy or with traffic, definitely surrounded by good people. San Pedro shows us our connection to nature; we see energy everywhere; we can sit with a flower and see her grow. It shows us all the stages of life in one day!

So, following from this, what are your thoughts regarding individuals in places like Europe, the States, Australia, et cetera, who are brewing and drinking San Pedro on their own, in their own homes, perhaps because they have no shaman to refer to? You often read accounts (on Erowid, etc.) of such experiments with teacher plants. Do you recommend it? What advice would you give?

La Gringa: Rubén always says that if we are drawn to work with sacred plants we should learn to work with the plant of the country in which we live. He says that each country has its own sacred plant, meant for the vibration of that country. I have to agree with that because when I have used the San Pedros grown in another country I have found them to be very different to those grown here. It's all about vibration. Peru holds very high vibration—not all countries do. Therefore, the San Pedro is vastly different. When I drink any medicine I obviously prefer that which has the best vibration.

Sadly, I never got to experience any of the sacred plants in South Africa because when I was living there I was not aware of them. Now if I ever moved to live in another country I would certainly investigate, study, and learn to work with its plants.

My advice to people who are preparing San Pedro in other countries would be this: if you haven't drunk sacred plants, whether San Pedro or ayahausca, don't do it on your own—make sure you have someone with you who has a lot of experience with it. As it should be with anything in life, these plants should be totally respected. They can knock you down, they can lift you up, many things can happen.

Personally, I am very grateful to Rubén for his teaching and guidance in using these plants. Before my training, I once prepared San Pedro for myself and some friends, not aware then of the effects of the different [numbers of] ribs, et cetera. It was a horrible, dark, and frightening experience for all of us. When I asked Rubén about it he said that I should crawl before I walk, that there was much I had to learn before I presume to just prepare it and drink. Mostly the medicine is light and love, but there are exceptions and it takes patience, respect, and permission to use the plant in a positive way.

I've asked this question of Rubén too: San Pedro is less well known than ayahuasca. Why do you think this is and do you think the situation will change? When? Why? How?

La Gringa: San Pedro was forbidden in the times of the Spanish conquest by the Catholic religion because when people drank this medicine it made them feel as if they were in paradise—in heaven—and heaven or hell existed within the Catholic religion as an afterlife, not here in this life. So the cactus was considered diabolical.

It was as a result of the Spanish that the name changed from wachuma to Saint Peter (San Pedro), as it is he who holds the keys to heaven. It was, therefore, forbidden to drink this sacred plant or even to talk about it. The punishment was death. Still today there are many local Catholic people who believe that because when they try San Pedro it makes them feel like they are in paradise that it must be a lie and evil. So the Catholics banned all use of it and even now many people still believe it is diabolical.

Wachuma is also possibly less known because with ayahausca the visuals are spectacular! After my first aya experience I, too, was incredulous and I am eternally grateful for the healings, teachings, and the gifts she gave me. Of course, aya can be life changing and my first drink was! Since then, 1993, aya has not been the same to me. But my lesson there is maybe to stop trying to recreate an experience, just have gratitude and move on.

Aya seems to be more of a "hook" to people, and many think that the more times they drink the more "notches" it puts on their belt. But it's not how many times you drink, whether it's aya or San Pedro; it's how much you integrate the lessons into your life. It's about becoming stronger, wiser, and living with peace, love, respect, and gratitude. It's putting wisdom into action daily. What's the point of drinking any sacred plant if we don't integrate it into our lives?

San Pedro is maybe less known as well because it is more passive and down-to-earth than ayahuasca. It teaches us how to live in *this* world, in balance and harmony. This is the world we are living in now so let's learn how to live here properly.

Maybe this [the "hidden" nature of San Pedro] is exactly the way it should be anyway, although I do wish that this medicine could reach those everywhere who really need it. I expect miracles from San Pedro and I see them in different ways each day. To me, San Pedro knows he is part of God and by drinking it we have the opportunity to experience God inside of us, too. Once you have had that experience you will never forget it!

Can San Pedro ever be used for bad? In ceremonies for example could it be used for sorcery? Do you know of any sorcerers who are doing this?

La Gringa: Rubén told me that when he went to learn from his teacher about San Pedro there was a long line of houses all belonging to wachumeros and his teacher's was the house at the end. His teacher was the only one in that street who was working with the plant for the light, the rest were all working with dark energies!

I believe that within everything there is light and dark. Whether it is medicine, food, accounting, law, there are always those who will use it for good or for bad, light or darkness. Yes there is dark magic but personally I haven't known anyone who has used San Pedro for darkness. How could they when this plant is pure light?

Author's note: Extracts from part 1 of this interview have appeared in articles I have written for *The Journal of Shamanic Practice* (U.S.) Winter 2009 issue, *Kindred Spirit* (U.K.) March/April 2009 issue, and the now-defunct *Shaman's Drum*. For information on how to retrieve these articles visit www.shamansociety.org, www.kindredspirit.co.uk, and www.shamansdrum.org.

4
Working Practically with San Pedro

Michael Simonato

I met Michael Simonato in 2010 when I was on a "San Pedro honeymoon" with my new wife; we had decided to drink *wachuma* with a number of different shamans and to see some of Peru. Since then, Michael and his wife, Maggie, have become good friends of ours and have also visited us in Spain.

Michael is a gentle soul and like many San Pedro shamans, he is quiet, unassuming, and caring. His medicine was strong and for most of the day my wife and I simply lay in his garden overlooked by magnificent mountains and cradled by the sky while Michael played the flute or puttered among the plants and flowers. We didn't talk all that much but we knew we'd met a fellow soul.

Michael is not Peruvian and I am always intrigued when people from outside a culture find their answers and their calling in a shamanic practice that is not indigenously their own. What calls them, what draws them to a particular teacher plant, why this medicine instead of another?

These are some of the questions I put to Michael. In the article that follows he answers them for us and tells us about his work with San Pedro, offering practical advice as well for those who would like to explore this plant for themselves.

BREAKDOWN

My heartbeat racing and neck muscles contracting, an invisible belt around my chest tightening, my breath diminishing to a rapid shallow breathing . . . Paranoia, suffocating. I am dying slowly, drowning in dread. Voices and sounds around me getting more distanced, disappearing, my mind dissolving into a dark space. Only the sound of my pounding heart remains. My peripheral vision blurs, hyperfocusing on a spot trying to hold on to the last anchor of reality.

I was twenty-three at that time and working at a local newspaper as a graphic designer. I was sitting by my computer working on an advertisement when it hit me. What I experienced was a panic attack, the first of many to follow. It felt like it lasted forever. I was terrified and I knew that this was just the beginning of a dark ride into the shadow landscapes of my soul.

What I didn't know was that I had also stepped over the threshold into a new world, my awakening. The panic attacks continued and made me socially crippled. I couldn't be in crowded places, stores, cinemas, buses, and my world continued to shrink until I was unable to leave my apartment. I was imprisoned in a world of terror.

Who was I before this occurred? In my eyes I was a handsome and confident young man. I was Superman. Practicing hard martial arts, pumping muscles, and feeling content with a fit, strong body. I enjoyed the sense of power and thrill in a full-contact fight. After my military service in an elite unit, I had joined the National Guard where I was a part of a small group of adventurous young men who trained in guerrilla warfare. I was always searching for new thrills and if I had continued on that path I would probably have ended up as a mercenary somewhere.

All of that confidence went out of the window with my first panic attack, and I couldn't function anymore. As the attacks got worse my mind started to change. It was like new dimensions were added to the reality I used to know.

The nights became a parallel reality. I had nightly visits by aliens performing surgeries or some kind of research on me. I thought that was it—I had lost all sense and would become permanently insane.

I had spontaneous out-of-body experiences and lucid dreams, so clear that when I went to sleep I woke up on the other side somewhere in a mountain landscape where I was met by an indigenous man. He took me to his little house where we sat in front of his fireplace sharing moments of silence. He told me stories while we were staring into the fire and gave me an amulet after each visit, a gift to bring back.

Both of my realities merged and there was a time when I couldn't define what was happening in dreams or in an awakened state. I wasn't even sure if I was still alive or if I had died and passed on from the physical realm. My perception of reality continued to drastically change. Even outside of my intense, vivid dreams I started to see spirits and energies. I could see auras around objects and people and I could feel other people's physical and emotional pain.

What I understand today is that I had a spontaneous awakening. The rise of an inner fire must have triggered my pineal gland to release a large amount of DMT, which opened the gates of perception into other dimensions.

RECOVERY

I knew I had to look for help but I didn't know where to begin. I went to see a psychiatrist whose only solution was to put me on antidepressants. I accepted this temporary solution while I started to search for a better aid. At one point while browsing the shelves in a bookshop a book fell into my hands: *The Way of the Shaman* by Michael Harner. That book made sense and felt familiar to me.

My next purchase was a tape by the same author with recorded shamanic drum journeys. Later I found my own drum, which became my vehicle for many interesting inner journeys. It was easy for me to enter a trance state and journey with the drum, almost as if I had done it before.

The next book that came to me was *The Way of the Peaceful Warrior* by Dan Millman. This also made sense and I realized that I could use what I had learned from my background in martial arts to heal myself, using my determination and aggression to stay within my center when all mental and emotional hell broke loose.

Coming from that background it was a natural transition into meditation and Eastern philosophies. I had a great mentor and friend who was a master in soft martial arts, and the greatest lesson he taught me was that whatever you practice you become. He also taught me that my enemy is actually my friend who can show me my weaknesses by giving pain to my most unprotected spots. This presents great opportunities for us to learn.

I thought that the hard martial arts would free me from my anger and dread but they actually increased it and made my life worse. My mentor taught me instead that power comes from inner silence, not from an upset mind. Another great lesson was that when you fall apart let yourself fall; go into it without resistance and use the energy from that fall so you redirect it to your advantage. Everything is just energy and can be used constructively if we learn how to manage it. So that was the end of my path of fistfighting and the beginning of learning how to surf on the waves in the oceans of energy.

I found a good Chinese qigong teacher who encouraged me to practice for many hours every day. After three months of qigong training I was able to get off the antidepressants. I was still having lighter panic attacks occasionally but now I was able to deal with it. My mind became clearer and I became more grounded again.

I wanted to learn as much as possible and qigong practice took me to energetic healing and Taoist inner alchemy. I also studied traditional Chinese medicine. By the following year I had become a qigong instructor myself and studied various forms of healing bodywork. I realized that I had been cured from the panic attacks when I found myself comfortably standing in front of groups of up to fifty people and actually enjoying it. I met other teachers along the way in perfect synchronicity, and each of them helped me a lot by pointing me in the direction I had to go.

While studying massage and healing I met my next teacher, who was a Hawaiian healer. I went to Hawaii to learn more about their esoteric teachings and ancient healing methods. I was eager to meet a great kahuna to show me some secrets, and asked my teacher to introduce me to some. The only answer I got was a big laugh and, "Michael, the only kahuna you ever need to find is within your heart." She taught me to not look for God in spiritual teachers or temples but to just be with nature and listen as God speaks through that creation.

Well, we have all heard that before, that "we have all the wisdom we need deep inside our hearts," but what I wanted to know was how to get there, to find my inner teacher. However, it was a good reminder that a teacher is just a person who is more experienced within a specific area, but they are all still human with the same baggage as the rest of us. So I went deeper inside with the tools I had. One of the more useful techniques was meditation, especially ten-day vipassana retreats. However, I still felt there was something missing and I continued searching for the lost piece. Like so many other seekers I traveled around the world to far-distant places to find myself.

MY INTRODUCTION TO PLANT MEDICINE

I found that missing piece when I first visited Peru. I had lived in Southeast Asia for almost ten years, first traveling and later working in the hotel industry as a manager for a group of luxury spas. At one point, when it was time for my vacation, I decided to visit a place I had never been to before. Machu Picchu was one of those places so I booked my ticket to Peru. Browsing the Internet for other things to do there I came across websites about plant medicines and shamanism, so I decided to attend an ayahuasca workshop in the Sacred Valley.

My first ayahuasca journeys totally blew my mind. I visited the darkest and most celestial realms within, which I could have never been prepared for. My mind, the room, and the world completely dissolved and I felt as though I died over and over again. But there was something more to it; it felt like I had been there before, that there was something in that state of consciousness that was familiar to me.

At the same time as I feared going into the experiences I was intrigued to go even further and learn more. I was also introduced to wachuma and the first time I drank it, it really put me on my path. I had found the missing piece I was looking for. Finally I had a way to unlock the doors into my soul and learn through direct experience without having to buy into any belief systems or concepts, just drink the medicine.

I continued to drink ayahuasca and wachuma with different medicine people in the Amazon jungle and the Andean mountains. I am eternally grateful to my teachers for holding a safe space for me to heal and learn from the medicine. I dieted on microdoses of wachuma for several months at a time and started to take full doses by myself when I felt that I had established a good relationship with the plant.

My Peru visit became all about exploring the plants. I felt compelled to buy a ticket back to Peru even before I left. My life was changed and things began to unfold in a positive way. I became a freelance consultant and decided to work as little as possible to have more time to spend in Peru. I finally decided to make Peru my new home.

What I am sharing below is based on my subjective firsthand experiences in my relationship with the plants. Just to clarify, I do not claim to have any "scientific proof" to support my observations. To study sacred plant medicine is to me an exploration entirely based on direct experience. I encourage everyone to do the same: to establish a relationship with the plants with an open mind and a humble heart and ask them to reveal their healing benefits and wisdom.

My connection with wachuma deepens with each journey and there seem to be no limitations for how much more there is to learn. I have stopped counting how many times I have been with wachuma so far, since this is now an integrated part of my life. I am very comfortable with wachuma, even when I drink up to ten days in a row. I have also pushed the limits by taking up to five times the normal dose so I have a better understanding of how people feel in a deep, difficult journey. So far the plant has never given me more challenges than I can cope with.

I used to be lactose intolerant and extremely allergic to cats, which I could never find a remedy for. I also had bronchitis that would come on a regular basis. But somewhere along the wachuma path the allergies and bronchitis disappeared. I truly believe that other latent diseases have been and are constantly being prevented or wiped out by the medicine. I easily gained weight in the past and I don't anymore. It seems like the plant restores the protein metabolism and brings back the body to its natural shape, eliminating edema and excess body weight. I also used to be introverted but today I feel more sociable and I have a more positive and calmer mind than ever before. Of course there is still more to deal with but I am working on it. I know that wachuma is patient with my progress.

HOW OTHERS HAVE HEALED BY DRINKING WACHUMA

I have had the honor to witness great healings from all kinds of imbalances and diseases. I have seen people beat anorexia, lung disease, migraine, hemorrhoids, allergies, depression, and many other illnesses after just one ceremony. Mental disturbances such as paranoia and borderline psychotic and schizophrenic states may need more than one ceremony to rewire the pathways of the brain, however, and I encourage people with serious diseases to commit to at least three ceremonies to reach the root of their problems. Each journey with wachuma peels off a few more layers and takes us a little deeper.

It takes some practice to get past our fears and learn to consciously work with the medicine. I believe that the root of most diseases is a spiritual one. It is the feeling of being separated from nature, God, and oneness that makes us sick. Once we rediscover who we really are and that we are all connected as one living organism, a lot of our problems disappear.

I also believe that our problems are bound to a limited view. If we can expand our horizons and attain new perspectives, our problems diminish as we see the reasons behind them. As we step out of ignorance and awaken to our true being, we start recreating our lives in healthier ways.

HOW I PREPARE THE MEDICINE

When I look for cactus to work with I ask the plants who want to work with me to "appear" and I choose the ones who stand out and appeal when I see them. The medicine is stronger when it is prepared during the waxing moon or full moon. It is also stronger if I am under the effect of the medicine while I prepare it.

I cut and slice the plant in a meditative and respectful mood and I always replant a part of the plant I use so it can continue to grow. The bottom part will eventually produce offspring and the top part will continue to grow.

Cutting and slicing is stressful to the plant and creates heat when its self-healing instinct kicks in. To balance this heat I freeze the plant material. From a more scientific point of view this process also weakens the cell walls in the plant tissue so the alkaloids are released more easily during cooking.

I only use the greenest part as the white is said to contain iodine, which can give headaches and may also be harmful to the eyes in the long term. The white can be used as a shower sponge, however, as it is very beneficial for hair and skin. I let the brew simmer for up to twenty hours, depending on the thickness of the slices. I boil it on a low heat as it makes the brew thinner and prevents evaporating the alkaloids.

COMBINATIONS OF DIFFERENT CACTUSES

I mainly work with two species of the cactus family: Peruvian torch (*Trichocereus peruanus*) and San Pedro (*Trichocereus pachanoi*), but sometimes I also combine them with *Trichocereus cuzcoensis* or other cacti within the same family. I tend to select bigger, older *peruanus* and *pachanoi* plants as they provide the base for the brew. I also like to use the offspring from a mother plant of any additional local cactus at least twenty years old that grows in the area where the ceremony is to be held.

I combine all three when I want to work with a wide spectrum of energies, and the third cactus helps to connect with the energy present in that specific location. I call this combination "the Three Wise Men."

It was shown to me during a wachuma journey that the spikes, as well as providing a natural defense for the cactus, work as antennas or acupuncture needles along the meridians of the plant. The different length of the spikes, together with the geometric shape of the cactus, tunes the plant into different frequencies. I have also made combinations of cacti from the north and south of Peru. The plants tend to take turns, alternating and facilitating each other's specialities and the unique energies gathered from their natural habitats.

THE SIGNIFICANCE OF THE DIFFERENT STARS (RIBS)

The medicine differs with the age of the plant and how fast it has grown, the location, altitude, and so on. The different number of ribs also brings different frequencies and qualities.

Even-numbered cacti tend to be more "yin" in their nature and work on the physical body and the denser energy levels. Cacti with odd-numbered ribs are more "yang," with more active energy and usually bring more visual sensations. Looking from the top, the ribs form a "star," which is the term I prefer to use.

The Six-Pointed Star

I was sitting cross-legged on the floor peeling my first six-pointed cactus when my friend Matt, a Jewish rabbi, came by. He offered to help out with the peeling and I gratefully accepted. The six-pointed star looks just like the Star of David hexagram, so I found it amusing that a rabbi walked in and got his hands on it.

We discussed sacred geometry and Matt shared his knowledge of Kabbalah while helping with the medicine. I believe that the six-pointed star symbolizes yin and yang. Matt suggested that the six points can also symbolize the four directions, plus one point for heaven and one for Earth. That can also mean finding the center line within ourselves and expanding out in the four directions.

This is the same principle used by the Sufi whirling dervishes who spin around their center line for hours while in a deep trance and total communion with God. The hexagram in the Hindu yantra symbolizes the union of Shakti, the Divine Feminine, Mother Earth, with the down-pointing triangle. The upward triangle symbolizes Shiva, Divine Masculine, Father Sky. The two components are called Om and Hrim in Sanskrit, and symbolize man's position between Earth and sky. It is also the symbol for *anahata*, the "heart chakra."

In Tibetan Buddhism the hexagram often forms the center of a mandala and is called *chos-kyi' byung-gnas,* "the origin of phenomenon." The hexagram is also used by Christians and Muslims.

This medicine is primarily for balancing the masculine and feminine energy within ourselves. It also helps couples to connect on a deeper level as they surrender to their true essences. The six-pointed star is, therefore, good medicine to find equilibrium and the center within. Its affirmation is: "I am a divine expression of unity; I am whole."

The Seven-Pointed Star

This is a good "all-round" medicine. If I were to compare it with a car it would probably be a Ferrari convertible that moves fast around the turns. Its energy is more yang than yin. It connects peoples' hearts on a deep level and brings joy into their lives.

I use the seven-pointed star as a good introduction to San Pedro for those new to this medicine, and work with it for healing emotional wounds. I usually use this type in combinations with other plants when my intention is to work on thought patterns and emotional imbalances. Reconnection with the heart is the main property of the seven-pointed star. It also works as extra fuel when mixed with the mellower six- and eight-pointed stars, almost as a booster to enhance their beneficial properties. It also works as a catalyst to connect with the nine-pointed star's higher frequencies.

The archetype that I like to associate with it is the firefly as it tends to give more vivid visual sensations and is all over the place. Affirmation: "I am in one heart with all creation."

The Eight-Pointed Star

Having eight directions makes this plant more balanced than other cacti. One of my participants described its medicine as like a tank: unstoppable, strong, and single-minded in purpose. It usually takes you on a mellow journey, however, connecting the mind with the physical body to heal and balance physical or materialistic problems.

It is the most contemplative of the different stars, with a medicine that works slowly and consistently, like a plow through the mind. The eight-pointed star with its octagon shape reminds me of the *pakua,* the Taoist symbol for the eight forces of nature, holding the trigrams in perfect balance. The archetype of the medicine feels to me like an old dragon, wise and watchful. Affirmation: "I am present, grounded."

The Nine-Pointed Star

Nine is the number of initiation. In the Taoist tradition it is the number of the emperor. The vibration is high. It is a detoxifying medicine and your body may continue to release toxins for days following a ceremony with it. It raises your vibration to the highest possible level and may help put you on a new track where life rapidly unfolds in a lighter way that serves your highest good.

It is good medicine when we are standing on thresholds in the passage of life and a good aid for changing destructive life patterns. It opens the gates to the upper world and can allow you to see beyond your physical body, to observe your life from above as if through the eyes of the condor. Its medicine is usually more subtle and I recommend it for more experienced journeyers. I usually use the nine-pointed star at the end of a retreat program.

If I was asked to give it an animal archetype it would be the hummingbird. Affirmation: "Wake up, rise and shine!"

The Ten-Pointed Star

This medicine works on a very high level. It can be very subtle so I combine it with other stars to obtain the maximum benefit from it. I usually work with a brew of one-third ten-pointed star and two-thirds nine-pointed star to bridge the physical and celestial body. From here we have a good platform to connect with the Creator.

In one of the stronger ceremonies with a group of experienced people we drank a brew of ten-, nine-, and seven-star plants. We all shared the intention to journey deep, which supported the process of working on a high level. We were all shaking and vibrating that day and the energy was so high that the journey lasted for about fifteen hours. One woman received an initiation from the spirit of wachuma and started channeling powerful medicine songs (*icaros*).

Affirmation: "I am co-creating with God."

COMBINATIONS WITH OTHER PLANTS

When we add other plants to the brew, it enhances their medicinal properties as the spirits of these plants are facilitated by wachuma to reveal themselves in their full potential. I have experimented with different plants and this is what I have found so far with those I have used more extensively.

Uña de Gato (Cat's Claw)

This plant grows in the Amazon basin. Its medicine strengthens the immune system and heals the reproductive organs. On another level, the plant also helps to clear the first two chakras: the core. It is helpful in healing past sexual traumas as well as other issues with sexuality. Uña de gato is traditionally used by indigenous people for treating diseases including tumors and cancer. Scientists are currently working on using it to boost the immune system for HIV patients.

Chamomile

Chamomile has a sweet, soothing effect on the nervous system. It helps prevent spasms during strong wachuma experiences and it calms the stomach. It works on the solar plexus and heart chakra. It calms excessive yang (active) energy and brings a state of acceptance and trust.

Coca Leaves

Mother Coca brings clarity to a confused and distracted mind. I use it to keep a clear head during strong journeys. It also expands the bronchiole in the lungs, allowing more oxygen and prana (life energy) to enter the bloodstream.

Coca connects us to Pachamama (Mother Earth) so we can learn more about agriculture and healing directly from the plants. It clears and stimulates the upper chakras, the third eye, and the crown chakra, and can also help women to truly surrender to their feminine essence. In the past, tobacco—a strong masculine plant—was placed on the stomach of menstruating women as a way of suppressing the strength and power present during the moon cycle. However, using coca instead can help a woman to embrace her femininity and reconnect with her body and moon cycle. Western society, which offers birth control pills, painkillers, and hormone manipulation to skip menstruation for months at a time, disconnects and distances women from this natural cleansing time. Women are encouraged to use tampons so they can avoid seeing their menstrual fluid and do all the activities they normally do. Mama Coca can be a really powerful tool to correct this conditioning and allow women to embrace their physical bodies and the Goddess within.

White Sage

This sacred plant has been used for ages as a cleansing smudge and to clear the way for Great Spirit to do its work. It keeps the aura clear and seals holes to block out unwelcome energies. It is a great ally for energetic protection and cleansing.

Palo Santo

This is South America's equivalent to North America's white sage. It is used for cleansing and raising the vibration in energetic fields. It deters negative energies.

I use a small amount of palo santo in the wachuma brew to repair and cleanse the aura. It is like cleaning wounds on an energetic level.

OTHER USEFUL PLANTS

Calea zacatechichi

This Mexican herb is used for conscious dream work. I don't mix it in the wachuma brew but a pinch of the dried plant can be chewed at the end of a ceremony before going to sleep. It can help you to stay aware during the dream state so you continue to work with your subconscious processes.

Datura and Brugmansia

Putting one to three flowers under the pillow may give more vivid dreams and reveal subconscious processes through these dreams. Flowers and leaves can also be placed on chakras and body parts in hands-on healing.

Valerian

Some people may find it difficult to sleep after a day with wachuma. They may be a little overwhelmed from the intense mental work and download of information. Depending on the medicine and the person's intention, the journey may last anywhere from eight to fifteen hours. I find it helpful to take ten drops of valerian tincture in water or chamomile tea as a sleeping aid before going to bed.

Bach Rescue Remedy

During a ceremony I sometimes give a few drops of this remedy to someone who is going through an experience of recalling memories of strong trauma from the past. It helps them stay calm and surrender to the process. Any flower essence if used correctly can be very powerful during or after a wachuma journey. For example, a few drops of lavender on your pillow is another natural sleeping aid.

Floral Bath

I make my mixture with water from a sacred place, such as a water temple or fresh water source from the Sacred Valley. I combine it with *ruda* (rue), white sage, and palo santo for their cleansing properties. I sometimes cook the core part of the San Pedro cactus and add this to the mixture, too. The white part of the cactus is very good for the hair and skin. It is an alkaline antiseptic and can treat dandruff and other hair and skin conditions. It also helps to keep people connected to the plant over the nights during a series of ceremonies. The floral bath is done in the evening before going to sleep. An extra component to the bath is to use a piece of San Pedro's white core as a sponge.

THE CEREMONIAL SETTING

I open my *mesa* (altar) by giving thanks and prayers and calling in my spirit helpers. I thank our Mother Earth and Grandfather Sun, Taita Inti, for bringing life, for keeping us warm, and for bringing the light.

I thank our Grandmother Moon, Mama Kia, for bringing light into our darkness. I also call on the four elements, which are the four pillars of all creation. I ask the element of Earth to show us our life purpose and to heal our physical body. Then I call on the element of Water, our blood, to cleanse our bodies and souls. I thank the Water for teaching us about the flow of energies and the flow of life and I ask it to heal our emotions. Then I call on the element of Air, the winds, our breath, the breath of life, which carries our prayers and intentions. I ask the Air to teach us to communicate in a respectful way and to create beautiful music as medicine. I ask the element of Air to heal our minds. Finally I call on the element of Fire, our spirit, the element that transforms energies from dense to higher frequencies and awakens us. I ask the Fire to heal our souls.

I thank the sacred mountains, the Apus, the creator God, Great Spirit, and I thank the sacred medicine of the plants for healing us and helping us to wake up from this dream. I thank our spirit helpers, guardians, doctors, wisdom keepers, ancestors, animal spirits, our totem animals and allies, and the saints, prophets, bodhisattvas, and buddhas, all the awakened ones, the ones who have walked before us.

I thank the great circle of medicine people, healers, teachers, and everyone who wants to heal and make the world a better place. I pray for a healthy Earth with nutrient-rich soil, fresh air, and clean waters. I pray for harmonious coexistence and for peace. I pray for the children who are waiting to come and that all beings may be free of suffering and happy.

I thank the participants for coming to do this work for themselves and for all their relationships and to co-create with God to give birth to a better world. I then invite them to share their prayers and specific intentions for the journey. We also invite the souls of friends and relatives who need healing to enter our circle. Ingesting the medicine of wachuma binds us together in sacred space throughout the day. I think it is important that everybody who participates in the circle drinks the medicine, unless there is any medical reason that contraindicates this, and I always drink at least a threshold dose with the participants. I think it is essential that the person who is leading the ceremony drinks the medicine to be on the same page and in tune with the circle.

In ceremony we are one people who come together to heal and each participant brings their own unique qualities of love, compassion, and support. My role is to hold a safe space for the participants to do their work with the medicine and to be of service when they need assistance. The point is to let participants learn from their direct experience and find their answers within. I don't interfere with their process unless necessary. I also ask each participant not to disturb anyone else's process. But every ceremony is different and it sometimes happens that all may sing and play together, which is a beautiful way of connecting and creating a healing space.

The purging may be intense at times with cathartic reactions of crying, vomiting, or even laughing hysterically with pure joy. I let participants go through their own process and stay on standby if they need support, offering comfort once they have gone through what they needed to.

At the end of the ceremony we return to the circle to share what we have learned and to close the mesa. Sharing experiences can be an important part of people's healing. I close the ceremony by cleansing the space and participants with smudge, making a silent closing prayer, and giving thanks for the day.

ADVICE FOR THE JOURNEY

It is important to have an intention when participating in a ceremony. However, the answers we seek may not always be what we have expected, because the medicine may redirect our experience to the root of our real problems. This we need to accept.

It is best is to stay centered throughout the day without getting attached to any of the experiences we have, but instead staying open and paying attention to whatever may come. If you find yourself stuck in a loop or a mind trap, thinking the same thoughts over and over again, snap out of it! Same thing if you find yourself enchanted by beautiful visions so much so that you drift away too far: get back to your intention and work!

The mind, which so often acts out of fear, will sometimes try to distract you from getting closer to the core of your being. This distraction may come as doubts, fear, ridiculing your process, or judging yourself or others. This fear doesn't want to die, so it will do whatever it can to hang on. Don't be fooled by it. Be strong and persistent and detach from it.

Wachuma is not just another recreational drug. When we drink it we go on a mission to learn important things about ourselves, to heal ourselves and others, and to awaken to our fuller potential. The spirit of the plant will only reveal its secrets to sincere and humble seekers. You need to build a good relationship with it in the same way as you build good relations with animals and humans. Our whole life experience is very much determined by our relationships. Everything is alive and everything has spirit and that spirit is what connects us with the oneness of all creation.

In preparation for a journey certain dietary restrictions are also important, such as abstaining from alcohol, drugs, and meat the day before and after the ceremony, and to fast on the day of the ritual itself.

Some traditional shamans also insist on abstinence from sex. I think that sex between partners in a harmonious and established relationship isn't necessarily contraindicated, but the man should avoid ejaculating if having sex the day before a ceremony. The reason for this is that men lose vital energy by emptying the semen. I actually think it can be beneficial for couples to be intimate before a ceremony, however, if they want to work on strengthening their relationship. On the other hand, if you intend to work on personal issues only, then it's better to maintain your own space and not take on energies from your partner before you work with the medicine.

The work during ceremony requires glucose as fuel for the brain, and the body may need extra water to help flush out toxins that get released in a purge. Fruit should be at hand from three hours into the journey together with herbal tea and drinking water throughout the day. However, we eat as little as possible, as eating can be a trick of the mind to suppress emotions and disturb the medicine and its work.

On a deeper three-day retreat we drink three doses of wachuma per day and don't eat at all, and drink only the minimum amount of water unless medical conditions are contradictory. This is the ultimate way for profound inner work as it keeps the body's systems open and breaks down the mind's defenses so we surrender more deeply to the medicine, but it is not for the beginner. An intense journey like this may also require up to three or sometimes six months of integration work so that things fall into place before the next medicine journey.

POSTCEREMONY INTEGRATION

Integration work after (or between) ceremonies is essential to be able to successfully function in our daily lives. We must work to understand what the medicine has shown us and how to use the lessons in everyday situations. Wachuma helps us to heal diseases and to make us aware of our harmful thought patterns of negativity, delusion, and ignorance. The medicine gives us the keys and a little push, but we must use our free will and determination to complete the work.

Some of our discoveries may feel abstract and difficult to comprehend, because we experience them in an altered state of consciousness. Writing, drawing, painting, singing, or other creative expression is therefore helpful in the integration process. It is also a good idea to set up an action plan based on the insights you have received about how to get where you want to be, and it is best to stay away from situations and people who don't support or resonate with your process until you have established a new platform to act from. When we are strong enough and feel solid enough to face the world and exercise our new way of being, we should then do so and enjoy the dance of life.

Wachuma is very clear in pointing us in the right direction, but we need to walk by ourselves to get where we want to be, and there is no point in continuing to drink the medicine if we don't seriously want to do the work. We won't get any further, and instead we will build up piles of unfinished tasks. The teaching of wachuma is to take one step at a time and to find a resolution so we don't need to struggle with the same issues over and over again.

A FEW LAST WORDS

I wish for as many people as possible to have the opportunity to meet this beautiful medicine in the correct way. Most pharmaceuticals only treat symptoms that appear on the surface, but wachuma and other plant medicines can heal our souls and cure the reasons for diseases and suffering.

Wachuma reconnects us with the core of our being and brings us back to oneness with all creation. It helps us to awaken from the haze of illusion and ignorance, to see beyond the fear and conditioning that have formed our ego, bringing us home to our true nature and helping us peel off the layers of pain and fear surrounding our hearts. It opens the doors to deeper love and understanding.

Wachuma wants to bring us back to the lost paradise of Earth and invites us to join the joyful dance of life.

It is an exciting time we are living in now. Humanity is awakening to a higher consciousness and the sacred medicine of our elders is becoming more accessible to modern civilization. This may play a vital part in the reawakening of many confused or lost souls in our modern world. With this transition comes the responsibility to work with wachuma in a responsible way, not to abuse it in the same way as we have tobacco, marijuana, poppy, and other sacred plants. We must be mindful and treat plants as living beings, not just commodities to be bought, sold, and manipulated.

We must take full responsibility for our lives with our hearts and minds open, walking humbly with an awareness that we are part of a bigger picture. We are all one.

Thank you wachuma, sacred medicine, for bringing us home.

PART TWO

The Western Mind

Life lived in the absence of the psychedelic experience is life trivialized, life denied, life enslaved to the ego.

TERENCE MCKENNA

THE WESTERN PERSPECTIVE on San Pedro will inevitably be different from that of the shamans working in Peru, immersed in the culture and seeing the breakthroughs achieved each day by their patients as a result of the plant and its healing powers.

Westerners have different needs and often different intentions than Peruvians. While it is typical for the latter to approach ceremonies with very practical questions, concerns, and healing needs, it seems that Westerners arrive with the baggage of their culture and with many doubts, fears, anxieties, and emotional issues to work on.

Wade Davis and Peter Furst have written about San Pedro ceremonies they attended where Peruvian participants had questions about their businesses and how to improve them, or wanted to know who had stolen money from them, or had a definite health issue, a problem located in the body that they wanted San Pedro to cure. By contrast, the participants who join me for ceremony in Europe or who arrive from other Western countries to attend my healing trips to Peru seem sick at the level of the soul. They are grieving, uncertain, lost, or confused and, in whatever particular way it manifests, they are unhappy and no longer in love with life or with themselves. Shamans call conditions like this soul loss. And when the soul is missing it is not just a spiritual, emotional, or mental crisis (although it is all of these things too), it can lead to very real physical problems.

After years of working with people like this—and feeling many of their afflictions myself —I am convinced that this is a cultural as much as a personal issue. In the West we often have no one "real" to talk to, we have lost our communities, our families are broken, and we have become disconnected. This can only make our problems worse, for when overwhelmed by grief, anxiety, or loss, where is the *anam cara,* "the soul friend," we can confess to and relieve the pressures within us that are making us ill? From where can we take good, objective advice or counsel that does not have an agenda of its own or a fee at the end of it?

Having witnessed many of the healing miracles that San Pedro can perform and that La Gringa also mentions, I am convinced of something else too: that the Western world desperately needs the help of San Pedro—to reconnect us, to make us whole again, to let us know we are loved so we are able to truly give and receive love.

Thankfully, we are beginning to take a new interest in the potential of this plant, so perhaps the day is not so far away when San Pedro will be better known and more available to those who need it. In this section we hear from some of the Westerners who are assisting the spread of this knowledge.

Eve Bruce, M.D., was a board-certified medical doctor in the United States with more than two decades of experience and memberships in numerous medical societies, including the American College of Surgeons and the American Board of Plastic Surgeons. She has appeared on "Medical Breakthroughs" for CNN Headline News, the Learning Channel, Lifetime Live, and the Discovery Channel and has been featured in magazines such as *Harper's Bazaar, Health, Natural Health,* and *Healthy Living.* She then had a healing breakthrough of her own, and became a shamanic initiate as the first non-Quechua woman to be inducted into the Circle of Yachaks or Birdpeople Shamans of the high Andes. In the article that follows she speaks of her journey into shamanism and of the plants that have helped her to heal and heal others: ayahuasca and San Pedro.

David Luke, Ph.D., is a British university professor carrying out pioneering work with San Pedro in the study of ESP states and precognition. It is his firm belief that the cactus is able to overcome the effects of the "reducing valve" of the brain, removing our filters to information in order to expand our consciousness. In his article he reviews the evidence and reports on a unique experiment of his own into precognition.

Morgan Maher is a writer for Daniel Pinchbeck's *Reality Sandwich* new consciousness magazine. Here he conducts a wide-ranging interview with me that covers the history of San Pedro, its healing potential, its similarities and differences to ayahuasca, the "message of the plants," and the role of teacher plants in human evolution.

5

The Anaconda and the Hummingbird

Sacraments of the Lowland Rain Forest and the Highest Mountains

Technologies for Ascended Wisdom and Consciousness

Eve Bruce, M.D.

The dwelling of my Father
Is in the heart of the world
Where all love exists
And there is a profound secret.

This profound secret
Is within all Humanity
If all will know themselves
Here, inside the truth.

I have taken this drink

It has incredible power,
It demonstrates to all of us
Here in this Truth.

I have climbed, I have climbed, I have climbed
I have climbed with joy
When reaching the Heights
I encountered the Virgin Mary.

I have climbed, I have climbed, I have climbed
I have climbed with love
I have encountered the Eternal Father
And the Redeemer, Jesus Christ.

Daime force, Daime light
Daime love!

Daime . . . the teacher of all teachers.

HYMN FROM SANTO DAIME FOUNDER
MESTRE IRINEU SERRA*

It has been postulated that the beginnings of spirituality—the notion that there is a great deal more beyond this physical life—began countless eons ago with the assistance of plant entheogens. Evidence of this shift in consciousness can be found in our ancestors' artistic renditions of their visions on cave walls. Graham Hancock in his book *Supernatural* eloquently explores this, meticulously detailing the "otherworld" through accounts of visionary experiences from ancient times to the present, comparing current visionary descriptions with the images found in rock art.[1]

---

*Epigraph translated by Benny Shanon in *The Antipodes of the Mind: Charting the Phenomenology of the Ayahuasca Experience*. —R.H.

This "otherworld," it would appear, has changed over time, developing alongside of the everyday world that some call "reality." Frequented by our ancestors long past, these other dimensions were found to be healing and informative. Indeed, the world beyond our gross receptive bodies appears to have long provided a path to being able to transcend, transform, and expand our existence by giving us powerful, pragmatic tools that can be used to assist in both basic survival and in pondering the mysteries of our existence.

Cave paintings of forty thousand years ago involved abstract images and patterns, and are in essence the same as the visions that we see today when communing with these plant teachers. Although we were anatomically fully evolved some two-hundred thousand years before this time, the fact that there was remarkably no change noted in what is found in archaeological remains through the vast reaches of human existence before the beginnings of rock art, and an exponentially rapidly changing vista of human patterns of existence and thought since then, is a magnificent testimony to these plants usefulness to us.

And yet at some point this otherworld became co-opted by religious intermediaries in an endless power play. Direct communication and communion with the otherworld was forbidden in the "developing" world, first by vilification and law, and then by the most effective method of all—ignoring its existence. The rise of the material world at the altar of science has removed this otherworld from our lives and placed it in the realm of the ridiculous, of fantasy, explaining it away by the chemical reactions in our very material brains. The imaginal has become synonymous with the imagined.

Whatever your stance on this, it seems clear that from the time of our earliest musings on the nature of life, humans developed ways of interfacing with these mystical realms, and that at some point this most democratic leveler of communities and wisdom became relegated to the few. Despite rapid advances of material knowledge in the way of science, many find themselves disconnected and lost. Where did we make a turn that took us away from our connection with and empowered assistance from the divine nature of life on this planet?

Luckily for us there are still pockets of peoples who have evolved along a more connected and sacred path of oneness, for if there is a universal shamanic cosmology throughout Mother Earth it is that of our interconnectedness, of the great web that links us all—whether embodied, disembodied, or never embodied. This is the notion of ecstatic oneness—the *samadhi* state explored in the yoga sutras (with the assistance of plants through the use of soma), and in many parts of the world this state is attained and sustained through the use of sacred plant medicines—the entheogens.

For over fifteen years I have been honored to have had the mission of taking groups to these pockets of indigenous peoples in remote communities so that we might vision with sacred entheogens. As witness to hundreds of peoples' communions, along with my own personal relationship with these plant spirits, I have been blessed with great access to the mysteries of how they interact with and heal us, and to the knowledge that in some ways no two interactions are the same—and in some ways they are all exactly the same.

As physical beings our spirit is aware of the world around us through our body's tightly gated and censored sensory organs and their pathways, all of which are highly limited as to which spectrum of energies we can perceive. We all know of the existence of the ultraviolet and infrared light spectrum and are also aware that with the limitations of our eyes' perceptive abilities we are not able to see these light rays. We are also aware of the existence of sounds that are above the frequency that our ears can hear. We are familiar with and comfortable with the fact that we can only perceive a fraction of what is around us, and that in addition to this limitation, at any point in time we can only be aware of a small fraction of that which we are capable of perceiving. This small portion of the All is our consciousness—our "reality." How arrogant can we be to even hypothesize that our very limited sensations can begin to know the whole of reality even in the physical world, let alone the nonphysical.

Some of us are blessed to have spontaneous openings in this shell of our beingness, those magical moments when we know we are simultaneously both huge and miniscule, both a vital miracle of immense universal source and an impossibly small part of this vastness. Both part and whole. And so we strive for ways of reaching beyond our limited world to find that experiential peek at infinity, of methods to enhance our perception of the "supernatural"—and thus to expand our reality—to remind ourselves of our nonphysical existence and of the web of connectedness. We search for any way that can reach out and expand our consciousness—meditation, ascetic practices, fasting, chanting, drumming, repetitive dance movements, hyperventilation.

One of the oldest and most consistently useful methods known to man—and to animals I might add—is through the use of entheogenic plant medicines.

As a physician and scientist I am continually amazed by how consistently useful these plants are. I am also aware of how—in a way—they are also inconsistent. In other words, the experiences of people using these sacred medicines always hold something of profound usefulness for each person, enabling them to open to their interconnectedness with the All, to expanding their notion of reality and by doing so to raising their consciousness by the similarities in visionary patterns, scenarios, and information. Also by the repeatedly experienced songs and even dances that each plant gifts to us with relative frequency. These are the consistencies and these consistencies cross wide cultural and environmental boundaries. As mentioned above, these consistent patterns even span the length of millennia as seen in European, Australian, and African rock art of some thrity-five thousand to forty thousand years ago. Are these patterns in the plants themselves or in us as receivers of and sifters through these visionary gifts? In our brain's anatomy? In our brain's chemistry? Or in the otherworld that we have trouble perceiving without the assistance of these teacher plants.

And then there are the inconsistencies.

It never ceases to amaze me from a biochemical point of view that when taking a group of people for ceremonial, entheogenic consciousness expansion and healing, on any given day, with everyone taking the same brew and being in the same place with the same shaman and the same energies, each person has a completely different experience—both physically and nonphysically. This might be explained by individual physical, emotional, psychological, and spiritual differences, but the inconsistencies do not end there. The next time this same group of people imbibe the same recipe in the same place with the same environmental conditions each will have a completely new experience compared to their last. As the Shuar say, you get what you need.

I have extensive personal experience with ayahuasca in both the Upper and Lower Amazonian regions, and with San Pedro in the Andes. In describing my ayahuasca experiences, it should be noted, I will tend to use examples from the Shuar perspective as it is in a Shuar community of the Upper Amazon that I have spent most time. In addition, this community is remotely located in an area with no roads or electricity, resulting in less cultural pollution and a more traditional outlook. My Shuar elders or Uwishins (shamans or "wise ones") are from a very long lineage of uninterrupted teachings going back into prerecorded time. I have also, however, spent a great deal of time with ayahuasceros from the lowlands and have found remarkably similar reverence and practices.

The miraculous beauty of plant entheogens fills me with awe. In this chapter I have been asked to talk about these two sacred medicines—ayahuasca and San Pedro. This will by no means be a complete treatise of the subject, but rather an exploration into the essential nature of these two sacraments.

When befriending someone new you spend time with them and get to know them. Similarly, when befriending a plant spirit, or indeed any Earth spirit, the native way is to sit with them, getting to know the plant, developing and nurturing this new relationship. In other words, to begin to know the spirit of the plant, begin by sitting with it and communing with it as you would in the early stages of any relationship.

Ask questions of them: Who are they? What is their name? Where do they live? Where do they come from? Who are their friends? You begin to share stories and songs. Your life stories. Your accomplishments and your role in your communities.

Begin by getting to know each other body-to-body. Understanding that our essential energies are not disconnected from our life-form. Get to know the vessel in which our new friend's spirit lives, the physical form that is home to the spirit on this planet. Sit together in its house if you are able to do so, in the plant's natural surroundings. Ask questions. Listen and share. Learn its names, how it is called to by those who hold it most sacred—the plant shamans, called the *vegetilismos*, or *vegetilismas*, if female. Who are this plant's other friends and how does it connect with them? What is its part in the community? What is its contribution to the world (in the case of a plant spirit this story will be long and measured in millennia)? As you sit with it, listening and communicating over time, your relationship with it will deepen. As you continue to share with this being, gaining mutual trust and understanding, it is sure to tell you more and more—its songs, its stories, and its gifts. Let us begin.

AYAHUASCA

Ayahuasca (also known by the names *caapi, yaje, natém, dapa, mihi, pinde, la purga*) is a Quechua word variously translated as "the vine of death" or "the vine of the soul," also "the vine of the dead" or "the vine of the ancestors." This naming tells it all. It is thought by the Shuar to open the head, to create an opening through which a new life vision can seep and the old can die. It is through this opening that, it is said, one can see true reality.

Ayahuasca is not a loner or a dry being. It is literally a hot, wet soup. Not brewed from a single plant, it is the dance of several plant spirits together.

The hanging forest liana *Banisteriopsis caapi* vine's woody trunk is prepared and combined with the *chacrona,* that is *Psychotria viridis* and/or a host of other plants—the light. This combines the heaven-seeking vine with the Earth-based lower plants, as well as bringing together the four elements of fire, water, earth, and air in the preparation. Into the cauldron the Shuar Uwíshins will place the carefully cut vine, layered with the leaves of the plants of their choice, which are counted out between the fingers of their hands. Water to cover and place over an open fire. The brew is cooked for a full day, although each ayahuascero has his or her own recipe (added to the *Banisteriopsis* vine you will encounter most commonly *Psychotria* various species, although numerous others may join in the dance including *Brugmansia* species, *Diplopterys, guayúsa,* and others too numerous to recount here).

Biochemically, the effects on the imbiber are also a dance and depend on a unique sparring between the mixture of plants and the person's own body. The vine *Banisteriopsis caapi* contains harmine MAOI's, or monoamine oxidase inhibiters. Without this inhibition of our stomach's monoamine oxidase, the DMT of the chacrona would be rendered orally inactive. The dance between the plant spirits and our stomach allows the light to enter our being.

The plants of ayahuasca also grow in a "soupy" landscape. The primary jungle of the Upper and Lower Amazon is a hot, wet, and soupy mix. The very air is a soup. The home of these plant spirits is richly dense and abundant, filled with countless entities. It is a deeply sensuous and sensual medium where life and fecundity create a veritable soup for the senses. This is not a subtle forest but filled with loud smells, sounds, tastes, textures, and sights. This is a place where plant spirits live in close community with the spirits of thousands of animals and disembodied entities. The vine, snakelike, winds its way up the trees in an uncertain course, and its very life depends on its relationship to these trees and the myriad other creatures surrounding it in this mutually supportive and destructive landscape. Although life abounds in this environment, the vine can be quite slow growing. It is not unusual to see a twenty-year-old vine growing in the remote jungle.

Out of this soup the disciples of ayahuasca arose. The nature of this dance of just the right spiritual elements points to a divinely inspired and spiritually guided birthing. It has been said that due to the immense complexity of the jungle's vegetation and the sheer number of species, the random selection by chance of just the right combination of plants to create the effect that we find used in the ayahuasca sacrament, even over time, is mathematically impossible. If you ask the Uwíshins they will tell you that they talk to the plants. The plants teach them how to be used and this has always been the way.

The location where a particular vine is harvested (that is, the location where it is found and the surrounding spirits with which the vine has grown up) is thought to have a great deal to do with its potency and its unique spiritual essence. For example, an old vine found growing in a remote and quiet area away from human settlement is thought to have a more powerful spirit and a more potent effect. Amongst the Shuar the essence of a particular vine is often described by which god or goddess it is aligned with. I have often seen an ayahuascero come from a foraging session leaping with excitement at having found and harvested a vine of the Goddess Tsunki, foretelling and expounding the virtues of the upcoming night's ceremony with this particular plant sprit.

Ayahuasca has many stories, and I will recount one that I was told by a Shuar grandmother.

It is said that in ancient times, when Étsaa ascended to the sky to become the sun god, the people became saddened and lonely at night time. Étsaa sent Ayumpúm on a bolt of lightning to help them.

Ayumpúm is the god of thunder and whenever you hear this crashing sound you know that he is near. It was Ayumpúm who taught the people which plants to pick and how to prepare the sacrament of natém (ayahuasca). Through this divine gift they were made aware of all spiritual entities that inhabit the night.

From that day onward it is said, the people were never again sad or lonely. From that day onward they learned to prepare ayahuasca at night time to keep them aware and connected to the spirits that lived all around them.

The ayahuasceros traditionally are the healers of the people, of the land, and of the communities. They are the Uwíshins and Pajés of the jungle. Steven Rubenstein in his book *Alejandro Tsakimp: A Shuar Healer in the Margins of History* describes the mission of an Uwíshin in this way: "Shamans are not supposed to act solely to augment their own power. They exist to help others."[2]

I have experienced several ways that ayahuasca is used by the Shuar to help others, both as a part of everyday life and as a catalyst involved in rites of passage and vision quests. For example, ayahuasca may be used for medicinal purpose at the time of a healing or in lesser amounts on a regular basis for a medical condition that requires continued use. For visioning and healing, the concentrated form is more frequently used by the Uwíshins. At adolescence, for example, an entire family will participate in the initiatory ceremony using either ayahuasca or *aaikiúa* (datura) and follow the young man or woman's vision for their future by dreaming it together. Before visioning in this way there are preparatory practices that can be challenging and lengthy. These can include fasting from all food for periods of days to weeks combined with strenuous physical exertion and the snorting of strong sacred jungle tobacco, *Nicotiana rustica*. This *dieta* is not simply fasting from foods, but also going into nature and separating from daily chores and situations. By purifying your body and surroundings you are prepared to concentrate on the otherworld and to receive visions by coming into a deeply quiet and contemplative attitude and space within.

Less frequently, *natém* (ayahuasca) is used in the *natémamo* ceremony. In this instance the preparation is thinner and less concentrated such that literally gallons are drunk by each person until a great purging occurs, followed by extremely strong healing visions. The natemamo ceremony is performed when a family or community has experienced a challenging event requiring a cathartic purge, such as a death or other major upheaval. At the onset of the evening's ceremony, the communal drum is beaten and can be heard for miles. Upon hearing this call those who wish to partake with the family are summoned.

The purgative nature of ayahuasca is deemed a gift. An important part of the healing experience, the emetic properties are highly appreciated. To put this into context, know that in many rainforest cultures vomiting is part of one's daily cleansing practice. In contrast to our Western mind where, as nausea builds, we begin to think that we are getting sick, these peoples think of this process as getting well. The Achuar arise well before dawn and communally drink gallons of *guayusa**[3] in order to vomit as part of their everyday morning ablutions.

Ayahuasca's visionary potential is essential for the practice of the Uwíshins. On the other hand, although the Uwíshin shaman will always use ayahuasca during his healings on others, the person being healed may or may not take the brew, at least amongst the Shuar.

The healing ceremonies by the shamans include chanting as well as brushing with plants. Phlegm is a complex concept that is difficult to translate into English; however, suffice it to say that unwanted energies are extracted by sucking. Amongst the Shuar this practice is enhanced by the use of *tsentsak,* or invisible darts. These can be seen by the Uwíshins when under the influence of ayahuasca, who will scan the patient, sending his own darts in to search out offending darts or other unwanted energies, which are then extracted by sucking. The energies removed will concretize into palpable items or "phlegm," which are then discarded. The physical part of the healing is generally not lengthy and does not detract from the visionary healing potential of the plant spirit experienced by the patient.

---

*Guayusa is a rainforest plant that, like all plants, has many uses and functions—not just one as we are commonly taught to view plants in the West. One use, as suggested here, is as a purge in order to purify for the day. Another is as an aid to "lucid dreaming" and for this reason guayusa may also be known as "the night watchman's plant" as it enables those who drink it to remain aware of their surroundings even when they are sleeping. —R.H.

An important part of the traditional ayahuasca session is the music. Each ayahuascero has his own songs or chants (*icaros* in Quechua). The shape and direction of the entire experience seems to be guided by the songs of the ayahuascero. Other senses, such as scent, will also drive the experience.

The spirit of ayahuasca is known to strongly impart a sense of unity with the All. Commonly the Uwíshins or other ayahuascero will be aware of all the visions of those who are participating with him. This attribute was even recognized by scientists, and in fact the first alkaloid isolated from the *Banisteriopsis* vine was termed "telepathine."[4]

Another universally experienced gift from communion with this plant spirit medicine is a sense of connection to and love of nature. Many, after first-time communion, describe to me that they felt forever changed in their relationship to Mother Earth and Father Sky, and devote their lives thereafter in some way to honoring all life on this planet.

How the spirit of ayahuasca comes to you in vision or how you sense this spirit is highly variable. In general it is thought that a plant spirit will come to you in a form you are able to relate with in vision. Ayahuasca is said to often show herself in the feminine form, although the Tukano will describe ayahuasca as Father Aya or Grandfather. Mestre Irineu Serra, the founder of the Santo Daime Church, describes his first encounter with the spirit of ayahuasca as a female—La Reina de la Floresta, or the forest queen.

Although ayahuasca visions are individual and varied, classically she comes in the guise of potent animals such as jaguars and as light beings from the celestial realms. And as snakes: if there is one vision that is most associated with the spirit of ayahuasca it is of the snake—the anaconda.

Primordial snake, asleep for centuries in the fundamental waters of my material body, associated with instincts, primordial fears, my first water-demon . . . I might not see you but still you are there.

. . . I fear you every time the internal wind blows, bringing me your voice . . . like you, I too would like to be close to the Earth, to feel that my heat is that which she gives me to and to emerge from her womb at night to bathe in the moonlight . . . to see values change in the world, from within my immobile ophidian blue eye, with my physical eyes closed as only animals divest of the rigid-rational wrappings of the brain are able to see: forwards and backwards further than time and distance with ears capable of hearing the voice of the serpent-mother the way Eve heard it, speaking from within oneself without words, directly to the cells, distrusting even the gods. . . .

THE ICARO OR SHAMANIC SONG
BY DR. JACQUES MABIT DESCRIBING
HIS AYAHUASCA VISION[5]

The course these visions take can be, like the vine itself, serpiginous. Winding through your consciousness like a snake, there is a sense that you might get lost in the randomness of the direction that your visions take—that is if you let it. The Shuar will remind you to be strong, to capture your strength by following the vision trail. A session during which you are able to focus and follow the trail of the visions, finding the inner power to confront terrifying entities, which then reveal to you their gifts, is especially welcomed and is said to impart *arútam*—Shuar for the vital warrior life force.

After the sacramental session the Uwíshins will ask you to consecrate your healing by committing to certain sacrifices. It is said that the path to the sacred is through sacrifice, words with similar etymological roots coming from the word for an oath or obligation. The sacrifices asked of you will vary widely; however, they often include prescriptions for a period of abstinence from certain foods and activities such as spicy foods, meats, alcohol, and sex. After my first experience with ayahuasca I was asked to abstain from sex for six weeks although I was never again given such a lengthy prescription.

As mentioned above, an ayahuasca ceremony in traditional usage is devoid of major fanfare or ritual at the time of drinking and is more of an internal experience with dreamtime revealing to us our truth and expanding our reality. It is most often held at night; however, there are ayahuasceros in the lowlands who hold ceremony during daylight hours.

No discussion of ayahuasca would be complete without mention of more recent initiates—the Churches of the Santo Daime, the União do Vegetal (UdV), and the Barquinha. Disciples of these churches have taken the sacramental use of ayahuasca throughout the world, even to upper-middle-class suburban neighborhoods of Europe and North America. These relatively recent syncretic churches coming out of the deep Amazonian rainforest regions are centered on the sacramental tea itself.

In the early 1930s a Catholic Brazilian *siringueiro,* or rubber tapper, of African ancestry, called Raimundo Irineu Serra, or Mestre Irineu, after instruction from local shamans in the sacred use of ayahuasca, was given visions by the spirit of the plants along with instructions for his new church movement.

> Irineu's first significant vision was of a Divine Lady, sitting in the moon, who told him he must retreat into the forest for eight days with only ayahuasca to drink and only *macacheira* (boiled manioc) to eat. During this retreat Irineu had visions of the "Forest Queen" who told him that he must start a new faith in which the ayahuasca drink (to be called "daime," meaning "give me" in Portuguese) would be central. She would show him how the Daime was to be used as a sacrament and guide him through the initial hostilities he and his followers would face.
>
> MICHELLE PAULI, *THE SANTO DAIME—HOW IT BEGAN*[6]

The Santo Daime religious ceremonies (called *trabalhos,* or works) are Christian based and consist of differing sessions—meditative, festive, healing, and commemorative. Depending on the type of work, they involve the singing of hymns, dancing, and visioning. The use of the sacramental ayahuasca is central to these ceremonies, which serve to move energies individually and communally, resulting in personal and communal spiritual evolution. Women and men are separated and there is a hierarchy of disciples within the church. The *feitio,* or preparation of the tea, is also segregated and is a beautiful ceremony. The women collect the leaves of the chacrona singing to the plants and give them to the men. The men collect and cut the vine, which they then pound in unison while chanting hymns. The *padrinho* then begins to prepare the tea.

The UdV has similar origins in the rainforests of Brazil in 1961 by another siringueiro, Gabriel do Costa; however, this church claims spiritual lineage back three millennia. The Barquinha is a syncretism between the Santo Daime and Umbanda, an Afro-Brazilian religion that embraces the skills of mediumship. Both the Santo Daime and UdV have active congregations throughout the world.

SAN PEDRO

San Pedro (also known by the names *achuma, huachuma, wachuma, giganton, aguacolla, mescalito, Cardo Santo,* and *el Remedio*) by comparison has been given the name of an apostle of Christ. Saint Peter in popular mythology is the keeper of the keys to heaven and over the preceding centuries, in common parlance, the essence of this plant spirit has been depicted using the name of the founding rock of the Christian Church. As the biblical story goes, upon Simon's first meeting with Jesus he was renamed Cephas (in Latin *Petra* or Peter)—the rock.

The San Pedro plant itself, *Trichocereus (Echinopsis) pachanoi,* is a tall, straight, firm cactus. It stands alone and grows hard, straight, and very tall in the mountains of the Andes. The physical form of this plant conjures the images of an erect phallus, and indeed one of the names by which it is known is *pene de Dios*—literally "penis of God."

Fast growing in a high, dry, and arid landscape, San Pedro firmly and resolutely reaches upward toward the celestial realms, perhaps taking with him the keys to those very gates of heaven. It is a plant of great beauty day or night, and in fact it unfolds its sweetly aromatic flowers only at nighttime.

Interestingly, similar to the ayahuasca mythology, there is at least one story from the Bolivian highlands, recorded by archaeologist and anthropologist Mario Polia, associating San Pedro with lightning, as determined by Bonnie Glass-Coffin.[7]

You are probably familiar with the story of the condor and the hummingbird. This story associated with San Pedro tells of cooperative ascension whereby the highest flying bird, the condor, flew with the hummingbird on its back as high as it could go into the celestial realms. The hummingbird through the condor's assistance was able to go the remaining distance and reach heaven. Thus it is that we can only get so far in our striving for connection with God, falling short each time we attempt to reach the divine realms. With the help of the hummingbird (aka San Pedro) and working in unity we too can reach the heights of heaven where San Pedro holds the keys.

It is worth noting that this same story has been twisted in the Western psyche from a tale of cooperative unity to a tale of sub-terfuge—the ancient Celtic tale of the eagle and the wren. As the story goes, the eagle flew skyward, higher and higher with all his might, trying to reach heaven but unable to make it all the way. Unbeknownst to him, the little wren had hidden himself in the eagle's feathers. When the eagle tired, getting as high as he could go, the wren flew out—easily becoming the first to get to heaven. Thus this crafty bird reaped all the glory while ignoring the eagle's determination and hard work. Is it a wonder then that in Britain on Wren's Day in times past the birds were slaughtered and impaled by young boys who would wander through the towns, waving this show of their prowess and asking for handouts? I find myself wondering whether the original stories about the eagle and the wren were more cooperative, and I pray that we in the West can return to a less competitive stance in our search for communion with our celestial guides.

Here is a more feminine story told of the San Pedro spirit, known as *aguacolla* in Ecuador, from Glass-Coffin: "It seems that aguacolla before becoming a plant was a queen, first born, beautiful and attractive (and it is therefore that) the plant used to give tribute to the princess, the queen and the moon." It is noted by her that on the north coast of Peru, the moon and sea were considered more important deities than the sun. Glass-Coffin also equates the ancient use of San Pedro with connection to the ancestors through whom control of the subterranean waters are sought for the fertility of the land.

San Pedro, in contrast to ayahuasca, stands alone. Although other sacred plant spirits may accompany the spirit of San Pedro in its ceremonial healing work, it is in general a solo practitioner. The brew of San Pedro is made from the green chlorophyll-containing outer portion of the cactus decocted to a concentrated, green, slimy, gelatinous drink. Like any herbal decoction, the whole plant's physiological and biochemical effects are much more complex than that of its isolated component chemicals, in this case the alkaloid mescaline. It is a devoted plant spirit that works in a characteristic dedicated yet individualistic way.

Similar to ayahuasca, you get what you need. Each person and each session with the plant spirit is widely varied and appears to be tailored to the spiritual, physical, emotional, and mental needs of the person in that time—and of course all of these needs are connected. Just as we are looking at the physicality of the plant to get to know its spirit, so too our own physicality, external and internal, at any given moment gives clues to our spiritual condition and vice versa.

The San Pedro cactus grows in segments. When foraging for plants, besides speaking to it, note is taken of its number of segments. This number is traditionally thought to correspond to that plant's spirit—to its personality, energies, and thus to its utility in healing for various purposes. Seven-segment plants are most common and are used for group ceremony. For individual healings, however, one might hunt for a plant whose spirit has the qualities that your patient needs—the rare four-ribbed plant being the most potent and complex spiritually.

San Pedro, more often than ayahuasca, is also used for its nonvisionary healing properties. Perhaps because of this healing potential, ceremonial practices in which lower concentrations are used are prevalent. In addition, many practices involve lengthy participatory healing sessions that render the healing from a purely visionary internal experience less attainable to the participant. In many curanderas' traditional healing practices it would appear that the visions in and of themselves are not crucial to the healing process. Deemed more important by many healers is the spiritual communion with the sacrament that will heal and advance the patient's soul life. Having said that, as opposed to Shuar healing practices where the patient may or may not drink ayahuasca, during a San Pedro healing ceremony all participants generally partake of the *remedio* (the brew).

The plant grows alone in high and often dry landscapes. It is found behind many old churches from the sixteenth and seventeenth centuries, and indeed on the walls of some chapels you will find the painted images of the San Pedro cactus. One chapel that I have frequented high in the mountains of Ecuador has a beautiful depiction of the baby Jesus arising out of a San Pedro plant. From these murals one can assume, despite the many written church treatises condemning its use, that the isolated and contemplative monks in the Andes seemed to have found the holy nature of this plant and used it to enhance their mystical experiences with Jesus and with their other divine guides.

We know that San Pedro has been revered for more than six thousand years. Images of San Pedro are seen on numerous archaeological specimens. Evidence of its sacred use has even been found in preceramic cultures in areas of Peru from as long ago as 4000 BCE. Within the archaeological remains of the Chavin culture of the northern Peruvian highlands are found several depictions of San Pedro with mythical beings as well as with images of jaguars, hummingbirds, and deer. One

Chavin excavation even found ancient "cigars" made from the San Pedro plant. The San Pedro motif is also found in archaeological digs of other cultures such as the Salinar and Nasca.

In visions, many have recounted to me that the spirit of San Pedro often comes to them as a male, but this is not always the case. Whether you imagine a plant spirit as male or female is likely to say more about you than about the spirit itself; however, what is apparent from the descriptions of people who have been with both San Pedro and ayahuasca is that San Pedro is commonly described as the more gentle spirit. Just as in Tibetan Buddhism compassion is thought of as a male attribute, San Pedro's teachings are frequently seen as coming from a male entity. Although in the end these teachings are just as challenging and difficult in substance, the plant tends to reveal them in a softer and more cogent manner than the teachings from the harsh and exacting spirit of ayahuasca. The teachings from San Pedro are also more often described as direct and clear as opposed to the dreamlike and circuitous teachings of the spirit of ayahuasca.

The San Pedro cactus is said to be of the wind and is indeed an airy plant that grows high up in the mountains, as opposed to the earthy, wet, crowded conditions under which the plants that make up the spirit of ayahuasca grow. This high mountain air is home to the cactus and is also seen in the stories that recall San Pedro as being associated with the four winds, invoking the sacred spirit of the four cardinal directions and of the breath of the icaros. In addition, this rarefied clarity is translated into the visions and teachings that come from communion with San Pedro. It is this essential air quality of the spirit of the San Pedro that people describe as providing a sense of clear lucidity to the entire San Pedro experience.

As a generality, everything about San Pedro is gentler when compared to ayahuasca. Although the purgative effects are sought after and enhanced by some curanderas, the vomiting is not considered an essential part of the healing from San Pedro, and when present is usually much milder. Prior to the ceremony the preparation (or *dieta*—to be contrasted with diet) for San Pedro communion is also traditionally gentler than that for ayahuasca. The purpose of the dieta is to obtain a lightness of being such that your energies are clear and open. This is achieved by the consumption of light foods and by abstinence from sex and alcohol for at least a day.

Although the experience as a whole, in the emotional, mental, and spiritual sense, is often perceived as being gentler with San Pedro than with ayahuasca, the ceremonies that accompany the traditional use of San Pedro are often a great deal more harsh and challenging than ceremonies with ayahuasca. As mentioned before, the use of ayahuasca traditionally allows a more internal experience whereas many traditional San Pedro ceremonies are lengthy and filled with physical activities that detract from the internal visionary experience. It is difficult to say, however, how much this has to say about the essence of these two spirits or whether it has more to say about the extremely isolated communities where the plants of ayahuasca are found, compared to the more structured and less isolated cultures in the lands where San Pedro calls home, and where cultures have, through time, syncretized with the cosmology and practices of the Christian Church.

It is not uncommon for a San Pedro ceremony to last the whole night long and to involve repeated and lengthy requirements of the participants, necessitating much physical stamina and concentration. I personally find that this detracts from my process of communing with this beautiful plant spirit, and yet it must be said that I have also found great benefits are to be gained from these healing ceremonies that are combinations of ancient Quechuan Incan tradition and Catholicism. On the *mesa* of the curandera are numerous *huacas* (power objects and sacred items) that invoke and hold the spirits of the *Apus* (spirits of the mountain peaks) and other holy places. Often literally rocks, these huacas are essential spirit tools for the work of San Pedro who was, as pointed out before, known as the Rock of the Christian Church.

Icaros, or songs, hold a particularly important function in San Pedro ceremony. As with ayahuasca ceremonies, many participants experience the songs as a guiding force for the entire process. They also serve as prayers or songs of intent and guide ceremonial energies and focus them where needed, whether for protection, for easing anxiety, for healing, or setting the pace and quality of the visions.

Through chanting the curandero is believed to communicate with the spirit realm and mediate the healing. The singing voice as embodied song could be seen as constituting a relational bridge among clients, curandero, and spirits—concrete and magic at the same time, which seems to synthesize the essence of the integral health beliefs.[8]

HEALING EXPERIENCES

What of my own relationships with these plants? It would seem that it is indeed true that "you get what you need"—or perhaps it is just that I am a topsy-turvy soul, for my own experiences with these two plant spirits were not always the same as I have previously outlined or as commonly described by the majority of participants.

When I first met the goddess of compassion ayahuasca (for she often comes to me as a woman) she was so very gentle, and generous, and loving. It came at a time when I was at the culmination of years of difficult challenges—of living deep in shadow. Already in the midst of a death of sorts—finally separating from my addict husband of twenty years and all the whirlwind of hell that his addiction created for me and our children—I was exhausted, in deep despair, sick and numbed to anything like possibility or hope. I had already been through so many of life's hard initiations and was plodding on the best I could. I guess at that time in my life I just needed to come into the light and to be held. She held me.

For years I communed with her in this gentle way, all the while surrounded by others undergoing seriously challenging sessions. I could hear their struggles nearby and I came to know that theirs was the more typical interaction with ayahuasca—the taskmaster of transformation through fire. I was surrounded by people diving deep into their shadow selves. Yet throughout these years when I was with her, I was filled with an all-encompassing sense of loving and of being loved. My journeys were emotional and beautiful. Uplifting and empowering, warm and supportive—I experienced true oneness with the All. I was taken down tunnels to golden thrones, shown luminous, numinous gardens and cosmic miracles.

In one session that stays clear in my consciousness and remains a part of me since that time, I danced and sang in a clearing in the jungle under a starry night sky. All night I found myself in dialogue, back and forth, with the full moon and the stars. I remember the moment that I suddenly became aware that this was what I was doing, that I was speaking to them and being answered, in Spanish.

"Why are we speaking Spanish?" I asked. "Well, we could speak Shuar, the language of the people of this forest, but you don't speak Shuar very well. And English is not spoken by the people here at all. Spanish works." All night I found myself dancing a dance with simple steps, over and over—I knew not why. And I was given downloads of deep wisdom and clarity, much of which is still coming to me in conscious awareness.

Many years later I was in Washington, D.C., at a Christmas Eve ceremony of the local Santo Daime. It was my first festive Daime experience. I was shown where to stand and how to dance. It came as no surprise that the steps I was shown were the same that I was shown by the vine so very far from there in that clearing in the jungle. Are these the steps that are held by the spirit of ayahuasca and that she also taught to Mestre Irineu? Perhaps.

These were my early years in relationship with Mother Ayahuasca. Not that I didn't have physical challenges. I did a great deal of purging in these early sessions. But for years she gave me a gentle and sweet form of emotional, psychological, and visionary love and support.

Then at some point in my life I guess I needed to dig deeper. I had lost sight of and denied my shadow. She does not abide this in her disciples. At that point she wanted me once again to dive into the darkness of my being. To search out and uproot unproductive patterns of behavior and thought. It was at this communion that our relationship took a sharp turn. She poured me into a blender and turned me inside out.

Over and over again in the ensuing years my times with her became so mind-numbingly hard that I began to beg her to have mercy, to stop, to just let me be. But she is too loving for that. She kept me in that alchemical fire, time and again. Perhaps I have too much shadow. Perhaps I am a slow learner. But time and again she took me to the depths of my psyche and of the world's psyche. It was dark. It was painful.

During those years, even when I was far removed from her, just the memory of her smell and taste brought the darkness and pain back to me like a sword impaling fear into my gut and brought unbidden tears to my eyes. Yet even in the depths of despair, even while pleading with her to stop, I never lost faith that she does indeed love me and she would never ask more of me than I could handle. And that I would always get what I need.

And during these times I learned to pray more productively. To better communicate with her my conscious needs, to commune in a gentler way. I must have finally burned in the fire. Polished enough for her—at least for now. I found peace once again with my wise Mother Goddess.

And San Pedro? My relationship with San Pedro began in the opposite way. Perhaps it was simply that it was a later time in my life, during the time when I needed harsh lessons. San Pedro presents me with a male energy, authoritative and firm. My experience with this deity began quite the opposite to that of my honeymoon with ayahuasca (and perhaps opposite to that of most peoples' experiences). For at first it was he who was the harsh taskmaster.

There were many times when he took me to places that I really did not want to go—showed me things I didn't want to see. I came out of each session drenched with sweat and torn asunder. Although the physical effects were far gentler and easier than those with ayahuasca and the messages more direct and clear, the overall effect of these journeys was one that brought me to my knees. And one day he too shifted.

The past several visits from this deity had been filled with loving kindness, at once very different and very much the same expression of love and of oneness as with ayahuasca. Ayahuasca's love comes to me messy and fiercely—an emotional and sensual feeling—whereas San Pedro's love comes as a higher, more intellectual, heady, and airy love—at times cutting—but always clear and compassionate.

These healings for me have been profound, life changing, and long lasting. I could say with deep sincerity that I do not know if I would have survived without these plant spirits. Certainly not in a good way.

And so we can see that sitting with the Anaconda and the Hummingbird, with these powerful plant teachers, we catch a glimpse of the immensity of their contribution to us as human inhabitants of this planet. We are blessed to have the opportunity to commune with them, to avail ourselves of their ability to retune our receptive capabilities such that we can soar higher and higher, raising our consciousness and expanding our source for knowledge. Over time we have evolved varied methods for communion with these plants that are unique to the essence of the spirit of each, as well as our changing environment, needs, and cultural ethos.

For me, the messages from each plant are much the same. An experiential knowledge of ecstatic oneness, of samadhi, has been strong with both plant deities, and yet the flavor of the messages, the personalities of these spirits, are totally different. I love them both with all my heart and trust them with my life and soul. To me all of the gracious entheogens that we commune with are the best healers on the planet and—dare I say—could be the saviors of our species should we allow them to be.

What can we see for our future as a community of life-forms on this planet? What do these plant spirit deities hold for us? What is their compassionate gift?

Einstein once said that if you find yourself with a result that is not what you expect or want, go back and look at the premise. The result of our lifestyle and relationship with this Earth is heading us down a dark and dangerous passage. What is our premise for this lifestyle and disconnectedness? What brought us to this very limited view of "reality"? Of scientific "proof"? Of our dominion over and separateness from nature?

It is indeed a miracle that the plant kingdom, despite the fact that we as a culture have increasingly disconnected from both spirit and nature, is always at the ready and willing to heal us, to take us where we need to be, to show us the path, to guide us. To give us what we need. And of all times in human existence we sorely need help now. For the good of our descendants and all our relations we need these sacred plants now.

Let us reach out to the Anaconda and the Hummingbird. Let us go back to our beginnings when we first communed with these plants and through their gracious help find that we are more than what we can feel, see, taste, and hear. Let us go back to the time when we entered those deep caves and created symbolic art to communicate our visionary spiritual experiences. Let us once again listen to these wise and compassionate plant spirits and rethink our premise of life as spiritual beings living in this limited physical plane. Let us expand our understanding, our reality, and our consciousness and find a new premise on which we may thrive and live in ecstatic oneness. The plants will lead us. *Yomimsamwhe.*

NOTES

1. Graham Hancock, *Supernatural: Meetings with the Ancient Teachers of Mankind* (New York: Arrow Books, 2006).

2. Steven Rubenstein, *Alejandro Tsakimp: A Shuar Healer in the Margins of History* (Lincoln, Neb.: University of Nebraska Press, 2002).

3. For more on this plant see Ross Heaven and Howard G. Charing, *Plant Spirit Shamanism: Traditional Techniques for Healing the Soul* (Rochester, Vt.: Destiny Books, 2006).

4. Richard Evans Schultes, Albert Hofmann, and Christian Ratsch, *Plants of the Gods: Their Sacred, Healing, and Hallucinogenic Powers* (Rochester, Vt.: Healing Arts Press, 1996).

5. Available at www.takiwasi.com/docs/ard_ing/about_the_ikaro_or_shamanic_song.pdf, accessed June 27, 2012.

6. Available at http://csp.org/nicholas/A16.html, accessed June 27, 2011.

7. Bonnie Glass-Coffin, "Shamanism and San Pedro through Time: Some Notes on the Archeology, History, and Continued Use of an Entheogen in Northern Peru," *Anthropology of Consciousness,* vol. 21, issue 1, Spring 2010, 58–82.

8. Susana Bustos, "The Healing Power of the Curanderos' Songs or 'Icaros.' A Phenomenological Study" (Ph.D. diss., Spring 2004).

6

Notes on Getting Cactus Lodged in Your Reducing Valve

San Pedro and Psychic Abilities

David Luke, Ph.D.

I'd spent the best part of a week on rickety buses going up and down mountains, skirting and scooting round precarious precipices and back and forth across a number of small towns in southern Ecuador.

It had started out as a shamanic healer hunt but was fast becoming a manic wild goose chase. Armed with a few leads—some locations and numbers—I had emptied several bags of coins into phone boxes to little effect because the healers I was pursuing did not, as a rule, make much use of modern telecommunications. I joked with myself that this forsaking of telephony was possibly due to their mastery over psychic abilities, the likes of which I was hoping to test.

Under the auspices of an ambitious scientific research project, I had traveled to South America in an attempt to conduct controlled experiments with people under the influence of the psychedelic San Pedro cactus, in a bid to test the claim that the use of certain psychedelic substances could induce the ability to transcend space and time and to know and foresee things through nonordinary means. In essence, I wanted to know if the use of San Pedro could facilitate clairvoyance, telepathy, or precognition, the abilities, respectively, of accessing hidden information, communicating mind-to-mind with others, or obtaining knowledge from the future. Collectively, these three supposed phenomena have been termed extrasensory perception (ESP) or simply psi.

I finally caught up with a mestizo healer on my second visit to his remote village and traversed the extra few miles up the mountain with my partner to his secluded wooden shack. No running water, no electricity, no neighbors, just spectacular views out over the Andes. He greeted us very hospitably and we began talking about participating in a San Pedro ceremony with him and the possibility of conducting some psychic tests, all of which he happily agreed to. Everything was going well until I pointed out that—well equipped with batteries—I would like to use my laptop computer to do the tests. The healer looked at me sternly and marched me over to the edge of the clearing surrounding his small house. Overlooking the valleys and mountains he told me how his family owned all the land we could see on this side of the mountain and how his ancestors had lived here for hundreds of years in much the same way as he did now: as part of Nature. Standing behind me, he then lifted a huge conch shell to his lips and blasted me with a resonant bombardment of sound. Turning me around ninety degrees with his hand, he repeated the sonic assault, doing the same maneuver twice more until I had been thoroughly trumpeted in all four directions and had greeted the four winds. Sledgehammer for a nut, I got the message: there would be no use of computers during his San Pedro ceremony.

It's thus I found myself some weeks later, rather than testing twenty people for their possible psychic abilities, holed up in a room alone in front of a computer for eight hours, deeply nauseous and in a definite altered state of consciousness, doggedly running twenty psychic tests on myself. I'll return to this odd experiment later, but will first discuss why anyone should even want to test for the ESP-inducing capabilities of a spiny succulent angiosperm.

THE CACTUS OF THE FOUR WINDS

The Andean San Pedro cactus (*Trichocereus pachanoi*) was used as a sacred power plant (i.e., as a sacramental) for at least two thousand years before the Spanish conquistadores arrived in the sixteenth century, according to the archaeological evidence. Some finds may be much older. The Peruvian site of Chavín for instance, home of the Chavín people, has stone etchings that attest to the central role of psychedelic plants in that culture (Burger, 1992) including but not limited to the San Pedro cactus (Jay, 2005). The site itself dates from between 1500 BCE and 900 BCE, and reverence for the cactus among later Andean cultures has been identified from ceramics from the Cupusnique, Salinar, Nazca, Moche, Lambayeque and Chimu people, dating from the time of Chavín to the arrival of the Spanish (Glass-Coffin, 1999).

Written accounts following the arrival of the Spaniards indicate the way in which the cactus was used by Pre-Columbian Andean people. Of interest to the project under discussion is that most of these include some report of the parapsychological effects of the plant. Juan Polo de Ondegardo, a sixteenth-century Spanish officer stationed in Cuzco, Peru, described how the natives using the cactus "take the form they want and go a long distance through the air in a short time; and they see what is happening" (Sharon, 1978, pp. 112–13), probably indicating out-of-body experiences and "traveling clairvoyance." Juan Polo de Ondegardo continued that when they take the plant, "They serve as diviners and they tell what is happening in remote places before the news arrives or can arrive" (Sharon, 1978, p. 113), clearly demonstrating de Ondegardo's belief in the healers' cactus-induced psychic abilities.

The following century a number of accounts of San Pedro's use appeared among missionaries posted in the Andes. In 1631 Father Oliva described the ritual use of *achuma* (San Pedro), noting that "they [ceremonial participants] see visions that the Devil represents to them and consistent with them they judge their suspicions and the intentions of others" (cited in Sharon, 1978). Peruvian healers, called *curanderos,* in recent years continue to consume San Pedro to know people's intentions (Glass-Coffin, 2000). It's clear though at that time that such activities were treated as suspicious and sacrilegious by the early missionaries, and in 1653, a few years after Father Oliva's account, nothing having changed, Father Cobo (as cited in Sharon, 1978) wrote an equally biased and pious report of the effects.

> This is the plant by which the devil deceived the Indians of Peru in their paganism, using it for their lies and superstitions. . . . Transported by this drink, the Indians dreamed a thousand absurdities and believed them as if they were true.

Such negative reports stemming from the period of the Inquisition between the fourteenth and seventeenth centuries are hardly surprising; nevertheless, the witch hunts did not totally eradicate the use of San Pedro, despite the attempt. In the less punitive years after the Inquisition, numerous cases of "pagan idolatry" can be found in the records, such as the trial of Marco Marcelo in 1768, who described how when he drank San Pedro "he came into full awareness and patently saw with his eyes the sick person's [bewitchment] . . . and he also recognized the sorcerer who had done the [harm]" (cited in Glass-Coffin, 1999).

Despite continued persecution for the best part of five hundred years, the shamanic use of San Pedro continues to this day, representing an unbroken magico-religious tradition spanning more than three thousand years (Sharon, 1978). According to Dobkin de Rios (1977) the use of San Pedro as "a revelatory agent" to determine the source of witchcraft and misfortune affecting a patient is currently its predominant function, although more recently healers may typically diagnose the cause of illness as being due to the person's thoughts and behaviors rather than external agencies such as sorcery (Heaven, 2009). For instance, a curandera interviewed by Glass-Coffin (2000) saw that those living life without conscious awareness and in emptiness were prone to illness, though she specifically used the word *daño* (harm), which traditionally is associated with an illness caused by sorcerers (*brujos, maleros*) through witchcraft (Sharon, 1978). *Envidia* (envy) is unanimously given as the reason for such witchcraft, possibly as a result of continued post-Columbian poverty, scarcity of resources, and subjugation of the Andean peoples by the dominant class, according to the Peruvian psychiatrist Mario Chiappe (cited in Sharon, 1978).

Aside from daño, other maladies traditionally diagnosed by San Pedro curanderos include *mal aire* (bad air, usually emanating from tombs or ruins of sacred places) (Dobkin de Rios, 1968), *mal suerte* or *saladera* (bad luck, to the point of lethargy and pessimism) (Dobkin de Rios, 1981), *susto* (soul loss, manifesting as lack of self-efficacy) (de Feo, 1992), *mal puesto* (hexing or cursing), *mal d'ojo* (the evil eye), and *bilis, empacho,* and *pulsario* (rage, pain, and sorrow, caused by a blockage of energy) (Heaven, 2009).

Both diagnoses and treatment for such maladies are made by the curandero under the influence of San Pedro during an all-night ceremony in which the healer enacts magical battles to heal the patient. Typically the patient also ingests the cactus brew (Dobkin de Rios, 1968) as it is also considered a medicine or even a panacea in its own right and may also help the patient have revelations regarding their own maladies (e.g., Heaven, 2009; Sharon, 1978) though traditionally such revelations are usually made by the healer.

THE CACTUS OF VISION

Once known as achuma, these days the cactus is known by a number of pre- and post-Columbian names such as *huando hermoso, cardo, gigantón, huachuma* (Sharon, 1978), *chuma, pene de Dios* (penis of God), *El Remedio* (Heaven, 2009), and *aguacolla* (Shultes and Hofmann, 1992). It was first described and classified in 1920 by the botanists Britton and Rose, who gave San Pedro its Latin taxonomic name, *Trichocereus pachanoi,* and noted that its distribution remained within Andean Ecuador. More recently, it has been found to be indigenous to

Bolivia and northern Peru, typically growing at two to three thousand meters above sea level, although it has also been found in coastal regions (Sharon, 1978), and as far south as Argentina (Shultes and Hofmann, 1992).

The main active principle of San Pedro was originally identified by the French ethnobotanist Claudine Friedberg (1959) who found that the fresh plant matter contains about 0.12 percent mescaline (3,4,5-trimethoxy-β-phenethylamine), an alkaloid of the phenethylamine family (Shulgin and Shulgin, 1991). Dried *T. pachanoi* is reported to contain about 2 percent mescaline (Stafford, 1977), although a review of published analyses shows that reports vary from between 0.33 percent to 2.37 percent mescaline in the dried plant (Erowid, 2001). Nevertheless, this makes it somewhat weaker than its northern Mexican and southern United States cacti cousin, peyote (*Lophophora williamsii*), which contains about 8 percent mescaline by dry weight (Bruhn et al., 1978), although some reports suggest that dry peyote only contains between 1 percent and 6 percent mescaline (Crosby and McLaughlin, 1973).

Louis Lewin first described the extraction of a mixture of alkaloids from peyote in 1888, but it wasn't until 1895 that Arthur Heffter isolated four pure alkaloids, one of which he called Mezcalin, now known as mescaline (Ott, 1996). Then in 1897 Heffter (1898) did what any great explorer would do and tested the alkaloids' psychoactivity on himself; he heroically ingested it thereby identifying mescaline as the main active chemical because its effects differed from that of the plant itself. It is this self-experimentation technique that later led Albert Hofmann to discover psilocybin and psilocin as the psychologically active principles of the psychedelic *Psilocybe* genus of mushrooms, a discovery made well in advance of the large pharmacological companies who had been working on the problem for some time by testing the chemicals on animals (Luke, 2006). In 1919, the chemist Späth then identified mescaline's structure as 3,4,5-trimethoxy-β-phenethylamine and confirmed this by synthesising the compound (Ott, 1996).

Returning to San Pedro, besides *T. pachanoi* there are thought to be more than twenty-five species of *Trichocereus* that contain alkaloids (Crosby and McLaughlin, 1973), and at least eleven of these species contain mescaline (Ott, 1996). Most of these close relatives of San Pedro are not used as ethnomedical plants, however, because the alkaloids are in trace quantities, the exception being *T. peruvianus* (Peruvian torch), which is supposedly much stronger and thought to contain almost as high concentrations of mescaline as peyote (Ott, 1996; Pardanani et al., 1977), although other reports suggest this is an exaggeration because some analyses report no mescaline in *T. peruvianus* and yet more than 2 percent in some samples of *T. pachanoi* (Erowid, 2001). Nevertheless, despite mescaline being the primary active principle of peyote and both San Pedro and Peruvian torch, there are a number of other alkaloids present that are not the same—so although the psychopharmacological effects of these cactuses are roughly analogous, they are not entirely equivalent (Bruhn et al., 2008).

Peyote is known to contain over fifty alkaloids (Anderson, 1980), mostly mescaline and tetrahydro-isoquinoline alkaloids, albeit in trace quantities, as the total alkaloid content is only about 8 percent of the dry weight (Bruhn et al., 1978), most of which is mescaline. *T. pachanoi*, on the other hand, consists mainly of mescaline and related phenethylamines such as tyramine, hordenine (a stimulant with antibacterial and antibiotic properties, also found in peyote), 3-methoxytyramine, 3,4-dimethoxy-β-phenethylamine, 3,4-dimethoxy-4-hydroxy-β-phenethylamine, 3,5-dimethoxy-4-hydroxy-β-phenethylamine, anhalonidine and anhalinine (Crosby and McLaughlin, 1973).

A recent study (Bruhn et al., 2008) has also discovered the presence in San Pedro of three new phenethylamine alkaloids: lophophine (3-methoxy-4,5-methylenedioxy-phenethylamine), which is also psychoactive and is closely related to MDMA (3-methoxy-4,5-methylenedioxy-amphetamine, commonly known as Ecstasy); lobivine (N,N-dimethyl-3,4-methylenedioxy-phenethylamine), a relatively mild psychoactive compound also related to MDMA; and DMPEA (3,4-dimethoxy-phenethylamine), which is a nonpsychoactive compound.

These three new alkaloids were also found to be present in peyote, and at higher concentrations than in San Pedro, yet it is thought that they have very little direct psychoactive effect in the quantities they are naturally found at relative to mescaline, although they might have a synergistic effect with mescaline (Bruhn et al., 2008). Demonstrating great insight, having previously synthetically created lophophine, Shulgin and Shulgin (1991) noted its similarities to mescaline and predicted its psychoactivity and its likely presence in peyote (*Lophophora williamsii*), hence the name given to it by Shulgin and Shulgin (1991) even before it was found to occur naturally. This discovery calls into question the artificial rather than natural status of designer drugs like MDMA, which are artificial or only potentially natural.

ARTIFICIAL PARADISES—OR NATURAL CHEMICAL UTOPIAS?

A similar difficulty of distinction arises over whether the states induced by psychedelics are natural or artificial, though early writers clearly placed them in the latter camp, such as the medic Havelock Ellis, who was the first person in the United Kingdom to write about his experience with mescaline in an article titled *Mescal: A New Artificial Paradise* (Ellis, 1898). However, these days it is known that there are a number of naturally occurring psychedelic substances in the human body, so experiences such as synesthesia and clairvoyance that are induced by the ingestion of psychedelic substances like mescaline might also occur spontaneously, as they are known to do, through the action of "endogenous" (made within the body) chemicals.

It is highly likely that all altered states of consciousness, including potentially ESP-conducive states, involve alterations in brain chemistry and so psychedelics like mescaline have an important part to play in helping us understand the neurochemistry underlying those states. Taking this further into the realm of parapsychology, several psychedelic-neurochemical models have been proposed based on the specific neurochemical action and the subjective paranormal experiences occurring with certain substances, such as ketamine and DMT (e.g., Jansen, 1997; Roney-Dougal, 2001; Strassman, 2001). Advancing on these models it is entirely feasible that genuine paranormal phenomena are mediated in the brain through the action of specific endogenous psychedelic molecules such as DMT (Roney-Dougal, 2001). This does not simply imply that neurochemicals are the sole cause of paranormal phenomena, but they may rather just be a part of the process. As the novelist Aldous Huxley once said in relation to mystical experiences and the use of psychedelics—they are the occasion rather than the cause.

CLEANSING THE DOORS OF (EXTRASENSORY) PERCEPTION

Aldous Huxley was also prominent in promoting the influential French philosopher Henri Bergson's (1896) nascent parapsychological theory of the brain as a filter of memory and sensory experience.

In this model the brain acts to reduce the wealth of information available to our awareness lest we become overwhelmed by this mass of largely useless data, which is irrelevant to the survival of the organism. Bergson suggested that if the filter was bypassed people would be capable of remembering everything they had ever experienced and able to perceive everything that is happening everywhere in the universe (i.e., clairvoyance).

After being given mescaline by the pioneering psychedelic researcher Humphry Osmond (who coined the term *psychedelic* in correspondence with Huxley), in 1953 Huxley then applied Bergson's theory to psychedelics by suggesting that these mind-manifesting drugs override the reducing valve of the brain, allowing man access to both psychic and mystic states. A notion that Huxley (1954) eruditely paraphrased with the quote by the English poet and mystic, William Blake, "If the doors of perception were cleansed, every thing would appear to man as it is, infinite."

Huxley's rather basic conception of the influence of psychedelics on the paranormal function of the brain never received a more formal operationalization of the specific drug action involved, but recent research into the neurochemistry of psychedelics lends some support to this simple notion. For instance, Vollenweider and Geyer (2001) propose that information processing in cortico-striato-thalamo-cortical (CSTC) feedback loops in the brain is disrupted by psychedelics, thereby inhibiting the "gating" of extraneous sensory stimuli and subsequently inhibiting the ability to attend selectively to salient environmental features. Furthermore, psychedelics are also thought to induce a simultaneous neurochemical overload of internal information in the cortex. It is thought that these combined overload effects, of information coming from both inside and outside the organism, are at least partly responsible for the psychedelic experience with these drugs, which are known to induce greatly altered or amplified incoming sensory information (Vollenweider, 2001).

Research into the neurobiology of psychedelics in humans has only just resumed after decades of dormancy, so the current understanding of the action of these substances in the brain is limited. One of the few studies to have been conducted, however, also offers some unexpected support for Huxley's reducing valve theory.

Looking at the blood flow around the brain following the ingestion of psilocybin, it was expected that certain regions of the brain would have more activity given the overwhelming intenseness of strong psychedelic experiences, and yet, counterintuitively, there was no single brain region that increased in activity and the brain's activity was reduced overall (Carhart-Harris, 2011).

This disruption of the sensory gating function by psychedelics and their reduction in brain activity could also underpin the neurochemistry of ESP (Luke and Friedman, 2010). Indeed, like psychedelics, psi experiences and psi phenomena have variously been conceptualized in relation to an inhibition of the ordinary sensory inhibition system, often related to states of elevated psychosis and creativity, such as with the psychological concepts of latent disinhibition (Holt, Simmonds-Moore, and Moore, 2008), transliminality (Thalbourne, 2000) and boundary thinness and schizotypy (Simmonds and Roe, 2000). It may be noted that psychedelics have also been long associated theoretically with both creativity (e.g., Dobkin de Rios and Janiger, 2003) and temporary psychosis (e.g., Osmond and Smythies, 1952).

That the special neurochemistry of psychedelics is central to psi is supported by a wealth of collectively compelling personal accounts from users as well as anthropological, clinical, and survey reports. There is also a body of preliminary experimental research that presently remains equivocal and generally methodologically flawed but is nevertheless promising (for a review see Luke, 2008). Of these numerous psychedelics mescaline is one substance in particular that according to the historical, anthropological, and personal accounts to follow, is known to induce psi experiences.

Putting the "Psi" back in Psychedelics

Traditionally, the sacramental use of mescaline-containing cacti was restricted to the New World (i.e., the Americas) where these plants are endemic and included the use of peyote among the Kiowa and Comanche people of the southern United States, through to parts of northern Mexico where the Tarahumara people of the state of Chihuahua and the Huichol people, originally of the state of San Luis Potasi, make use of peyote and other putative mescaline-containing cacti (Schultes and Hofmann, 1992). Archaeological evidence suggests that the use of peyote has continued for at least five thousand years (El-Seedi et al., 2005) and ever since the use of peyote was first documented in the mid-sixteenth century by the personal physician of King Philip II of Spain, Dr. Francisco Hernández, it has been reputed to induce prophetic qualities. "It causes those devouring it to be able to foresee and to predict things" (quoted in Schultes and Hofmann, 1992, p. 134).

Further south, San Pedro has been used traditionally by the indigenous people of Ecuador, Peru, Bolivia, and even Argentina for the same type of magico-religious practices, such as divination, as those of their northern American cactus-using "cousins" (Schultes and Hofmann, 1992), as discussed earlier.

More recently, anthropological research also attests to the capacity of San Pedro, and therefore probably mescaline too, to induce or facilitate psychic abilities. Sharon (1978, p. 45) reports that a Peruvian folk healer (curandero) he studied and studied with used San Pedro, like other curanderos, to induce what the healer called "the sixth sense, the telepathic sense of transmitting oneself across time and matter. . . . It develops the power of perception . . . in the sense that when one wants to see something far away . . . he can distinguish powers or problems or disturbances at great distance, so as to deal with them." This psychic enhancement apparently occurs because "San Pedro is the catalyst that activates all the complex forces at work in a folk healing session, especially the visionary and divinatory powers of the curandero himself" (Sharon, 1990, p. 117).

Similar reports of actively using other mescaline-containing cacti for "psi" (e.g., clairvoyance) also appear in the historical and anthropological literature, as with the use of peyote among the Huichol (Slotkin, 1956), Chichimeca, Zacatecan, Tamaulipecan, and Tarahumari people of Mexico and among the Apache, Comanche, and Kiowa in the United States (for a review see Le Barre, 1938). This literature is backed up by experiential reports from nonindigenous mescaline users like that of the French researchers who gave mescaline to six subjects, one of whom temporarily developed very detailed and accurate clairvoyant abilities and was able to describe the contents of a nearby room (Rouhier, 1925, 1927). Similar reports exist among parapsychology researchers themselves, such as Rosalind Heywood (1961) who, after taking the mescaline given to her by psychical researcher John Smythies, believed that psychedelics could help researchers understand spontaneous psi experiences.

The same sentiment was reported by the man who coined the term *psychedelic,* Humphry Osmond, after his own mescaline experiences in 1951. Osmond (1961) also reported that in 1957 he and his fellow researcher Duncan Blewett, both under the influence of mescaline, successfully transmitted telepathic information in an informal experiment to such a degree that an independent observer became acutely panicky at the uncanniness of the event.

Similarly, during mescaline self-experimentation Langdon-Davies (1961) claimed to have demonstrated traveling clairvoyance and successfully identified thirteen correct targets from a pack of twenty-five zener cards where each pack contains an equal mixture of five distinct symbols, the odds of correctly identifying thirteen or more symbols by chance alone being 1 in 2,500, which is truly quite improbable.

Reflecting the growing popularity of psychedelics in 1960s alternative culture, a member of the Byrds musical group claimed to have experienced telepathy with other band members under the influence of mescaline (Krippner and Davidson, 1970).

Nevertheless, merely consuming mescaline is no guarantee that an experience of ESP will follow, as the Oxford philosophy professor H. H. Price (1964) demonstrated in a self-experimentation guided by Humphry Osmond. Similarly, parapsychologist Charles Tart described in a letter how, when he was given 500 mg of mescaline (a reasonably large dose) by Austrian psychologist Ivo Kohler in 1959 and was supposed to perform an ESP card guessing test, he was far too absorbed in cosmic revelations and the overwhelming beauty of the universe to actually engage seriously with the task (Tart, personal communication, May 13, 2011). Nevertheless, other parapsychologists have reported personal ESP experiences with the use of mescaline (e.g., Millay, 2001).

Despite there being a good body of survey research to substantiate the induction of paranormal experiences with psychedelics generally (for a review see Luke, 2008) all but one of these surveys omitted to investigate the effects of mescaline in particular. One in-depth drug and experience survey, however, revealed that mescaline did indeed give rise to reports of telepathy and precognition among those using it, yet the primary "transpersonal" experiential features of ingesting mescaline cacti were the perception of auras (as also reported by Tart, 1972), the experience of encountering the plant's spirit, and a sense of unity (Luke and Kittenis, 2005). Other less common experiences reported included dissolving into energy, powerful long-lasting religious awakenings, out-of-body experiences, clairvoyance, death-and-rebirth experiences and/ or past-life memories, psychokinesis (influencing objects or people with one's mind), encountering a divine being, encountering a (nonanimal) intelligent entity, and the sense of the loss of causality (where A causes B) (Luke, 2009). Many of these experiences have also been reported elsewhere under the influence of San Pedro (Heaven, 2009).

Individual reports and surveys of people having psychic experiences with mescaline under nonexperimental conditions may be provocative and interesting but are scientifically limited given what is known about the ways in which individual experiences do not necessarily indicate genuine paranormal phenomena. This is because individual experiences may be prone to misperception, misreporting, memory errors such as confabulation, or may be merely chance coincidences (Pekala and Cardeña, 2000). Nevertheless, the various individual reports collected may be actual cases of genuine psychic phenomena occurring under the influence of mescaline, but without controlled experimental testing there can be no certainty.

Reviewing the extremely scant experimental literature, then, there are few studies that have been conducted that can be considered. Humphry Osmond's co-worker John Smythies (1960, 1987) reported a preliminary study with one volunteer using mescaline in a psychometry experiment whereby the task is to describe the unknown owner and their environment when given a personal object belonging to them. Although the participant was unable to discern the targets under adequate blind, "remote-viewing" style conditions, informal questioning about the target location typical of psychometry tasks elicited promising responses. Similarly using mescaline, a series of pilot studies with three participants "failed in card-guessing tests but showed encouraging success in tests with free material, particularly token objects" (Rush and Cahn, 1958, p. 300). Likewise with mescaline, presumably in self-experiments, Breederveld (1976, 2001) reported success in consistently winning above chance at roulette experiments in casinos using real money, although the mescaline condition was only one of several mostly successful methods, perhaps indicating that either Breederveld's methodology was flawed or that he had some psychic talents anyway.

Nevertheless, Breederveld's success echoes informal reports concerning the pioneer psychedelic researcher, Al Hubbard, who after supposedly developing his psychic ability through the use of LSD (Osmond, 1961; Stevens, 1988) became somewhat notorious for winning on gaming machines in casinos, his reputation being such that he was politely escorted out by the management when he reached a certain limit of earning (Krippner, 2006). Overall, it can be said that the research literature is very positive about the informal use of mescaline for inducing ESP; however, there are as yet no clear reports of well-controlled and statistically sound formal experiments so it certainly begs further investigation.

UNCORKING THE GENIE'S BOTTLE

It's thus that I found myself some weeks later, rather than testing twenty other people for their possible psychic abilities, holed up in room alone sat in front of a computer for eight hours, deeply nauseous and in a definite altered state of consciousness, doggedly running twenty psychic tests on myself.

I had prepared about 30 grams of dried slices of San Pedro by powdering them in a coffee grinder. The actual mescaline content must have been somewhere between about 100 and 700 mg, according to the concentrations reported for *Trichocereus pachanoi* (Erowid, 2001), with about 200 to 400 mg of mescaline considered to be a standard dose (Shulgin and Shulgin, 1991). Effective doses are thought to be in the 150 to 1,500 mg range, although the maximum safe dose is proposed to be 1,000 mg (Ott, 1996). Once the effects took hold I was quite pleased that the actual dosage was probably at the weaker end of the possible mescaline content range due to the necessity to be able to function in this state enough to run my experiment on myself and yet still have a visionary experience.

Having prepared the cactus I then also prepared myself and the experiment. I had fasted since the previous evening to reduce nausea or vomiting and to maximize the potency of the plant. I had also organized all the materials I would need for the ESP tests: a pile of questionnaires, a clock, a Dictaphone, and a laptop with a large collection of preformulated video clips.

The procedure was fairly straightforward: once I was under the influence of San Pedro I would close my eyes and attempt to visualize "the target," then write down anything that appeared in my mental imagery and any feelings or insights associated with it. At this point I had no idea what the target actually was, of course. Once I had written down my impressions of the target I would then complete a series of standard scales relating to my state of consciousness: how easy it was to visualize, how confused I was, how paranoid I was, whether I saw bright colors, that sort of thing. I would then turn to the computer, on which I had a large collection of one-minute video clips from films, none of which I had seen before and which were arranged into a number of pools, each of which contained four clips that an independent researcher had previously selected so they were as different from each other as possible. I had twenty of these pools lined up and so aimed to run twenty trials of the ESP task. Under the influence of mescaline it really would be a trial too.

After writing down my impressions of the target from my mescaline-enhanced visualization process, it was planned that I would then watch a pool of four video clips for the first time, having no idea what the clips were beforehand. Once I had watched all four it was then necessary to rank them according to how closely they corresponded to the mental images I had just had. Then comes the weird bit: I would then select which of the four film clips was to be the actual target by running a random number generator that would choose a number between one and four in a manner that, according to ordinary linear conceptions of reality, cannot be predicted. Thus one of the four clips would become the target after I had made my selection, but also completely independently of my selection. Making the target selection after my attempted divination of it made this psi task a test of precognition rather than telepathy or clairvoyance—which if successful would demonstrate the ability to access information from the future without recourse to inference or other ordinary means of prediction.

This precognitive ability might also be also called prophecy, premonition, or prescience. Ordinarily, attempting to guess the randomly selected target from one of four clips would produce a success rate of 25 percent by chance alone so that only one in every four of the clips I selected would be ranked as the most similar to my mental imagery if purely random processes where at work. Over a series of twenty trials like this it is therefore expected that the correct target would be selected just five times by chance alone.

The Experiment

Skipping breakfast in the morning, I prepared the 30 grams of San Pedro for consumption by powdering it. Like peyote, San Pedro is known to taste extremely bitter and be very difficult to eat or drink without wanting to vomit. Nature has a way of ensuring that you have to be pretty serious if you want to eat these cacti.

Having prepared myself mentally and made my propitiations to the spirits in my own way, I poured the emetic powder straight to the back of my throat in 5-gram batches every five minutes or so and washed it down with orange juice as quickly as possible, taking care to get as little of the repulsive pulverulent anywhere near my taste buds. I started at 10:15 a.m. and within half an hour I had consumed an entire handful of the green-grey dust without any tears, but was beginning to feel increasingly nauseous. The nausea continued in waves, getting worse for a while and then finally abating so that by 2:30 p.m., more than four hours in, I finally noted "less sick now and actually enjoying this at last."

Despite feeling sick I began testing at 12:08 p.m. I would start the experiment with a dummy test run that would not form part of the official count, just to make sure I could function properly and do what was required. Attempts to use the Dictaphone left me overwhelmed by the fiddliness of technological endeavor required to actually get it to work and, feeling sick as a parrot, I abandoned it in favor of a written account.

I closed my eyes and let the visions come. A swirling liquid cocktail of imagery poured through my mind, morphing and reforming before I could fully comprehend the scene, constantly coalescing and dissolving again, and then occasionally forming something I could hang on to and actually name. Every time an image formed that was distinct enough to describe linguistically I would open my eyes and write, though my descriptions were pretty much limited to primitive machine-gun grunts of nouns and occasional adjectives. "Ancient Greek scene. Eyes. (Visuals too vague and fluid). City at night on a lake."

Given that the mental imagery was getting quite diverse I opted to stop there. Turning to the laptop I then opened the folder for the dummy trial and played the first film clip, wondering what would come up. I leapt, somewhat startled, as the speakers suddenly let rip with a strange animal cry and the screen displayed a monster swinging a large club toward me. There was the sound of crushing metal as a warrior in a distinctly Greek helmet adorned with a plume of Mohawk-like stiff hair fell backward, his shield crumpling under the blow of a Minotaur's mace. A fight to the death between the human-bull beast and the hero continued for an intense sixty seconds, ending quite abruptly just short of the decisive moment and recklessly derailing my utter absorption in the scene.

I laughed rapturously as I suddenly remembered what my reason for viewing the clip had been, having been so completely engrossed for the last minute that I had totally forgotten during that time what my sense of purpose was. Oh wow! I really laugh. I will have to watch at least another 80 clips throughout the day, a mind boggling thought.

I then watch the other three dummy clips and write "12:22, test run complete, very engrossed in clips, laughing at how lost I am when the clip ends." Looking back at what I had originally written I also see that although the "city at night by a lake" was absent from any clips, the "ancient Greek scene" fitted perfectly with the first clip and this gets me excited enough to almost make the nausea worthwhile. I didn't bother to run the randomizer to see if this was the target this time, this being just a dummy run.

Into the Magical Realm:
Skeletons in Space on the Great Mechanical Star

Now it's time for the first proper trial. I make a note of my increasing nausea and the fact that my fingertips feel odd and press on. Eyes closed, I dive into the swirling vortex of imagery again and fish around for something tangible. "12:32 p.m., rotating, like [heli-]copter blades, space, more mechanical stuff, spacecraft, space skeletons." A pause in imagery occurs, then "water, submarine, big rig but underwater." Quickly then I complete the measures for gauging my state of consciousness, noting merely that I was 28 percent of the way between being "normal" and "extremely altered," and that my closed-eye mental imagery was somewhat increased compared to normal.

Turning now to the video clips I begin the judging phase of the first trial. Clip one starts. Enter Luke Skywalker and Princess Leia in the classic escape scene from *Star Wars*. Luke and Leia have gone through a doorway onto a ledge overlooking a large drop inside the Death Star. "How do you get the blast door closed?" asks Luke. "They're coming through" shouts Leia and shuts the blast door. They are suspended on a ledge inside the huge machine that is the Death Star. They look around to try to find a way across the huge vertical chamber in front of them. Suddenly laser fire comes in from the front and slightly above. Stormtroopers have appeared at an open doorway across the chamber and are firing on our heroes. Luke shoots one of them and they back off for a moment.

"Here, hold this" says Luke, handing Leia the gun. He then pulls out a small metal device on a string from his utility belt as Leia engages the Stormtroopers above in a gunfight. Luke pulls out more and more string from his belt as the blast door behind them begins to open a crack at the bottom. "Here they come!" shouts Leia.

Lots of smoke now and more laser fire. Leia shoots one of the Stormtroopers above. Luke steps forward and hurls his metal device and string into the air and we see a small grappling hook consisting of three metal blades on a metal stem as it spins around a pole above and secures the end of the string line. Luke pulls the string tight, Leia grabs hold of him with her free arm, gun in the other, and kisses him quickly "for luck" as he looks at her somewhat shocked. They launch into the air as the Stormtroopers behind them start to come through under the blast door on their bellies, shooting as they emerge. Luke and Leia glide across the large chamber on their impromptu string swing just in time and land safely in another doorway on the other side, casually tossing the string aside as they run to safety amid a hail of laser fire . . .

Wow! The clip ends. I must have whooped with excitement a couple of times watching the clip even though I had seen it many times before over the years. George Lucas sure knows how to pack a lot of adventure into sixty seconds—a duration that actually seemed timeless as I had once again been utterly transfixed.

The next two clips were much less intense: a cartoon sequence of hippos dancing a ballet, followed by a clip of a flock of seabirds flying across a brown-orange sky. Then finally a clip from the film *Legend* of a large blue and ugly hag emerging from a swamp and proposing to eat our armored hero (a very young Tom Cruise), who cowers behind his shield and tries to flatter the hag out of killing him. "You don't intend to eat me do you?" he asks. "Oh indeed I do," replies the hag. This last one I found particularly intense but as it ended I dragged myself out of my absorption in the story and back to the experiment.

I begin to review and rate the four clips in light of my prior mental imagery and rank them in order of their similarity to my visions. It's then that I realize how closely my imagery matches the first clip, thematically at least, and quite literally in some ways too. "Rotating, like [heli-] copter blades, space, more mechanical stuff, spacecraft, space skeletons. Water, submarine, big rig but underwater." Certainly the association with space, spacecraft, and "space skeletons" was completely obvious with the *Star Wars* clip, and writing now I see how the Stormtroopers themselves have helmets that look like futuristic skulls—all white save for the black eye patches and the thin black mouth. Indeed the completely white and chunky uniform gives them a real sense of being some kind of techno or space skeletons, and I now see that this was probably a guiding principle in their ultimate cinematic design when the film was made.

It doesn't get any better than the Death Star either in terms of a place where space skeletons might hang out or in terms of the "more mechanical stuff" as the whole thing is supposed to be one big mechanical planet. As for the "rotating, like [heli-]copter blades" Luke's metal grappling hook even looked like helicopter rotors.

This was pretty convincing for me and even though clip one was also like a big rig and somewhat like a submarine, I didn't need to find a match for the other bits of my visualization. I happily ranked this clip number one with some sense of confidence (42 percent). The final elements, "water" and "underwater" tied in with the hag emerging from the swamp clip, which I ranked number two, and the hippo emerging from a paddling pool, which I ranked number three. Having virtually no correspondence with my previous mental imagery, I ranked the birds clip fourth.

Now began the moment of truth. I had recorded my choices and now had to randomly determine which was the actual target clip. I opened the randomization program on the computer and ran the automated selection of a number between one and four, corresponding to clip 1, 2, 3, or 4, respectively. The computer presented number one as the target so *Star Wars* was the target clip! I had got it right and against the odds had successfully selected the correct clip. I then watched the clip again so that my viewing of it might echo back in time and help my past self reach forward in time and select the right clip in the future—

a kind of paradoxical confidence trick symmetrically across time to ensure that my past self would select the right one.

Riding the increasing wave of nausea—and also now the exaggerated sense of meaningfulness and oddity that I was feeling—I was pleasantly surprised and pleased at my performance. Unfortunately, guessing just one clip in a batch of four does not really convince anyone that it was just due to psi though, so I continued the whole process another nineteen times, finally finishing the experiment eight hours after ingesting the first inedible mouthful of purgative powder. This was to be a long and strange trip indeed.

PUTTING THE CORK BACK IN THE BOTTLE

I won't describe the entire experiment or the details of the results—that will be published in a scientific journal—but suffice to say that the experiment was a success in the end.

By the end of the twenty trials I had successfully selected the target in advance eight times out of twenty, which equates to a 40 percent hit rate compared to a chance hit of 25 percent. This figure is slightly better than the average 32 percent hit rate found with the Ganzfeld altered state classically used to experimentally test for psi (e.g., see Radin, 2006), but although my score is better than chance it is not particularly extraordinary based on just twenty trials.

However, the method by which I had planned in advance to analyze the data is slightly more refined. This method considers the rank assigned to each clip in relation to the probability of assigning that rank. In this way it would be expected that, out of a range of between one and four, the target would be ranked as 2.5 on average according to chance. The actual average target rank of all twenty trials was 2.0, indicating that my overall score was safely above chance. The important bit for scientists is that the probability of getting this score is less than 5 percent, or looking at it another way, less than 1 in 20, which is the standard level at which scientists accept that the results are meaningful.

This means that if I had selected my targets merely by chance we would only expect to get these results if we ran the entire experiment twenty times. The thought of that makes me feel quite queasy, anticipating that nausea for hours on end again another twenty times. So chance must take a back seat to improbability and the results as they are must be considered to be what scientists call "statistically significant"— that is, the experiment, this time at least, must be accepted as successful in demonstrating precognition.

One problem, however, is that we cannot be certain that it was San Pedro that caused these significant results, because perhaps I have reliable precognitive abilities anyway even without San Pedro. This is a possibility, of course, but it should be noted that my ability to visualize a scene in my mental imagery was definitely enhanced by the cactus and it was the relationship of this visualization to the clip that led to my accurate choices.

A better experiment would have had an identical series of comparison tests where I didn't take San Pedro but rather a dummy version of it—this is what we call a placebo-controlled condition. But a placebo study is just wishful thinking because it really isn't easy to fake a San Pedro experience with a nonpsychedelic substance. Sure, I could have eaten something to give me stomach cramps, but how to induce the sense of meaningfulness and the increased mental imagery? I would surely have known that the placebo was bogus.

One possibility, almost never used in research, would be to use deep hypnotic suggestion to artificially reinduce the same psychedelic state without the use of the cactus, combined with a suggestion to make me think that I had actually taken the cactus rather than being hypnotized. This kind of hypnotic reinduction of psychedelic states has been demonstrated experimentally at least once (Hastings et al., 2000) but inducing selective amnesia requires especially suggestible participants. This approach has other problems as well, but I won't continue with this line of attack because all scientific research has its limitations, and there are always methodological issues to surmount. What is really required is that somebody else replicates my research findings, otherwise, currently, they can only be considered preliminary at best—but, nevertheless, very promising.

For me, stepping away from the endless scientific debate that could engulf the experiment I have described and talking in a purely nonscientific way, the sense of awe and surprise at getting many of the targets correct speaks directly to my sense of truth. It's not just getting them right either, because improbable statistics alone do not convey much meaning, but rather the degree to which my mental imagery under the influence of San Pedro repeatedly matched the specific target for the trial.

The *Star Wars* example is typical of the hits I had, but to give another example, on one occasion I wrote "desert, dunes, sands of time" and the actual target, which I had also chosen, showed a sidewinder snake elegantly traversing the sand dunes of a desert in its unique and perplexing sideways motion: A parable perhaps for the equally sideways movement through time and space that is embodied by psi.

One of the oddest things, though, was that on several occasions I would visualize an image of something that I would write down in a simple form, such as "broken body," and then three or four of the clips would all have elements clearly related to that specific imagery. On these occasions I tended not to pick the target directly as was hoped, but nevertheless it seemed as though I were visualizing all four of the coming clips in some oddly synchronistic and codified way. What this strange twist means I am still in the process of digesting.

One thing that is clear is that the mind is certainly a maze to get lost in. And from my own experience I am amazed at the apparent accuracy of some of my imagery and that which can be found in the literature from those healers that work with plants as a way of life. I am no shaman or healer, I am just a scientist, but the personal significance to me of this research leaves me indebted to those curanderos, healers, vegetalistas, and shamans who have kept these interspecies relationships alive for millennia in the name of their community and for the sake of their environment (Krippner and Luke, 2009).

It would serve us well in the West to remember that science is only one path to truth and that thankfully there are many others, because, as the saying goes, the universe is not only stranger than we imagine but stranger than we *can* imagine.

REFERENCES

Anderson, Edward F. 1980. *Peyote: The Divine Cactus.* Tucson: University of Arizona Press.

Bergson, Henri. 1990. *Matter and Memory: Essay on the Relationship of Body and Spirit.* Translated by Nancy Margaret Paul and W. Scott Palmer. New York: Zone Books. (Original work published in 1896.)

Breederveld, Heyme. 1976. "Towards reproducible experiments in psychokinesis II: Experiments with a roulette apparatus." *Research Letter of the Parapsychology Laboratory of Utrecht* 7, 6–9.

———. 2001. "An adventure in casino gaming." *Paranormal Review* 19, 34.

Bruhn, Jan G., Hersham El-Seedi, Nikolai Stephanson, Olaf Beck, and Alexander T. Shulgin. 2008. "Ecstasy analogues found in cacti." *Journal of Psychoactive Drugs* 40 (2), 219–22.

Bruhn, Jan G., Jan-Erik Lindgren, Bo Holmstedt, and James M. Adovasio. 1978. "Peyote alkaloids: Identification in a prehistoric specimen of *Lophophora* from Coahuila, Mexico." *Science* 199, 1437–38.

Burger, Richard L. 1992. *Chavín and the Origins of Andean Civilisation.* London: Thames and Hudson.

Carhart-Harris, Robin L. 2011. "Using fMRI to investigate the effects of psilocybin on brain function." Abstracts of papers presented at Breaking Convention: A Multidisclipinary Meeting on Psychedelic Consciousness, University of Kent, 5.

Crosby, D. M., and Jerry L. McLaughlin. 1973. "Cactus alkaloids XIX: Crystallization of mescaline HCl and 3-methoxytryptamine HCl from *Trichocereus pachanoi.*" *Lloydia* 36 (4), 416–18.

De Feo, Vincenzo. 1992. "Medicinal and magical plants in the northern Peruvian Andes." *Fitoterapia* 63 (5), 417–40.

Dobkin de Rios, Marlene. 1968. "*Trichocereus pachanoi:* A mescaline cactus used in folk healing in Peru." *Economic Botany* 22 (2), 191–94.

———. 1977. "Plant hallucinogens and the religion of the Mochica: An ancient Peruvian people." *Economic Botany* 31, 189–203.

———. 1981. "Saladera: A culture-bound misfortune syndrome in the Peruvian Amazon. *Culture, Medicine, and Psychiatry* 5, 193–213.

Dobkin de Rios, Marlene, and Oscar Janiger. 2003. *LSD, Spirituality, and the Creative Process: Based on the Groundbreaking Research of Oscar Janiger, M.D.* Rochester, Vt.: Park Street Press.

Ellis, Havelock. 1898. "Mescal: A new artificial paradise." *Smithsonian Institution Annual Report* 1887 (pp. 537–48). Washington, D.C.: Smithsonian Institution.

El-Seedi, Hesham R., Peter A. De Smet, Olaf Beck, Goran Possnert, and Jan G. Bruhn. 2005. "Prehistoric peyote use: Alkaloid analysis and radiocarbon dating of archaeological specimens of *Lophophora* from Texas." *Journal of Ethnopharmacology* 101 (1–3), 238–42.

Erowid, Fire. 2001. "A look at the mescaline content of *T. peruvianus* and *T. panchanoi.*" *Erowid* Extracts 2, 20–21.

Friedberg, Claudine. 1959. "Rapport sommaire sur une mission au Pérou." *Journal d'Agriculture Tropicale et de Botanique Appliquée* 6, 439–50.

Glass-Coffin, Bonnie. 1999. "Engendering Peruvian shamanism through time: Insights from ethnohistory and ethnography." *Ethnohistory* 46 (2), 205–38.

———. 2000. "The meaning of experience: Theoretical dilemmas in depicting a Peruvian curandera's philosophy of healing." *Method and Theory in the Study of Religion* 12, 226–37.

Hastings, Arthur, Ida Berk, Michael Cougar, Elizabeth Ferguson, Sophie Giles, Sandra Steinbach-Humphrey, Kathie McLellan, Carolyn Mitchell, and Barbara Viglizzo. 2000. "An extended non-drug MDMA-like experience evoked through hypnotic suggestion." *Bulletin of the Multidisciplinary Association for Psychedelic Studies* 10 (1), 10.

Heaven, Ross. 2009. *The Hummingbird's Journey to God: Perspectives on San Pedro, the Cactus of Vision.* Poole, Dorset: O Books.

Heffter, Arthur. 1898. "Über pellote. Beiträge zur chemicschen und pharmacologischen Kenntnis der Cacteen." "Zweite Mittheilung." *Archiv für Experimentelle Pathologie und Pharmacologie* 40, 385–429.

Heywood, Rosalind. 1961. "Personality changes under mescaline." *Proceedings of Two Conferences on Parapsychology and Pharmacology.* New York: Parapsychology Foundation, 67–69.

Holt, Nikola J., Christine A. Simmonds-Moore, and Stephen L. Moore. 2008. "Psi, belief in the paranormal, attentional filters, and mental health." Paper presented at the Bial Foundation Convention, Porto, Portugal.

Huxley, Aldous. 1954. *The Doors of Perception*. London: Chatto and Windus, Ltd.

Jansen, Karl L. R. 1997. "The ketamine model of the near-death experience: A central role for the NMDA receptor." *Journal of Near-Death Studies* 16, 5–26.

Jay, Mike. 2005. "Enter the jaguar: Psychedelic temple cults of ancient Peru." *Strange Attractor Journal* 2, 17–34.

Krippner, Stanley. 2006. "LSD and parapsychological experiences." Paper presented at LSD: Problem Child and Wonder Drug, an International Symposium on the Occasion of the 100th Birthday of Albert Hofmann, January 13–15, Basel, Switzerland.

Krippner, Stanley, and Richard Davidson. 1970. "Religious implications of paranormal events occurring during chemically-induced 'psychedelic' experience." *Pastoral Psychology* 21, 27–34.

Krippner, Stanley, and David Luke. 2009. "Psychedelics and species connectedness." *Bulletin of the Multidisciplinary Association for Psychedelic Studies* 19 (1), 12–15.

Langdon-Davies, John. 1961. *On the Nature of Man*. New York: New American Library.

Le Barre, Weston. 1938. "The peyote cult." *Yale University Publications in Anthropology* no. 19.

Luke, David. 2006. "A tribute to Albert Hofmann on his 100th birthday: The mysterious discovery of LSD and the impact of psychedelics on parapsychology." *Paranormal Review* 37, 3–8.

———. 2008. "Psychedelic substances and paranormal phenomena: A review of the research." *Journal of Parapsychology* 72, 77–107.

———. 2009. "Cleansing the doors of perception: Introduction." In R. Heaven, *The Hummingbird's Journey to God: Perspectives on San Pedro, the Cactus of Vision* (pp. 1–7). Poole, Dorset: O Books.

Luke, David, and Harris L. Friedman. (2010). "The neurochemistry of psi reports and associated experiences." In Stanley Krippner and Harris Friedman (Eds.), *Mysterious Minds: The Neurobiology of Psychics, Mediums, and Other Extraordinary People*. Westport, Conn.: Greenwood/Praeger, 163–85.

Luke, David, and Marios Kittenis. 2005. "A preliminary survey of paranormal experiences with psychoactive drugs." *Journal of Parapsychology* 69 (2), 305–27.

Millay, Jean. 2001. "The influence of psychedelics on remote viewing." *Bulletin of the Multidisciplinary Association for Psychedelic Studies* 11 (1), 43–44.

Osmond, Humphry. 1961. "Variables in the LSD setting." *Proceedings of Two Conferences on Parapsychology and Pharmacology* (pp. 33–35). New York: Parapsychology Foundation.

Osmond, Humphry, and John Smythies. 1952. "Schizophrenia: A new approach." *Journal of Mental Science* 98 (411), 309–15.

Ott, Jonathan. 1996. *Pharmacotheon: Entheogenic Drugs, Their Plant Sources and History,* second edition. Kennewick, Wash.: Natural Products Co.

Pardanani, Jasoda, Jerry L. McLaughlin, R. W. Kondrat, and R. G. Cooks. 1977. "Cactus alkaloids XXXVII: Mescaline and related compounds from *Trichocereus peruvianus.*" *Lloydia* 40 (3), 286–88.

Pekala, Ronald J., and Etzel Cardeña. 2000. "Methodological issues in the study of altered states of consciousness and anomalous experiences." In Etzel Cardeña, Steven, J. Lynn, and Stanley Krippner (Eds.). *Varieties of Anomalous Experience* (pp. 47–81). Washington, D.C.: American Psychological Association.

Price, Henry Habberley. 1964. "A mescalin experience." *Journal of the American Society for Psychical Research* 58, 3–20.

Radin, Dean. 2006. *Entangled Minds: Extrasensory Experiences in a Quantum Reality.* New York: Pocket Books.

Roney-Dougal, Serena. 2001. "Walking between the worlds: Links between psi, psychedelics, shamanism, and psychosis." Unpublished manuscript. Glastonbury, UK: Psi Research Centre.

Rouhier, Alexandre. 1925. "Phénomènes de Matagnomie expérimentale observés au cours d'une expérience faite avec le 'peyotl' (*Echinocactus williamsii*)." *Revue Métapsychique,* May–June, 144–54.

———. 1927. La plante qui faite les yeux émerveillés: Le peyotl. Paris: Doin.

Rush, J. H., and H. A. Cahn. 1958. "Physiological conditioning for psi performance." Abstract from the proceedings of the first convention of the Parapsychological Association, August, 1958, New York. *Journal of Parapsychology* 22, 300.

Schultes, Richard Evans, and Albert Hofmann. 1992. *Plants of the Gods: Their*

Sacred, Healing, and Hallucinogenic Powers. Rochester, Vt.: Healing Arts Press.

Sharon, Douglas. 1978. *Wizard of the Four Winds: A Shaman's Story*. New York: The Free Press.

———. 1990. "The San Pedro cactus in Peruvian folk healing." In P. T. Furst (Ed.). *Flesh of the Gods: The Ritual Use of Hallucinogens*. Long Grove, Ill: Waveland Press, 114–35.

Shulgin, Alexander T., and Ann Shulgin. 1991. *PIHKAL: A Chemical Love Story*. Berkeley, Calif.: Transform Press.

Simmonds, Chris, and Christine Roe. 2000. "Personality correlates of anomalous experiences, perceived ability, and beliefs: Schizotypy, temporal lobe signs, and gender." Proceedings of presented papers from the 43rd annual convention of the Parapsychology Association, 2000, Freiburg, Germany, 272–91.

Slotkin, James Sydney. 1956. "The peyote way." *Tomorrow* 4, 96–105.

Smythies, John Raymond. 1960. "New research frontiers in parapsychology and pharmacology." *International Journal of Parapsychology* 2 (2), 28–38.

———. 1987. "Psychometry and mescaline." *Journal of the Society for Psychical Research* 54, 266–68.

Stafford, Peter. 1977. *Psychedelics Encyclopedia*. Berkeley, Calif.: And/Or Press.

Stevens, Jay. 1988. *Storming Heaven: LSD and the American Dream*. London: William Heinemann.

Strassman, Rick. 2001. *DMT: The Spirit Molecule; A Doctor's Revolutionary Research into the Biology of Near-Death and Mystical Experiences*. Rochester, Vt.: Park Street Press.

Tart, Charles T. 1972. "Considering the scientific study of the human aura." *Journal of the Society for Psychical Research* 46, 1–21.

Thalbourne, Michael A. 2000. "Transliminality and creativity." *The Journal of Creative Behavior* 34, 193–202.

Vollenweider, Franz X. 2001. "Brain mechanisms of hallucinogens and entactogens." *Dialogues in Clinical Neurosceince* 3 (4), 265–79.

Vollenweider, Franz X., and Michael A. Geyer. 2001. "A systems model of altered consciousness: Integrating natural and drug-induced psychoses." *Brain Research Bulletin* 56 (5), 495–507.

7
Heaven and the Hummingbird

Morgan Maher

This is a revised and updated version of an interview that first appeared in *Reality Sandwich* magazine in 2009. The original can be found at www.realitysandwich.com.

As the use and knowledge of ayahuasca gains momentum across the planet, I contacted Ross Heaven, coauthor of *Plant Spirit Shamanism* and author of *The Hummingbird's Journey to God,* to discuss a somewhat lesser known plant, San Pedro, the role it can play in helping us "get to grips" with the world, its relationship with ayahuasca, and the cross-cultural use of plants for healing.

You've described your first encounter with San Pedro as less than spectacular. What was it about the plant and the experience that continued to draw you closer to it?

Heaven: I first visited Peru nearly fifteen years ago, ostensibly to drink ayahuasca, but an opportunity arose seemingly by chance to drink San Pedro too. It certainly wasn't part of my plans.

Ayahuasca was life changing, as it so often is for those who drink it. In my case it led eventually to me leaving my well-paid job, selling the semidetached dream home, and giving back the keys to the BMW so I could devote time to the needs of my soul and to what was real and important to me: working more closely with the plants and the healers I had met.

By contrast San Pedro left me cold—physically as well as metaphysically. I drank it as part of an all-night ceremony at a historic site just outside Lima with a traditional shaman working with what I have come to call "old-school" rituals. So I was first given a *contrachisa* (an emetic to get rid of the spiritual toxins in my body), then a *singado,* a tobacco and alcohol mixture that is snorted into the nostrils to clean your energy and bring good luck. It is acrid, acidic, and drips down your throat like battery acid. So there was plenty of purging (i.e., vomiting) from me that night. Then there were baths with cold floral waters, sprays with *agua florida,* gentle beatings with *chonta* (wooden sticks that are a typical feature of many San Pedro *mesas,* or altars) and calisthenics to perform too, all of it designed to loosen my energy and remove spirit intrusions. Almost as a footnote, I was also given San Pedro.

The night was freezing, I was tired, and with all that activity there was hardly a moment to even engage with San Pedro, yet alone feel and experience the effects of the cactus itself—very much in contrast to ayahuasca ceremonies where in the gentle warmth of the jungle you are only asked to sit and listen to the beautiful healing songs of the shaman and allow your visions to unfold.

That first experience with San Pedro could have turned me off it forever. I mean, why would you bother with all that drama for so little effect when ayahuasca is so profound and its ceremonies so healing and beautiful?

There was something about San Pedro though, some nagging feeling that it contained new answers for me. Perhaps I received more than I thought from that first ceremony, despite the best efforts of the shaman! But, if so, it was at a subtle or unconscious level. It was enough anyway to encourage me to seek out other healers and ceremonies, different approaches and different brews, until I finally found a *curandera* with a San Pedro that was of a wholly different order to the others I had drunk. That ceremony was an eye-opener. With that shaman, La Gringa, I realized during the course of a single ceremony what San Pedro had been trying to tell me for years.

There were two keys to this: firstly that while other shamans brew their San Pedro for eight or even four hours, La Gringa cooks hers for twenty so it is much more potent. More importantly, however, she has dispensed with the ritual dramas of the "old school" shamans I had been working with, so there are no distractions from the healing and visions the cactus brings. You are totally *in* the experience for several hours.

Her ceremonies are held in the daytime too so it is warmer, more comfortable and, more than that, you can see the world around you and it is alive with color, spirit, and beauty. You just can't do that in the darkness of all-night ceremonies. What San Pedro had been trying to tell me for years is that the world is beautiful, healing, and nothing to be afraid of, but I needed to meet its spirit directly and in daylight in order to hear this message and that had been more or less impossible in the other ceremonies I had attended.

Could you describe a particularly profound experience you've had with San Pedro?

Heaven: Well, on that first daylight ceremony I *became* San Pedro. Almost as soon as I drank it I began to experience little jolts of energy that felt like muscle cramps running through my body, and after a while of this I grew intrigued as to whether I would actually be able to see my muscles moving under my skin, so I held my arm up to study it. It was green, with ridges and furrows on it, and its hairs standing upright like spines. It took me some moments to recognize what it was or what it reminded me of so I knew I wasn't "inventing" or imagining it. It was only when I made the connection that I realized I *was* San Pedro! It had totally taken me over and the jolts of energy I was experiencing were the cactus checking me out muscle by muscle, cell by cell, and healing the areas of weakness it found in me.

I was fascinated, awed, and alarmed all at the same time—I didn't know whether I'd ever make it back to human form. But my other experiences with entheogens had taught me that at times like these you simply must trust the plant so I relaxed and let it do its work. From then on I felt blessed and honored to be in the hands of such a powerful healer.

I had a vision then where I saw and experienced myself cowering outside the walls of paradise in a world that was as empty as a desert, pleading to be let back in to the place where God was but always receiving a gentle but insistent "no." Even under the intoxication of San Pedro, I knew that this symbolized my relationship to the world: that I felt alone and abandoned by God—or love—and that this was the root of my failures and dis-ease.

The message of San Pedro was to face my fears with Dignity (capital D) and to understand that everyone on this planet feels the same aloneness too; it is the cause of all our conflicts and terrors, but actually the world is beautiful and ours, just as we are its. We belong to each other so we are never truly alone and there is no need to feel afraid.

As soon as I realized that, a bolt of energy hit me full in the back and in the shock of it I took the deepest breath that I can ever remember taking. I had been suffering from the breathlessness of altitude sickness for a few days (I was in Cusco at the time, which is about twelve thousand feet above sea level) but with that single breath I was completely cured. Furthermore, I somehow understood that I had got sick because I *expected* to—because I always did when I visited Cusco—and the power of my mind had created my current reality of illness while in fact there was nothing physically wrong with me. "The world is as you dream it," as the Shuar shamans say. With San Pedro, more so even than with ayahuasca, you can see how *literally* true that is.

Since then I have met people who have been cured of all sorts of diseases—cancer, paralysis, pneumonia, grief, paranoia—by drinking

San Pedro and arriving at the same conclusion that I did: illness is a state of mind and simply by changing our minds we heal ourselves.

That healing with San Pedro lasted for twelve hours and what I have described so far took maybe two, so there was a lot more to this journey than I have space for. The take-home messages, however, were that the world is a magnificent place where everything is allowed and there is no need to feel afraid or to manifest our fears as illness. We can walk the world with power, pride, Dignity, and courage instead, because "We are That" and we always have a choice.

You mentioned San Pedro as being "much better than ayahuasca for getting to grips with the world." Could you elaborate on this?

Heaven: My experiences with ayahuasca give me the sense that it frees the spirit from the body so that figuratively speaking (or perhaps literally) we can drift among the stars and see the order of the universe and the energy that underlies it, or meet others—plants, animals, and people—on a spirit-to-spirit, soul-to-soul level. The healing comes when we realize that everything is energy, that this energy (or its manifestation as blessings, power, and success or as illness and misfortune) can be changed, and that we are all connected. The emphasis, however, is on going *out*, moving beyond the limitations of the body and the ego-concerns of our minds so we can come to know this.

With San Pedro, however, the overriding sensation is of bringing the soul of the universe *in* to the body: a "drawing inward" so you understand your place in the world, the creative powers you have to shape and direct it, and above all, the beauty of your soul and the soul of the things around you.

With ayahuasca, for example, you may be lost in wonder at the magnificence of your spirit and the universe you are a part of, but San Pedro is often more beautifully and gently humbling, more direct: you realize that even though you *are* magnificent you are no more amazing or significant than a house brick (which is incredible and alive in its own way). But you are no *less* significant or wonderful either! Everything is equal, in balance, and perfect as it is.

The effect of San Pedro, then, is to teach you how to be "the true human" as one of my teachers put it, and how to be and act in the world—with Dignity and responsibility. If you like, it provides instructions for us in how to fall in love with the world again and with all that we are and have instead of voyaging outward to heal what we are not. As one of my participants expressed it having drunk San Pedro, "I wanted to fuck the Earth!"

For these reasons San Pedro is the perfect complement to ayahuasca and helps to ground our spiritual lessons in our bodies so that a code for living in the real world can begin to inform and empower us. With San Pedro we can *apply* the lessons of ayahuasca to the world and understand that we too are God.

Knowledge and use of ayahuasca is growing across the planet. Do you see a similar thing occurring with San Pedro? Why or how do you feel San Pedro has kept a lower profile than ayahuasca?

Heaven: It's an interesting question. Andean shamans say that San Pedro has a certain "mystery" to it, that you have to in some way "earn" your relationship with it. Maybe that's why it took me so long to develop my own connections to it. I doubt that their view is wholly true, however, since I've taken many people to Peru to work with San Pedro and they have got its message at the first ceremony they attended.

The old school San Pedro shamans do have a protective attitude toward the cactus spirit, though, and in some ways I think that the rituals they use are a sort of mask they put up to its power so that not everyone is immediately granted access to what they regard as its divine essence and teachings.

I'm not sure either that the time is right just yet for people to have full access to San Pedro, although that time will surely come. I think that the medicine for our times may still be ayahuasca so we can experience and explore other realities and develop our understanding of oneness. The next evolutionary step will then be to bring this understanding into our relationship to the world, and that is the job of San Pedro, but maybe we're not there yet.

It is a discipline, after all, to *apply* the lessons of these sacred teachers to the world we live in and act accordingly. Only the saints have managed it so far and most of us are not saints! So maybe we need to develop greater spiritual powers before that can happen. Ayahuasca is definitely an aid to that and an immensely valuable teacher. But give it a little time and when a movement has gathered of people who are aware of a deeper truth, then it may be San Pedro's time. But, of course, that does not preclude anyone who feels themselves ready from exploring San Pedro now.

How do you feel the spirits of San Pedro and ayahuasca differ or relate?

Heaven: The stereotype seems to be that ayahuasca is a female spirit while San Pedro is male. I've also heard it said that ayahuasca is serpentine, winding like a snake so we must track its meanings to decode what it is telling us, whereas San Pedro is "straight like an arrow" and takes you directly to the answers you seek.

Those, however, are just projections. La Gringa's experience is that ayahuasca is a male spirit and San Pedro is the female but, at the end of the day, of course they are neither. They are plant intelligences and energies. We may project on to them whatever we wish since we are the great creators and our minds can shape realities, but it doesn't change their essential natures.

My perception (or projection) of San Pedro's spirit is that it takes the form of a matador, sword in hand, drawing a protective line in the desert sand to signify our boundaries and the power contained within them. A proud and Dignified warrior-spirit. Interestingly enough, when I drank San Pedro with another person in the hills above Cusco she saw exactly the same thing. But I can't say that this *is* San Pedro's face. I am reminded of Don Juan's comment to Castaneda about Mescalito, that our allies take many forms (for Castaneda Mescalito was at different times a moth and a dog), and the form that they take probably depends on our own needs, psychologies, and perceptions, and is not a quality inherent in the plants themselves.

What have you discovered in regard to the cross-cultural use of plants for healing?

Heaven: My earliest experiences of plant spirit shamanism were as a boy on the borders of Wales in the British Isles, when I met and worked with an old sin eater and herbalist (a story told in my book *The Sin Eater's Last Confessions*, 2008). Since then I have traveled to different cultures to learn from the plants and shamans and it has always interested me that the techniques and approaches they use are so similar. Why that should be, and how a sin eater in Wales could know the same facts about which plants would heal a particular disease and then employ the same methods for working with them as a shaman in a small town in Haiti or a curandero in the rainforests or mountains of Peru was always a mystery to me. They'd never spoken to each other, after all, or learned each other's techniques. They didn't even know of each other's existence.

It's a question I've put to all of these healers and the answer has always been the same: "Their spirits told us. We asked the plants and they taught us how to heal."

The biggest challenge in this for the Western mind is to take what they are saying literally. For us it defies rationality that plants have intelligence, can communicate with us, and have a healing intention, so we tend to dismiss the shaman's words as a metaphor or a quaint misunderstanding of what Western materialist science "knows" to be true. But if we listen to what they say and allow, beyond our own paradigms and egos, that they may actually know what they're talking about, then our eyes are suddenly opened and we understand that they are gifting us a profound and fundamental truth. In Terence McKenna's words, that "nature is alive and is talking to us. *This is not a metaphor.*"

And then of course we have our own San Pedro experience and, to quote the Oracle in *The Matrix*, we know in our bones and balls that plants are conscious, aware, and intelligent, and much more evolved than us. They were the first citizens of this planet and have a wisdom that is ancient compared to our fleeting time on Earth.

The central cross-cultural instruction for working and healing with plants then is simply this: open your mind and *listen* and you'll learn all that you need to know.

The world is changing. The current "global" (by which we really mean Western or capitalist) financial crisis, property crash, and environmental problems we face are evidence for many that our take on reality just isn't working and people are, I think, inclined to look for new solutions that, paradoxically, they are finding in old ways. It is the shamanic wisdom-keepers who are providing the new (and ancient) truths that have real meaning and application.

Many people have found their answers in ayahuasca and in this sense have become the Earth's pioneers seeking new worlds of understanding and, like early explorers and navigators, returning home with their strange fruits and wondrous tales of adventure. The next step is for these truths to become more widely accepted as self-evident and employed in *this* reality so we can all grow from them. This step, I think, is the work of San Pedro and its time is approaching fast.

Considering the transition of the generally accepted name of the cactus, from the traditional *huachuma* (Andean), *achuma* (Bolivian), to the Christian influenced San Pedro, in what ways is the cactus already affected, effected, or deepened by cross-culturalization?

Heaven: I've been talking about old school shamans—those with lots of ritual as part of their ceremonies and lots of Catholic symbols and artifacts. My teachers believe that this format is directly related to the coming of the Spanish and their imposition of a new cultural identity on Peru and its ceremonies, including concepts of sin and punishment that never existed in the country before.

Before the Spanish, work with San Pedro was more natural and flowing and the plant rather than the shaman was regarded as the healer—very much like the ceremonies *we* now run in fact. These ceremonies are therefore a "backward evolution" or devolution, back to the first ceremonial form these healings would have taken, where the plant itself is the maestro.

Our ceremonies are less ritualistic, for example, take place in daylight because San Pedro takes power from the sun, and the brew is much stronger so the ceremony becomes an uninterrupted flow of communion with the plant spirit. This, according to those who know the history of Peruvian healing better than I do, is closer to pre-Hispanic rituals.

It is true that San Pedro ceremonies were undoubtedly altered by the beliefs and customs of other cultures, but strip these glosses away and allow the plant to speak for itself and its spirit remains as it ever was.

It is a strange God that San Pedro introduces us to though—at least as far as our Western mind-set goes. I was rereading Jim DeKorne's book the other day [*Psychedelic Shamanism,* Loompanics Unlimited 1994] and he says the same thing about other entheogens: that under the influence of teacher plants our quaint ideas about a loving father— God, Blake's "Nobodaddy," "old man in the clouds"—who will solve all our problems for us, must inevitably vanish as we become aware of a deeper truth.

What San Pedro shows us, for example, is that there *is* no great cosmic father outside of us; instead we are responsible for ourselves. That might sound like a heavy burden to some people but in fact there is great freedom and power in this because we are also freed from rules and empowered to find our own ways. I suppose that the intelligence of the universe that San Pedro guides us to is still "parental" in a sense, but in the rather different sense of a father who gives his sons and daughters the liberty—without judgment—to find their own solutions and make their own mistakes.

What San Pedro does, however, at a very personal level, is show us the consequences of our choices. The outcome in most cases is that we naturally choose, without force or coercion, to act more lovingly anyway because when we understand the power of our thoughts, words, choices, and actions, and the connections between us there is simply nothing else we can do. Nothing else would make sense.

So again, while San Pedro has no dogmatic pronouncements to make or any download of rules we must follow, the outcome of our work with this plant is personal change so that we *do* evolve and become more compassionate beings. It is a beautiful process but one that can be very different to those we may have experienced with other plant teachers, and it is certainly a different order of truth to our experience of "normal" daily life.

What are your thoughts on the issue of sustainability regarding these plants?

Heaven: I suppose it is a judgment I choose to make but it bothers me when I see "spiritual tours" being advertised where you can visit Peru for a week and stay in a five-star hotel, go on a Machu Picchu trip, explore a "mystical portal," do a little yoga, and, as part of the tourist experience, have an ayahuasca or San Pedro ceremony as well.

An itinerary like this belittles the visionary and healing experience and is therefore wasteful of these plants and our human energies and potential. It is not in keeping with the spirit of ayahuasca or San Pedro. On the other hand if—even by chance—a tour like this can reach one person and inspire them to truly heal or to find out more about the truth of their lives and the world around them, then I suppose there may be a deeper purpose to the sacrifice than we know.

On the trips I run we work with healing centers that exist to preserve the rain forest and its traditions. For every drink of San Pedro a new plant is sown and another shaman is allowed to maintain and practice his art.

But that is just my choice. The lesson of San Pedro is that in the widest scheme of things there really is no right or wrong and no rules to follow, only actions and consequences, so we cannot impose our views on others. They must decide for themselves.

My feeling is that we reap what we sow but we should also sow what we reap. If we do not we may deprive ourselves of the very healing we need at an important time in our evolution, since these plants will not be available to us for long.

Has San Pedro, or any other plant, offered you advice regarding the ecological crisis or the so-called planetary crisis?

Heaven: Well of course, there is no "planetary" crisis. There is a *human* crisis but that is a different matter. My experience with teacher plants tells me that our planet, as a self-sustaining organism, has a liking for but no particular attachment to human life, and as a self-healing and homeostatic system it has ways to cure itself of the downsides of our presence if that becomes necessary and it will, quite rightly, fight for its own survival if need be.

Some of the environmental and economic shifts we are seeing now may be evidence of that correction but while we regard them as problems, to the Earth they may simply be the sore throat and runny nose of a cold that is a healing response to a virus that is screwing up its system. Even if all human beings were, like so much mucus, wiped off the face of the planet tomorrow, the Earth would survive and so would its other species.

Another analogy is an ant nest. As human beings we're not going to go out of our way to destroy a colony of ants, but if they start to become a nuisance in our own backyard or interfere with our quiet enjoyment of our own lives we certainly have that power and probably wouldn't give it a second thought. To the Earth we are the ants and we must remember that.

Perhaps it is ultimately not in our destiny for the human race to be more than a footnote to the pages of history, but that too is a matter of choice, negotiation, and cooperation between ourselves and the planet we are a part of.

If we intend to survive then we need to *really* learn the ways of cooperation, consideration, and compassion and not just give lip service to them—and to understand the deeper truths of the world and ourselves.

This is certainly the message of the plants and particularly of San Pedro. But then again, when have human beings ever listened to reason!

My belief—I hope not too pessimistically—is that human beings have a limited time on Earth and I'm relaxed about that. We all came here with the clock ticking after all. No one gets out alive. For our children's sake though, I would love us to be able to change and I'm sure it's possible but it relies on us making appropriate new choices about how we see, feel, and act in the world. San Pedro can help with this, but it requires that people with the power to make changes choose to drink and explore its wisdom—and to be all they are capable of being. This of course means all of us.

PART THREE

San Pedro Healing

Remember who you are
Remember where you came from

PUMA*

---

*Puma is a shaman who lives near Cusco. He began training as a healer as a young
boy after he was struck by lightening, a sure sign of a shamanic calling in the Andes.
"Remember who you are, remember where you came from" is a mantra he often repeats
to participants during *limpias,* cleansings prior to San Pedro ceremonies. He means by it
that all men are "Princes" and all women "Princesses" and that we all came from God.
Indeed, we *are* God and capable, therefore, of healing ourselves and others by simply
embracing this truth with the aid of teachers like San Pedro. —R.H.

WE BEGIN this section with an analysis of some of the themes that tend to emerge during San Pedro healing, a sense, that is, of what participants in ceremony feel, experience, and learn about themselves and the world around them, and the ways in which healing can flow from this. It's a little bit of number-crunching that serves as an introduction to the process if you've never drunk San Pedro before; or if you have, you might recognize some of your own process in the figures.

The numbers alone, however, cannot really give you a true sense of a San Pedro healing, which is by its nature personal, individually meaningful, and intimately connected to the life stories, the past and the present, of those who drink it. The anecdotes, in this respect, usually contain more truth, more "juice," and more sense than the statistics. For this reason I have also included the accounts of four ceremonial participants, told in their own words, three of whom have drunk San Pedro with me. We hear from the following:

Tracie Thornberry was born in Australia and moved to Peru in early 2009. She is a drug and alcohol counselor and teacher. After recovering, via spiritual and plant shamanic methods, from a history of addiction herself (in her case to heroin and alcohol) she spent several years researching various rehabilitation and recovery methods before deciding to settle in Peru to pursue her studies with plant medicines.

Based on the results of this research, Tracie founded an addictions treatment center in Iquitos where she offers traditional Western counseling alongside the use of ayahuasca and San Pedro, and says that she is able to achieve superior results to those available from Western therapies alone. In her article she discusses her journey into and escape from addiction and the role that teacher plants have played in this, as well as her research and healing work with addicts.

Alexia Gidding is a United Kingdom-based counselor, therapist, and hypnotherapist who drank San Pedro for the first and second times during healing ceremonies with me in October 2009. As she recounts in this report, her first experience was anything but expected, but turned out to be one of the most important and healing (albeit also one of the most painful) of her life. Her story suggests one way in which San Pedro heals: by supporting us in what Alexia calls "a gentle but persistent way" to immerse ourselves fully in the reliving of past traumas that have not so much been dealt with as repressed. With San Pedro they can finally be released so that the poison they contain can also be let go.

Robyn Silvanen is a bodyworker living in the United States who first drank San Pedro with me in 2008. Hers is an interesting story of healing in the sense that not only did she experience the insights and emotional cleansing that is typical of San Pedro, but through the ceremonies she attended she has also, she says, been liberated from a number of physical problems and issues. Her life has changed as a consequence and many of her old, self-limiting, and debilitating patterns have been removed.

Daniel Moler describes himself as a "father, husband, writer, professor, artist, energy healer, dreamer, and friend." His philosophy, quoting Terence McKenna, is that "we have to recognize that the world is not something sculptured and finished which we as perceivers walk through like patrons in a museum; the world is something we *make* through the act of perception." In his article he describes a healing that he and his wife undertook with San Pedro to cure a "heart condition" and how at the end of it he was able to address his fears and anxiety, some of it resulting from post-traumatic stress disorder, to discover "how to love: without fear, without anticipating return" because "giving oneself to another endlessly and selflessly is the only true to way to heal, to evolve."

Sonna-Ra is a healer from New Zealand who, as she relates, had to make a decision to live instead of incline herself toward death in order to receive the gifts of San Pedro. That in itself led to the possibility of an extraordinary encounter with this plant, and through that to a new and more joyful relationship with life.

All of these accounts are in some ways typical of the San Pedro experience, although every experience is unique and there is often more to it as well, which is far deeper than even the words of these participants can convey.

8
San Pedro Healing
An Overview

~~~~~~~~~

Ross Heaven

Simon Ralli Robinson is a onetime student of mine who joined my San Pedro healing journey to Peru in 2008. Depressed and confused at the time, his experiences with San Pedro turned his life around, relieving him of decades-old grief and helping him to see the world in a more earthy and holistic way than his previous beliefs had allowed.

Simon was working as an online business manager for a gaming company prior to his ceremonies, but after drinking San Pedro he knew that he couldn't, and didn't want to, return to this job or his old life, so he left his company and moved away from Gibraltar where he had been living and began a master of science degree at Schumacher College in the United Kingdom. He now has a qualification in environmental science after writing his thesis on the healing potentials of teacher plants and spends his time between the United Kingdom and Bolivia.

Simon's healing journey is recounted in his own words and in some detail in my book *The Hummingbird's Journey to God*.[1] More recently, however, he has published a book of his own, *The Shaman and Snow*

White (Simon Ralli Robinson, 2011), in which he has collated a number of testimonials from those who have drunk San Pedro and had life-changing experiences of their own.

These are a few of these testimonials, which range from summary sentences to more detailed accounts. Collectively, they provide us with an insight into what a healing with San Pedro might entail and what the outcome might be.

1. A lovely experience. I found the spirits in the sky.

2. An amazing journey. It gave me some powerful insights.

3. What could I say that in any way does justice to the experience I have had? All I could think was to be silent and listen to the answers around me in every living thing.

4. I found answers that I had been hiding from and many that I needed. San Pedro taught me what it means to be at one with nature and to trust myself more. Seeing the Earth spirits and the Earth breathing—wow! Love is the answer to any question.

5. My life has changed unbelievably since my experience. . . . My view of the world is different, my intuition much stronger, and my relationships with people much healthier and more direct. I've reconnected with my dad and I've begun the process of healing, having been able to let go of things that don't belong to me and knowing that healing comes from within.

6. I have learned more about myself in the past month than I have in my entire school career. Retching out toxic thoughts and emotions is a new cleansing for me but I am closer to the source now. [I] learned a new patience for myself. . . . It was a big deal for me because it's so unlike anything I have experienced before but it's really opened my eyes to a new way of seeing the world and all it offers. I feel powerful.

7. The sky was incredibly gorgeous, laced clouds with light blue and sparkling. And there in the sky was the answer. Things were brought to my attention: my life, friends, family, needing

to simplify my existence. Lots of little worlds to explore, possibilities one can't ignore.

8. My experience was not a pleasant one. The physical reaction in my body was intense to say the least. But still there were lessons learned and beauty found. [Afterward] I had a big checkup at the doctor and had everything done: heart, blood, x-rays, the whole lot, and guess what the doctor said? Never in a million years when she met me did she ever think I would be well again. [But now] there is not a thing wrong with me. I told her about San Pedro and she said she would never discount my testimony as she had seen with her own eyes how well I am. . . . San Pedro saved my life.

9. San Pedro opened my channels of light and reminded me of how I need to focus my energies: not on addiction and depression but on moving forward and dropping little nuggets of love-light into the lives of every new person I meet.

10. I felt like a little girl again, which is good because our minds aren't so polluted when we're young and kids see things that adults cannot see.

11. Awakening is the only way I can describe it. I asked San Pedro for liberation and it gave it to me. . . . I saw the love and power in all things.

12. Incredibly life changing and healing. Every day I see a new life, I am connected with nature and awareness. I actually feared this connection [before and] had a hard time receiving the extreme energy that I feel with it. I have become in touch with or aware of the thought patterns that I was previously unaware of that were inhibiting my health and spiritual growth.

13. San Pedro—not at all what I expected. Feeling at one with the spirit of life, feeling myself to be everything around me, seeing so many levels of energy and consciousness. . . . I am awed, humbled, and blessed.

14. My experience was more inside myself but I experienced beauty

and love beyond words. I saw things I don't understand yet but that's okay. . . . The experience released my power that I feel growing inside me. I saw myself before I was born. . . . I see God in me. My power grows, it doesn't stop.

15. San Pedro [has] taken me so much further than words can ever reach and today I keep learning from it. My first San Pedro experience was very physical. I could feel San Pedro caressing every part, every cell of my body, it was a wow feeling. . . . I could not stop smiling for twelve hours. It was more than a happy feeling, it was a complete connection with everything around me, especially nature, sometimes love coming from the trees and plants, it was overwhelming . . . a connection with my own love and with the love of the universe and our beautiful planet. [I experienced] a complete rebirth. I saw myself as a newborn . . . giving birth to myself . . . confusing and beautiful at the same time. I believe San Pedro showed me myself in my purest state to understand who I am and that no matter what happens to me along the way I have to remember who I am regardless. I also believe San Pedro wanted to give me a fresh start, a new beginning, a second chance and to show me I am always able to change my life whenever I want . . . [and] that my future is far more important than my past and I need to let go of my past sufferings to put that energy of the moment into the future.

WHAT CAN WE DRAW FROM THESE COMMENTS?

In *The Antipodes of the Mind*,[2] Benny Shanon, Ph.D., distilled the essence of more than 130 personal ayahuasca journeys along with data from others who have drunk the brew in various settings. In all, about 2,500 ayahuasca sessions are covered, a figure that adds considerably to our understanding of the nature of this plant, its visionary effects, and the information it has to impart.

In *The Hummingbird's Journey to God* I began a similar analysis of the San Pedro experience, although the dozen accounts I included there, most of them conducted in a limited ceremonial context and with one shaman, pale into insignificance compared to Shanon's figures and the scientific rigor with which he collated and analyzed them. Still, it was interesting to see what common factors emerged from the accounts of those who had drunk San Pedro with me. What I learned was that there are indeed consistencies.

The issue of what we might call "truth versus fear" came up for about two-thirds of my sample. By this I mean that it appears to be a property of San Pedro that it supports and empowers us to address our fears almost as a form of initiation. By facing what was hidden but still disempowering for us, we emerge with a greater sense of courage and understanding, feeling healed and more in touch with what is "real" for us rather than allowing the illusion of fear to overwhelm us.

Fear may be expressed as "feelings of claustrophobia when women got too close to me," as one of my participants put it. His San Pedro vision "addressed that fear head on" and enabled him to arrive at a new truth: "that it was a good thing if we [men and women] merged . . . I wasn't losing myself because there was nothing really to lose."

Another participant, because of her childhood experiences, was afraid of intimacy and especially of connections with children. What she realized during her journey though is that "everything [even the traumatic times she had gone through] is exactly as it is meant to be." As a result of this realization she was able to move beyond fear to find love and, within a short time, to marry and have a child of her own. As she remarked, "San Pedro gave me my daughter."

For another it was a fear of abandonment. With the aid of San Pedro, however, this participant was able to work through her issue until she realized that it was not really fear she was experiencing at all but "my old patterns again." From there she could move on and conclude that "everything was just as it should be . . . there is never anything wrong. Nature and the Earth is in the perfect bliss of the moment."

It will be interesting to reflect on this notion of an initiation into and beyond fear as you read Alexia's account, which appears in chapter 10.

Another commonality among my participants was their realization of the importance of love. At least 50 percent of my respondents reported that they were able to emerge from their exploration of fear with a feeling of greater love for themselves, for others, and for the world as a whole.

Kane, for example, said that his greatest lesson was to learn to love himself and to appreciate the Earth for the love and care that it gave him. Another participant, Jamie, realized that "the truth *is* love, always has been and always will be" and that it is important to "give yourself entirely" to its pursuit and "never take for granted the love that is before you." Michael's journey enabled him to reconcile his differences with his parents and rather than continuing to resent them for their controlling and overprotective actions, to understand where their anxiety stemmed from so his "frustration toward them turned to love and compassion."

As Michael's words suggest, allied to love in many cases is forgiveness. Nearly 20 percent of my participants mentioned this specifically in their accounts, whether it was expressed in forgiveness for themselves, a parent, girlfriend, child, or some other significant person with whom there had previously been issues. Not surprisingly as well in view of this, the healing of relationships (including the relationship to oneself) figured in 92 percent of the accounts I received.

For some people, these healings concerned relationships of a more spiritual or "cosmic" nature. Both Tracie and Kyle commented on the connections between us all and between human beings and the planet as a whole. "I had an overwhelming sense of belonging to the earth," said Tracie. "Every living thing has its place and it is all of equal importance." While Kyle realized that "I am intrinsically a part of everything. Whatever I do in the world also happens to me; my individual body is a microcosm for the world at large."

Another of San Pedro's teachings is the understanding that "reality" is not something that inheres in the world but is created by us as a consequence of how we view it, and by our thoughts, ideas, actions, and words. Nearly 60 percent of people mentioned this, including Michael who wrote that "our thoughts are things and create our reality in the physical world. We have the power to create our own heaven or hell with every passing thought," and Tracie who realized "the power of words and even thoughts" to create reality so that nothing is "really real" unless we make it so.

Sixty-seven percent of participants mentioned that they felt more deeply and intimately connected to nature as a result of drinking San Pedro, including Kane who said that he "met Mother Earth" on his journey and expressed a desire to try San Pedro again, "this time to increase my awareness and communication with Pachamama, to assist and heal her."

For Michael this connection to the Earth emerged from the landscape in which he found himself. "The land was beautiful. . . . I became part of the Earth itself and had a feeling of complete peace. . . . I looked at the mountains and the valley to my left and felt their presence. They were alive; breathing just like me."

Finally, for my participants there was a sense, particularly in connection with nature, that the world is ensouled and enchanted, that God exists and that the true order of the universe is love. Forty-two percent of people mentioned God directly in their accounts or else his or her representation as "Pachamama" or "Mother Earth." Kane, as we have already seen, says that he "met Mother Earth." Jamie felt that she had to give thanks to God "who has brought me into this gorgeous moment of gift and privilege." Michael understood that "we are all part of God."

It is interesting to compare these findings to those in the testimonials that Simon has gathered.

OTHER ACCOUNTS

Of these, 40 percent mention the ensouled nature of the world. Comments range from seeing "spirits in the sky" to "seeing the Earth spirits and the Earth breathing" to the sense that "I am connected to nature and awareness." Others report "feeling at one with the spirit of life, feeling myself to be everything around me," sensing "love coming from the trees and plants . . . [and] the love of the universe" to quite simply, "I see God in me."

Thirty-three percent of Simon's group also mention an enhanced connection to nature, and this is implied in many other responses too. Comments include "San Pedro taught me what it means to be at one with nature," there are "answers around me in every living thing" and the sense of "complete connection to everything around me, especially nature."

In *The Hummingbird's Journey to God* I reflected on the fact that one of the gifts of San Pedro is to show us that reality is never a given but instead is what we make of it and that there are answers to be found in all things. Seventy-three percent of Simon's respondents discovered something similar for themselves. "I am closer to the source now [and have] a new way of seeing the world," says one. "[There are a] lot of [new] little worlds to explore, possibilities one can't ignore," says another. Others reflect that "San Pedro . . . reminded me of how I need to focus my energies: not on addiction and depression but on moving forward," that San Pedro was "incredibly life changing [and I am now more aware of my] thought patterns." "Awakening is the only way I can describe it" says another, through to simply "I saw things I didn't understand but that's okay."

Then there is the account of respondent number eight, whose medical doctor confirmed that she had moved from a position of ill health to one of total well-being following her San Pedro experience ("San Pedro saved my life"). If the world is indeed as we decide it will be, then our health must certainly be part of that too, and as this example shows, a change of mind and a new way of seeing the world and ourselves may be all it takes to create a physical change that can be confirmed by a blood test or an x-ray.

Also consistent with my own study is the issue of forgiveness and the healing of relationships that can emerge from this. Many of Simon's accounts hint at relationship changes, healthier interactions with others and with the natural world, and at the forgiveness of others or the self for wrongs committed. Twenty percent of them mention the latter directly. "I've reconnected with my dad," "I've learned a new patience for myself" and "San Pedro showed me myself in my purest state [and gave me] a fresh start" are some of the comments made. From this, as respondent number five puts it: "relationships with people [at least have a new potential to become] much healthier and more direct."

Again, just as I discovered, a greater sense of love, self-love, and connection is implied or suggested in most of Simon's accounts. One-third of his sample mentioned this directly. "Love is the answer to any question," "I saw the love and power in all things," "I experienced beauty and love beyond words." There is a lesson in this too for some, that to be well and happy they must retain a "connection with my own love and the love of the universe" as well as "dropping little nuggets of love-light into the lives of every new person I meet."

What I have called the initiation into and through fear is also present in these accounts, as it was for me and my own respondents. A third of Simon's group refer to it. "I found answers that I had been hiding from," for example, and "I actually feared this connection [to nature and awareness]." Others are less direct but it is suggested in comments like "I've let go of things that don't belong to me," "I need[ed] to let go of past suffering," and in the experience of "retching out toxic thoughts and emotions."

Other things are interesting from Simon's group, too. It is fascinating how often the words *power* and *powerful* are mentioned for example. "I feel powerful," "I saw the love and power in all things," "The experience released my power," "My power grows," "[I received] powerful insights." This sense of new power is also reflected more subtly in other accounts: "[I] trust myself more," "I am closer to the source now," "I am connected," and in the realization that "healing comes from within."

For me, these summaries bring us back to the work of Henri Bergson, the French philosopher who has been mentioned a few times now in this book and who proposed that the mind is capable of all things—including self-healing, deep insights about the truth of the universe, and knowledge of ourselves—but limits itself so that we are not overwhelmed by all of the data around and within us. As David Luke and other academics have suggested, plants like San Pedro can remove the mind's barriers to wisdom so that the doors of perception are cleansed and we see the world as it truly is.

Many of Simon's respondents hint at the same thing, most notably here perhaps in the words of respondent 10: "I felt like a little girl again, which is good because our minds aren't so polluted when we're young and kids see things that adults cannot see." As children, before our socialization into a more limited worldview, we were indeed more capable of imagination, "true hallucinations," creative daydreaming, and inspiration that many adults have lost. Growing into a more limited worldview gives power to the filters of the mind and channels our thoughts and perceptions—what we can see (or allow ourselves to see) and know—into a particular direction so we can survive within the social dream we have created.

But then a plant such as San Pedro may come along to remove these filters, leading us to realizations and remembrances that the infinite is present in every moment and that the world is vaster and richer than we have come to believe. Observations of the infinite are apparent in every account that Simon provides, in fact, and are present in comments like these:

"I found the spirits in the sky" [that is, under the influence of San Pedro that which is normally hidden is made more obvious to us or as La Gringa expressed it in her interview, "San Pedro shows you what is already there"]; "[There were] answers around me in every living thing"; "My view of the world is different, my intuition much stronger"; "It's really opened my eyes to a new way of seeing the world and all it offers"; "San Pedro opened my channels of light"; "Awakening is the only way I can describe it"; "I see a new life, I am connected. . . . I have become in touch with or aware of the thought patterns that I was previously unaware of that were inhibiting my health and spiritual growth"; "I experienced beauty and love beyond words. I saw things I don't understand. . . . I see God in me"; "It was a complete connection with everything . . . it was overwhelming."

SAN PEDRO AND OTHER TEACHERS

I cannot say that San Pedro alone is capable of enhancing our perceptions in this way. Many of the observations above are consistent with those that arise from ayahuasca, for example. As Benny Shanon remarks in *The Antipodes of the Mind,* "Universally, Ayahuasca makes people reflect about their lives and leads them to what they feel is an enhanced psychological understanding of themselves." It enables them to "gain deeper understanding." Reality, too, is often "conceived as constituted by one, non-material substance which is identified as Cosmic Consciousness." This is accompanied by a sense of "a force that is the ground of all Being and that gives nourishment and sustenance to everything. Often this force is characterized as embodying love." It is what I have described here as God.

What seems to distinguish San Pedro from ayahuasca, however, is its immediacy and presence. Many of my participants who have experienced both plants remarked, for example, that San Pedro does not take us "out of ourselves" as ayahuasca does. Rather, it is as if the plant possesses the body itself and compels us to see the world "through the eyes of San Pedro," in one participant's words.

In doing so it also removes us from our "heads" and the confusions of the rational and analytical mind, so we are more of the moment and in our bodies as well as present in the landscape we are a part of. What it reveals to us from this vantage point is the power and beauty of the world, the majesty of life, the soul connections between us, and the knowledge that we are a part of God and a vibrant, living nature.

THE SHAMAN'S VIEW

I have put these observations to La Gringa and asked her to comment. "San Pedro achieves healings like these because it is a master teacher," she said.

> It helps us grow, learn, and awaken and it assists us in reaching higher states of consciousness. Through it we learn the truth of life and reality: that our health and our sense of purpose and balance is simply a choice we make, that we have a destiny and are more powerful than we think. San Pedro also reconnects us to the Earth and helps us realize that there is no separation between us—you, me, the soil, the sky. We are one. It's one thing to read that of course but to actually experience it is the most beautiful gift we can receive.
>
> And so San Pedro teaches us to live in harmony and that compassion and understanding are the qualities of all true human beings. Through this it shows us how to love, respect, and honor all things. It shows us too that we are children of light—precious and special—and to see that light within us. Each person's experience of San Pedro is unique, as we are all unique, and drinking it is therefore a personal journey of healing and your discovery of yourself and the universe. But there is one thing that is always true: The day you meet San Pedro is one you will never forget. It will change your life forever . . . and always for the better.

But does San Pedro really change lives "forever" and if so is it "always" for the better?

Rick Strassman, in his studies of DMT (the active ingredient of ayahuasca),[3] was eventually disillusioned at the potential for this "spirit molecule" to create lasting and positive changes. "As the years passed," he writes:

> I began feeling a peculiar anxiety about listening to volunteers'

accounts of their first high-dose DMT session. It was as if I didn't want to hear them. These psychotherapeutic, near-death and mystical sessions repeatedly reminded me of their ineffectiveness in effecting any real change. I wanted to say "That's very interesting, but now what? To what purpose?"

His conclusion was "the deep and undeniable realization that DMT was not inherently therapeutic."

We might, I suppose, expect a similar outcome with San Pedro, that those who have gone through a "life-changing experience" would, over time, settle back into the routines of the mundane world and make few if any real advances in their lives. This does not seem to be the case, however. Rather, as the accounts of my participants (most provided weeks or even years after their San Pedro experience) tended to show, the spiritual effects of San Pedro remain with them and almost compel them to take action so that they put their realizations to use.

Some of the participants I am still in touch with today (now sometimes three years or more after their ceremonies) have, relatively speaking (that is, relative to the changes that most of us make) often made extraordinary advances in their lives. They tell me that they have left unsatisfactory relationships, moved house or country, given up unfulfilling jobs, changed careers or returned to college, patched up their differences with parents and lovers, and much more, all of it, they insist, as a result of what San Pedro has shown them. Some have also returned with me to Peru so they can repeat their experience and "top up" on healing or renew their intent to become different people. They have come to regard San Pedro as their "spiritual teacher."

Of those who drank with me back in 2008 in fact, and whose accounts I featured in my first book, five have relocated, five have given up their jobs and are now working or training as healers, two have written books on plant medicines and healing, and a further two have set up healing centers of their own. These are not insignificant developments, and all of them show a commitment to a new future that stems from their work with San Pedro.

Simon is himself an example of this. Having drunk San Pedro and received insights about his life and where it was failing him, he gave up his job, moved country, retrained in environmental sciences, and has also begun an apprenticeship with a curandero with the intention of becoming a shaman himself. As I mentioned at the start of this chapter, he has also produced a book of his own on San Pedro, ayahuasca, and healing. On the face of this at least La Gringa may be correct when she says that San Pedro can change lives.

NOTES

1. Ross Heaven, *The Hummingbird's Journey to God: Perspectives on San Pedro, the Cactus of Vision* (Brooklyn: O Books, 2009).

2. Benny Shanon, *The Antipodes of the Mind: Charting the Phenomenology of the Ayahuasca Experience* (Oxford: Oxford University Press, 2003).

3. Rick Strassman, *DMT: The Spirit Molecule; A Doctor's Revolutionary Research into the Biology of Near-Death and Mystical Experiences* (Rochester, Vt.: Park Street Press, 2000).

9
San Pedro and the Cure of Addiction

Tracie Thornberry

The future has several names. For the weak it is the impossible. For the fainthearted it is the unknown. For the thoughtful and valiant it is the ideal.

VICTOR HUGO

I wake up every morning with the same two words on my mind: "Thank you." At night before I sleep my prayer is, "Thank you." They are heartfelt and directed at this miraculous world we share.

I haven't always felt this way, and I still have days that don't go right, where I feel at odds with the world and the lesson is not getting through—but not often. Life for me now is nothing like it used to be, and this is due in large part to my introduction to the plant medicines of Peru.

I had a traumatic childhood, which led to a thirty-year relationship with drugs and alcohol. I have used just about everything, but my substance of choice was heroin. I used it on and off from the age of sixteen until my last dabble at the age of thirty-five. Every time I gave up heroin I did so using alcohol, and I continued to be an addict for another ten years.

I seesawed between alcohol and other drugs, always feeling quite proud of myself when I wasn't putting a needle in my arm and was letting the alcohol take up the slack instead. I always had a job, went to university as a mature student, earned a degree, and had successful relationships with good, sober men. So what was my problem? Why was I using drugs at all?

It took me years to realize that I even had a problem, and more years before I could feel my own emptiness. Then it dawned on me that I had nothing going on inside. Somewhere in the trauma of my childhood I had chosen not to feel, and in that choosing I had lost touch with myself. I mistook the highs and lows of addiction, the flush of infatuation, the pride of the pay packet, and the thrill of anything fast or dangerous as true feeling and emotion. I jumped out of a plane once and felt so high that I had to have several "bucket bongs" just to come down. Another time I bungee jumped in an attempt to cure a mind-splitting hangover. I was what therapists call a "high-functioning addict."

I've also had two successful seven-year relationships. One ended because of my heroin use and the last because of alcohol. I did a lot of running away.

I took a job in the Middle East once in a vain attempt to curb my drinking. I didn't drink as often but every time I did I drank alcoholically. When my contract there finished I thought I might try a "normal life" back home in Australia. I fell in love, moved in with him, and managed to drink his entire wine collection before we decided that our relationship wasn't working. I lost a job for the first time. My boss recognized my condition as he had a mother who was an alcoholic and he suggested I get help. I was devastated; no one had ever accused me of being an alcoholic before, so in fine addict style I ran away again.

I took another job in South Korea after checking whether Koreans drink. They do and it's okay for women. I thought if I stopped trying to limit myself I would eventually have enough, so now I tried a different tactic: moved there and threw myself into being an alcoholic with gusto.

I stayed in Korea for three years and in that time I was hospitalized twice, drunk and delusional, and was put into a mental institution where no one spoke English. It was terrifying. Some of the women there had been totally abandoned by their families and left alone for fifteen or twenty years. This was probably my lowest point, but I still had a few years of drinking to do before seeking help. I was scared of myself and for myself.

Then I got a phone call from home to tell me that my mother was sick and to ask if I could return to Australia straight away. My mother's illness turned out to be my salvation.

My mother lived on an idyllic South Pacific island called Norfolk. It is an external territory of Australia and duty free, which means cheaper alcohol and cigarettes than the mainland. I could easily maintain my addiction while caring for my mother.

I nursed her for six months and she recovered well enough to go back to work in her shop. I worked there part-time for her too and did some casual work in a restaurant. I felt safer being back on Norfolk even though I continued to drink and my behavior was sometimes questioned by my boss. But I no longer denied my alcoholism. This was me, like it or not.

I was forty-two, though, and it felt wrong to be living with my mother. I was seeing a man at the time, and we decided to get married. I was lucky. I married Tom, one of the most honest, decent, sober men I have ever met.

He cared deeply for me. I would often wake up in our bed with no idea how I got there and no car in the garage. Tom would come home from work and tell me that I had passed out somewhere and someone had rung him to pick me up. I was a pass-out drunk and would black out anywhere but Tom was never angry. He was just concerned that I might lose consciousness while I was driving and hurt myself or someone else. He would beg me, "Please don't drink too much today," but it was like asking a duck not to quack. We spent two and a half years like this. It's a small island; I was a drunk and everyone knew it.

Then one day I woke up and actually *woke up*. I realized that this was IT, my life, forever. I went straight to my doctor and asked for help. I'd been to NA (Narcotics Anonymous) many years earlier and I'd spent time in drug programs and even a rebirthing retreat, but I'd never been in a rehabilitation program, which is what my doctor suggested.

I looked at the options and chose a three-month program focusing on cognitive behavioral therapy (CBT). I wanted no part in a religion-based program as I had a problem with the concept of God. I thought, "Look at me, look at this sad world, how can there be a God?"

I completed the three-month program and came back to the island. I joined Alcoholics Anonymous and received support from many people. I found a stress-free job and promised my new boss I wouldn't drink. I lasted almost three months before I went back on that, and it was hard. I always wanted to drink and it was through sheer willpower that I lasted that long.

There had to be another way. I went back to the doctor and asked for the longest, hardest, most successful rehabilitation program available. He told me that the success rate was the same for all of them . . . 30 percent.

With a heavy heart I opted for the longest and toughest, the Salvation Army Bridge Program, which lasted ten months.

The Bridge Program has been running for about ten years and is one of the most successful rehabilitation programs in Australia. It, too, boasts a 30 percent success rate. Its rules are simple: for the first month there is no contact with friends or family and while I was free to leave the program at any time, if I left three times I wouldn't be allowed to return.

I started the treatment with nine other women. After one month we were down to seven, after three months we were down to five, and by the end of the sixth month there were just three of us.

It felt good to be in the magic 30 percent but I also knew that if I went back out into the world I would drink again. Our days were filled with group meetings, counseling sessions, and AA meetings, and the three of us attended lectures about Jesus on Thursday nights. The latter was voluntary but it got us out of rehab for a night and they supplied a baked dinner.

The Jesus lectures culminated in a weekend retreat where a major from the Salvation Army conducted spiritual healings. I believe now that despite my skepticism my addiction was lifted by God on that weekend.

Something changed in me when the major called in the spirit of Christ to heal me. I started crying and was so embarrassed by my tears that afterward I slunk back to my seat. No blinding flash, no hallelujahs, nothing—but a few days later my world changed.

My mother was sick again. She was flown to Sydney for an operation and I was given time to be with her. Every day I went to the hospital and every night I went back to rehab. Mum improved enough to travel back to the island and recuperate in peace. I didn't go with her. She died in the hospital one week later.

Again I was given time out of rehab to arrange the funeral. It was my first time home in seven months. The manager of the rehab called me into her office and told me that no matter what I did when I went home I was to come back and finish the program. She gave me a green light to do whatever I wanted, including drink, as long as I returned. My roommates were so envious! Of course we all knew that I'd be getting drunk and passing out.

And so I went home, worried about how I'd cope with the grief and the stress and whether I'd start drinking again—but nothing happened. I was calm. I buried my mother with dignity and had no desire to drink.

The desire to drink was gone, just like that. I was amazed. I stayed home for two weeks then went back to rehab to finish the program, feeling humbled and very grateful. I stayed for another three months and then graduated along with my roommates Rachael and Kim. We were the magic 30 percenters.

A common saying in AA and in rehab is that an addict has only three choices in the long run: death, institutionalization, or sobriety. Rachael, Kim, and I were the lucky ones who had made it and we were going to live free.

We had been through ten hard months together and we vowed to keep in touch. I went back to the island and my stoic husband; Kim went back to her family and her job; Rachael lived briefly with her mother and then found her own place. For a while we were happy.

Then within two months Rachael was dead. Cause: alcohol. She was a beautiful, lively, funny thirty-five-year-old and one of my main inspirations now for seeking an alternative treatment for addiction. Kim is thankfully still alive but hospitalized for alcohol-related issues. She tells me she has good days and bad. So much for the magic 30 percent.

Back home on Norfolk Island I made contact with a counselor, Kathryn, attended a weekly AA meeting, and resumed my job. I was again supported by the community and my fabulous employer, Margarita, who encouraged me to practice vipassana meditation and gave me time off to attend ten-day silent retreats. I began a course in drug and alcohol counseling with Kathryn as my supervisor and was sponsored by the local hospital. I studied and worked for the next two years researching different rehabilitation programs worldwide but no matter where I looked I could not find anything better than the 30 percent success rate that I already knew and had experienced using standard Western methods.

I knew from experience that intelligence, support, friends, and money should be but were not the answers, and had hardly any bearing at all on who got clean and who kept drinking or using drugs. So what was it? In my search for a cure I knew I was missing something and failing all of those things that I now knew I could rule out, I suspected that it must have something to do with "spirit," so I looked for an answer there.

I came across an article about the Takiwasi Centre in Peru. This is an addictions healing center claiming a 75 percent success rate and it caught my attention immediately. I looked at their program and the only significant difference I could see between their model and the Western therapeutic model was the use of plant medicines. They used tobacco as a purgative and a plant I had never heard of—ayahuasca.

I was so excited by the prospect of a greater success rate that I began looking for a way to get to Peru and experience the plant firsthand. I found Ross Heaven's website (www.thefourgates.org) and read about his Magical Earth program,* a journey he leads to the Amazon to work with the shamans there and with the medicine of ayahuasca. It sounded perfect for me. The group was not too big and the event looked safe and professional. All I had to do was buy my ticket to Peru and meet the group in Iquitos. I told Kathryn about it and she asked if she could come with me. Perfect. She had over twenty years drug counseling experience and would be a great research assistant.

We came to Iquitos and met the group, a fantastic selection of people from six different countries all on personal healing journeys. My introduction to plant medicines could not have been better. We did seven ayahuasca ceremonies in Iquitos and then traveled to Cusco for two ceremonies with *wachuma,* better known as San Pedro.

I could see immediately what was missing in the Western rehabilitation model: the connection to spirit, which both plants gave. Ayahuasca helped me find myself; San Pedro completed the process by reconnecting me with the world.

During my first San Pedro journey I took a walk in the countryside around the Temple of the Moon, outside Cusco. As I walked through the ruins of an ancient Incan village I felt connected not just with that place but to the Earth as a whole.

This feeling of connectedness is something alien to addicts who

---

*The Magical Earth is a healing retreat in the Amazon rainforest where participants take part in ayahuasca ceremonies and recieve healings and cleansings with other medicine plants as well as seminars and workshops on Amazonian shamanism. —R.H.

often share a common grievance that they feel "different" from their peers, their family, and indeed from society as a whole. Now, with San Pedro, I could see the life force of the mountains and feel the energy of the clouds, the Earth, and my fellow travelers. I realized that we are all the same: energetic, spiritual beings, that our very breath intermingles with those around us as does the energy of our thoughts and words.

This is how I described my experience with San Pedro a month or so after those first ceremonies:

Sitting atop the mountain I could see the Andes rolling away into the distance and I had an overwhelming sense of belonging, not just to this area, but to the Earth as a whole and of the importance of every curve of the mountain range, every boulder, rock, stone, and blade of grass. The life of the mountains felt ancient and slow while the life of the clouds seemed young and quickly changing but all of it was part of the same incredible tableau and all of equal importance.

I ventured down from the mountain, visiting trees and rocks and taking a closer look at some of the sites I'd seen from afar. I rested in a large rock formation shaped like a seat and felt cradled by the mountain behind me and welcomed by the valley ahead. I had such a feeling of peace and acceptance that I was almost reluctant to head back to the ceremonial garden.

Once there I drank some water and relaxed in a hammock to observe my fellow travelers. We had been advised not to talk to each other too much so as not to interfere in each other's journeys. I saw my friend on her knees, sobbing, and didn't intervene but watched quietly as she came to the end of her crying, rested—and then rose up with the broadest smile, calm and serene, released. Some people curled up into themselves while others took pleasure in the garden, photographing plants.

I guess about five hours in I started to get a bit restless so I tried talking with one of the people who hadn't drunk San Pedro and found that I was in full control of my words and thoughts. I could have a normal conversation but found that I was choosing my words carefully, realizing their power and that of my thoughts, and that I didn't have enough vocabulary to express how I felt anyway.

Through the eyes of San Pedro the world is an exceptionally beautiful place. Every living thing has its place and it is all of equal importance. Through it I realized, as Ross put it, that "we human beings are no more important or beautiful than a mud brick—but we are no less important or beautiful either."

I have come home with new eyes and can bring the beauty of the world to mind and into reality by just remembering that San Pedro experience.

This is the gift I believe that San Pedro can give to the addict who still suffers: to feel and sense their union with the Divine so they realize that every living thing shares the same energy. Ayahuasca showed me who I am, but San Pedro showed me where I fit in to the world.

I found a deep connection to myself and realized that within me and within all of us is the whole world. I can't do something to myself without it having an effect on everyone and everything. The sense of responsibility this brought seemed overwhelming until I realized that the only way I can possibly live is to be as kind and gentle to myself as possible, thereby sharing that kindness and gentleness with all else.

That trip I took to Peru was to change my life completely. I went home with a deeper understanding. I had glimpsed the interconnectedness of all that is and was set on a path, which not only excited me but gave me a sense of hope that I had finally found a way to improve the chances of release from addiction. I needed to do more research though and knew that the best place for that was Peru.

My husband and I had decided to end our marriage a year before so I went home and started the process of moving. It took six months. We finalized our divorce, I sold my share of the house, gave away my pets, quit my five jobs, and completed the addictions counseling course I had started with Kathryn. Then I bought my ticket to Peru and returned to Cusco. Apart from that I had no plans and put my trust in spirit to guide me.

I spent the next three months working with San Pedro, learning about it and through it to trust the ebb and flow of the universe. I took part in ceremonies a few times each week and it was my privilege to meet many amazing people from all over the world.

San Pedro has a way of making us feel small in the great scheme of things but at the same time vast and hugely important—as important as every other living thing. This can sometimes be a difficult concept for people to grasp as it seems to contradict itself, but to me it is a fact and one of the teachings of the plant.

I also learned from San Pedro that through our breath we are all connected and that nothing is expected of us in this lifetime except that we continue to breathe. There is no good or bad except as we label it so. Judgment is unnecessary, an illusion. Everything just is.

I don't know how many times I drank San Pedro, maybe fifty, and it was different each time. The awe-inspiring feeling of connection is always there but each time I would gain more insight into how to be in the world.

One particular ceremony was deeper than my other experiences. I had been watching my diet closer than usual because of a group we had visiting for ceremony that was led by David Wolfe, the raw food specialist. We had a number of ceremonies that week and I think in retrospect that it was the combination of the strict raw food diet and the energy of the group that gave me what was to be my deepest—and last—San Pedro ceremony.

I cannot find the words to describe what happened. I'd like to say I met God but those words mean nothing and don't even come close to explaining the illumination I felt during and after that ceremony.

I knew then that I'd drunk enough San Pedro. There seemed little point in drinking more, for how much more could I learn or see after that one singular moment of communion? I still attended ceremony and enjoyed being in the company of people who were drinking San Pedro but I never drank again. So much had been revealed to me I feel that it might take me the rest of my life just to process what I have experienced.

That last ceremony meant a lot to me as an addict as well. It proved that San Pedro is not a drug that I can never get enough of, but a sacrament and a living energy with lessons to teach and connections to foster and one that I can choose to meet with or not.

While I lived in Cusco I traveled regularly to the north of Peru for ceremonies and *dietas** with other plants too, including *ayahuasca, guayusa, ajo sacha,* and *bobinsana*. I met a number of shamans who were having success in treating addictions with plant medicines. The whole process was incredibly exciting to me. It was no longer just an idea that freedom from addiction was possible; it was actually happening for real people in Peru as a result of the plant medicines and shamanic practices there. I was amazed, awed, and ecstatic. After years of searching I had found what I had been seeking.

In Pucallpa I met the shaman Jose Campos who had been one of the original founders of the Takiwasi Centre. He agreed to help me in any way he could and offered me sound advice about the use of plants for healing.

In the village of San Francisco, just outside Pucallpa, I met another shaman, Mateo Arevalo, who is treating addicts in his home and having great success. He doesn't speak English or keep records, but through an interpreter he explained his process to me. He's a secretive man, and I had to promise not to pass on what he told me, but he opened my eyes even more.

Everywhere in Peru it seemed—from the mountains to the jungle— so many different shamans were having extraordinary success in healing addictions by using plant medicines. These were not "freak incidents" or isolated cases of breakthroughs by addicts. The results were consistent and far superior to Western achievements.

During one of my dietas[1] it came to me that I needed to do something practical if I was to put the information I was receiving to use. My

---

*Dietas—regimes for working with the spirits of plants—are an important part of the healing experience when learning from teacher plants and can be a journey of self-exploration and discovery in themselves, bringing greater self-awareness and understanding of our routines and habits. They also enhance the visionary experience. —R.H.

brother Mark is a long-term substance abuser who was living in North Queensland and battling to stay off drugs, so I invited him to Peru. One of my shamanic advisors had said to me, "Heal those closest to you first," so I took this literally and brought my brother over for healing.

They involve purification, retreat, commitment, and respect for our connection to everything. Through the exclusion of some foodstuffs and activities, the diet enables the participant to purify and take in the spirit or essence of the teacher plant and its healing powers.

Other jungle medicines are added to the diet in addition to visionary medicines, such as *ajo sacha* (for the ability to blend with the natural world according to Amazonian shamans), *pinon colorado* (a defense against evil sorcerers), and tóe (a dreaming plant that brings the capability of "spirit flight"). Some of these plants are sometimes also used as admixtures to both ayahuasca and San Pedro.

After that, life moved quickly. I wrote up an addictions treatment program using plants, therapeutic practices, and shamanic medicines that I called Tranquilo (Spanish for calm, peaceful, and quiet), found a place to rent just outside Iquitos, and had my first client booked before I'd even moved in.

I'm one person so I take one client at a time. That way I can give my clients 100 percent of my attention and be available to them twenty-four hours a day. I run a course anywhere from one month to three months, the longer being preferred. My first client could only stay for one month, but we made a lot of progress. In her words, "I know the shortness of my program was not ideal but in that time we were able to accomplish a great deal. I feel that I have a solid backbone now toward staying sober . . . my resolution is stronger than it's ever been before in my life." We are still in touch and I hope to meet with her again in Cusco and conclude her treatment with San Pedro.

My addiction treatment program also includes work with ayahuasca. I have talked with people who have taken San Pedro before ayahuasca and prefer that, but I start with ayahuasca instead to give my clients a chance to get to know themselves, to understand their strengths, and to develop their personal sense of truth and integrity. With these qualities clarified the message of San Pedro—that we are all one and not so different from each other—is much easier for them to accept and assimilate.

I believe that if an addict can experience the lessons of San Pedro, they have a greater prospect of staying clean and sober. The plant opens a doorway for them and allows them to heal themselves. It may not happen all at once but when a universal truth has been revealed you can never go back to not knowing it.

An outline of a month-long Tranquilo program looks something like this, although treatment is always tailored to the individual:

Week 1: Assessment, cleansing inside and out with purges, saunas, and plant baths, and the first ayahuasca ceremony

Week 2: Daily meditation and counseling sessions, second and third ayahuasca ceremonies

Week 3: Daily meditation and counseling, with three more ayahuasca ceremonies

Week 4: Three San Pedro ceremonies, with meditation and counseling throughout

The program is flexible so it can adapt to each person's needs. It is also nondenominational but I use Buddhist concepts and the practice of meditation as well as various plants. I love this work and the more people I can help the greater the healing I also receive, and the greater strength I therefore have to heal others. It's like the butterfly effect or the ripples in a pond—such is the connection between us all. Each person who comes to Tranquilo has the opportunity to heal. They then can also make a difference in countless other lives. When people remind me of the vastness of the addiction problem worldwide, I remember this and the importance of the individual in healing the whole.

I have also made a promise that for every Westerner I treat there will be a place on the program for an indigenous person to come for

free. This way I can give back to the community that has given me healing and the knowledge of the plants that I use in my work.

The real purpose of Tranquilo is to find out who you truly are and
all of the power, dignity, and beauty you have. The Western social system that I was born into and lived within drilled into me that I was
powerless and weak and taught me that evil exists and that society is
fragmented—but none of that is actually true. We are powerful, beautiful, and extraordinary. I know this through my work with San Pedro
and other plant teachers. There is no reason why we cannot find out for
ourselves who we are and where we are going, and no reason why any
individual cannot be fully empowered and healed.

We have also been trained in our culture that our individual differences should stand out so that we can call ourselves "younger," "older,"
"richer," "poorer," "smarter," "dumber," "prettier" . . . and to put others
into these categories too and treat them differently because they are separate from us. One of the most dramatic experiences we can therefore
have is to be with another person and see the ways in which they are
like us, not different, and to experience our connection: to know that
the essence of you and the essence in me is One. This is the message of
San Pedro and understanding follows.

We are incredible beings, made even more extraordinary by the
plants. Our aim then does not have to be for us to become something
so we can stand alone, but to be who we already are and to melt into
connection with all and everything by knowing that place where we are
accepted and loved.

San Pedro can give us this experience. We weren't born as addicts,
we were born as human beings and the whole process of becoming an
addict is learned. Its purpose is to cover our sense of separation and the
hurts we feel have been done to us in this game of life. But as long as we
keep ourselves separate from everything else we lend ourselves to being
enslaved.

If we only realized the truth of our relationship to each other,
however, to nature and the extent of our power, then the entire

manufactured structure of the society that causes these wounds would collapse like a house of cards. A new consciousness is already emerging that sees the world as a single organism, and reason will tell you that an organism bent on damaging itself is doomed. Plants open doorways to this new consciousness and give us back our connection to the world.

I spent thirty years of my life on the merry-go-round of fear and addiction, running away from who I am and not feeling one with anyone. Now I feel powerful, connected, joyous, and free—and I'm still working on it. In my program I try to share this with my clients and empower them to heal themselves. I'm not special, I'm exactly the same as everyone else, and if I can do it everyone else can too.

Plants are nonjudgmental; they don't care what you look like or how much money you have; their concern is for their and your well-being. Plants understand the interconnectedness of everything and by helping us realize our potential they give the world we share a better chance of survival.

We understand only 3 percent of what our DNA is for and call 97 percent of it (and therefore 97 percent of ourselves) "junk." Only 30 percent of addicts get clean in traditional rehabs, so are we to consider the others who don't as "junk" human beings as well? We would be dismissing a whole section of our population. Plants do not make such distinctions.

When people have woven their spirit into negative thinking they need to retreat for a while, pull their spirits back, and learn to walk straight again. Healing requires action. It is not a passive event. We are meant to draw on our inner resources, to find the material strength to leave behind outmoded beliefs and behaviors, and to see ourselves in new and healthy ways.

The conventional medical world is now recognizing the link between energetic or spiritual dysfunction and illness. Shamans (the original doctors) have always been aware of this link. Working with plant medicines helps us to recognize the self. To "recognize" means to "know again," implying that you once already knew who you are and had the answers within you.

I've been advised by the shamans I have met who treat addiction that it is not wise to consider plants as a miracle cure. I have also met addicts who have come to the Amazon with a miracle cure in mind only to find that they leave the jungle and the first thing they crave is a beer.

In some cases one or two ceremonies may do the trick, but don't bet on it. In my experience and in the experience of others, it takes time to assimilate the message of the plants. I believe ayahuasca can give us a deeply spiritual experience, but this needs to be integrated and understood to have a lasting effect. San Pedro aids this integration. As a follow-up to ayahuasca it allows a deeper understanding of the function and place of spirit in the world. While ayahuasca can be challenging, showing us our shadow as well as our light, San Pedro is always light, gentle, and profound.

While little has been written about the use of these plants to cure addiction it is well accepted in the shamanic community that they work, and I hope they will become better known in the world community too as more people are healed by them.

NOTES

1. For more information on dietas and other plants that may be part of them see Ross Heaven and Howard G. Charing, *Plant Spirit Shamanism: Traditional Techniques for Healing the Soul* (Rochester, Vt.: Destiny Books, 2006).

10
Healing an Abusive Past

Alexia Gidding

Sadly, from my experience of drinking San Pedro I have no accounts of conversations with plants or rocks or of being at one with the universe. Nor did I learn about the great plans of the universe or gain insight into cosmic consciousness or the patterns of life and existence. My experience was all about me . . .

While I was writing this account of my experience with San Pedro, I thought that maybe I should offer a short resume of my life as well to illustrate how San Pedro has impacted me. So this is my past life in a nutshell. I left home at fifteen to live with my boyfriend and at that point I entered a world of misery; I left my freedom behind and was literally kept under lock and key and not allowed out without his supervision.

Physical, emotional, and sexual abuse occurred on a regular basis. After several near-death experiences, losing eight babies, and many visits to the hospital for injuries and breaks to bones, various drug addictions were forced on me, which resulted in two psychotic episodes.

Finally I managed to escape him and create a place of safety for myself and my children. My life has turned around now in many ways and I'm safe and mostly happy. For some reason I have felt compelled to work with teacher plants and I have taken part in two of Ross Heaven's healing journeys to Peru—with no real clue why I was there except knowing that I had to follow my soul. The first of these journeys was to the Amazon to drink ayahuasca and the second was to the Andes a year later to drink San Pedro.

I knew that San Pedro would be different from ayahuasca and I felt calm and relaxed about drinking it. Within thirty minutes, however, I felt my body fill with overwhelming emotion, and I took myself off to a quiet place outside the garden—actually a ditch that surrounded the house. I appreciate that doesn't sound very glamorous, but for me it was perfect in many ways. I had to be alone, which was significant in itself. I had to be away from others so they would not see my suffering. I had to suffer alone. I always suffered alone.

I'm not sure how long I was lying on the floor cradling myself sobbing. It felt like a long time and I know that I have never cried like that before. I cannot really recall either what I was crying for; I just knew that it was about my past.

When my conscious mind returned I realized that I was sobbing and I struggled to sort myself out and desperately tried to stop it. As I resisted my emotions, however, I heard (or, rather, felt) a voice telling me to "let yourself cry, it's okay." It was such a soft and soothing sensation and I think this was the first time I really ever cried for myself and for what I had experienced, without judgment toward myself. Normally I would stop crying and be strong for my children and others. Now, however, I had no power to be strong. I could not move, could not stop crying. Any resistance was futile. I recall just collapsing in a heap again after trying to pick myself up. I fell into my own arms once again, feeling quite pathetic. Alongside the discomfort I felt at displaying such emotion for myself, there was a part of me that did not think I needed to cry for my past, that I should just get over it and that it was done and gone.

I couldn't stop, however. I just cried more. Yet it wasn't unpleasant. It felt strange to be so out of control of my emotions, but it felt safe and okay, even though I was afraid to let go for some reason I wasn't sure of.

This sobbing in the ditch is still a very vivid memory, and one I hold tightly to my heart. It was a moment of true love toward myself and represented a real sense of self-acceptance and an acknowledgment that my past had been incredibly painful.

This kindness to myself sadly didn't last, however. I forced myself up from the ground and made myself regain control over my legs so I could regain stability with my inner world. I feared being out of control; it reminded me of the many times in the past where I also had no control over my life, and I was determined never to let this happen again.

I made my way back to the garden and vomited violently for around three hours. The pain needed to be released and if not through tears and self-love, then it would be spat out in vomit. This, at least, was something I just couldn't control.

Finally the vomiting stopped. This seemed to open the gate to feelings of immense fear that really overwhelmed me. It felt as though these fears were being poured into my mind by the bucketful and I knew they belonged to me: all the fears I had experienced in my past and then repressed over the years. I wonder now if the crying and vomiting had broken down the walls of my own prison, leaving me feeling vulnerable and exposed, but newly open to the environment and to others.

But then the environment around me began to seem strange and surreal and the people there all looked unhappy. I felt that I had to get away from them again or they would infect me, so I left the garden once more. I needed to be alone, away from others. I had to protect myself.

I understand now that San Pedro was showing me how I wouldn't let other people get too close to me and that their infection was actually an infection within me: my own fear that others would understand me and then hurt me.

San Pedro forced me to acknowledge that part of me who was still young and frightened, locked inside a prison of memories and pain. As I rested in the mountains I remembered a series of violent, terrifying, sad, and lonely experiences from my early teens and twenties. I had worked incredibly hard over the years to let go of that pain, fear, and hurt and the patterns of behavior and thoughts they had created in me. For the previous eight years I had been incredibly focused and felt mostly happy and content with myself and the world. And yet I realized now that on another level there was residual stuff within me, deep, deep down, which I had kept locked away from others and even from myself, and it was very painful: nasty, dark, dirty, and cruel.

Still sitting outside, now upright against the Andean mountains, I felt safe and I spent time just observing what seemed like an internal amphitheater within my mind of my past. I felt some annoyance at this as I didn't want to keep revisiting it, and slightly paranoid and frightened at the imagery that was being presented to me. I thought that San Pedro was being unkind in even showing it to me again. But then I heard a soft voice or a feeling that seemed to come from beyond me: the voice of San Pedro that said, "You can let go of this now. There is no need to stay here anymore. Let yourself out and you won't need me anymore."

At this point I knew I just had to give up and surrender. I knew I could not fight anymore. And then it was as if my younger self walked right out of me, out of what were once the strong thick walls of a prison to a place of safety, which ironically was also me. I was shown memories of a particular ordeal in which I was tortured for hours, beaten and terrorized. I felt my life slip away into bizarre and altered states of consciousness. I knew something seriously had left me or changed within me. I'm not completely sure which and I really don't care. What was important was that I was now able to observe this in my mind with no fear or hurt and without a single tear.

Now I have written this and I still feel no painful emotions anymore. I do not even hold any anger toward those who hurt me. I have forgiven them and moved on. I have even offered thanks to them for playing their parts in my life. They gave me hard and painful but wonderful gifts. The real issue was with me because I had not forgiven myself or even allowed myself to grieve for what I had lost: not my faith in humanity but my teenage years.

Above: San Pedro altar at the Temple of the Moon, showing a mixture of Catholic and spiritual symbols

Right: San Pedro growing in Huaraz, a short bus ride from Chavin de Huantar, said by anthropologists to be the birthplace of the "San Pedro cult."

San Pedro brew and rings at the Temple of Condor Heart in the mountains above Cusco. The brew is to be drunk and the rings exchanged as a part of a wedding ceremony

Puma, curandero and diviner, once-struck by lightning, performing a blessing with agua de florida ("flower water"). (Photograph by Darryl Guy)

Above: The author and a participant at the heart of the Temple of the Condor, a ritual site above Cusco. (Photograph by Darryl Guy)

Below: The San Pedro mesa used by Andean shaman La Gringa, laid out prior to the ceremony.

Above: The author's mesa, a hand-woven Qero fabric, at the start of a San Pedro ceremony. The keys represent St. Peter who also appears in the center as a lithograph.

Below: San Pedro participant at a ceremony in La Gringa's garden at the Temple of the Moon. The cactus before him represents an average dose drunk in ceremony.

Above: A nighttime ceremony in Spain with the mesa

Right: The author at Chavin de Huantar, next to one of the obelisks that depict the San Pedro experience

Below: La Gringa (right) with Andean musician and sound healer Carlos at the beginning of a San Pedro ceremony at the Temple of the Moon

Mummified skeletons of shamans and others at an open graveyard just outside Nazca. (Photograph by Sarah Coleman-Heaven)

Left: Andean shaman Chaska (left) performing an energy healing during a San Pedro ceremony

Below: Andean shaman Chaska performs a limpia (cleansing)—using feathers, sound, and the smoke of Palo Santo ("holy wood")—for a participant prior to a ceremony

Above: The Temple of the Moon, an ancient ritual site above Cusco

Right: Author Ross Heaven standing before a wall at Chavin de Huantar decorated with tenon heads representing the spirit beings and guardian animals summoned by San Pedro. (Photography by Sarah Coleman-Heaven)

Everything I had done to try to heal myself in the past had been aimed toward me being functional, but I see now that the result of this was only to bury my pain and guilt deep within myself.

I felt fragile for the remainder of the day and I told myself that there was no way I would ever drink San Pedro or go through that again. I spoke to the shaman Puma about this the following day and he said that my vibrations were very high and there was no need for me to take San Pedro again. I must admit to feeling relieved and very pleased that the experience it had given me was purposeful and there was no need for me to repeat it.

Despite this knowledge, however, there was something within me that knew that I did need to do it once more. I think it was to prove to myself I was okay and that my soul was cleansed of the past.

I remained undecided about drinking again until the last few minutes of the ceremony, then at the last minute I drank San Pedro again. This time I had the most wonderful experience and felt so connected to myself and totally at peace. In the past when my life had been unbearable, during beatings or an intense emotional grilling, I would leave myself and visit what I called my Magical Land. The day I drank San Pedro for the second time I found the Magical Land finally within me. I'm overwhelmed to know that it does exist and to realize that this magic existed in my soul all the time.

As my experience shows, San Pedro isn't always pleasant to drink and you may face things you prefer not to see. It will, however, show you the things you need to pay attention to, in a kind, albeit persistent, gentle, but practical manner.

In conclusion, I did feel immense pain throughout the process of the first ceremony, but in truth and as a therapist myself, I do not know of any other approach that would have cleansed my soul in the way San Pedro did. I reflect on that experience now with love and huge respect for the wonderful sprit of San Pedro, and I know that I will return to it to continue my learning in a wider sense.

11
New Insights, Emotional and Physical Healing

Robyn Silvanen

I had decided to travel to Peru to work with *huachuma* (San Pedro) because I had read that it could help a broken heart to experience joy again, and sometimes even alleviate a physical disorder. I'm always looking for a miracle, whether I need one or not, so it was inevitable that I would find myself eight thousand kilometers from home drinking this amazing cactus juice.

I had brought with me in my thoughts a quote by Einstein that you cannot solve a problem from the same level of consciousness that created it. In other words, take a quantum leap into the next dimension, and while you are outside of time take out your emotional "garbage" and heal yourself. And that's what I felt happened during the ceremonies I took part in, all of which were guided with compassion for all beings and respect for the spirit of the plants.

I was part of Ross Heaven's November 2009 workshop in Peru called "the Cactus of Vision," which he had organized with the *curandera* La Gringa. My biggest fear was that my delicate grasp of reality would slide off into paranoia, or that my body would find the plant useful for purging and nothing more, but neither of those things happened.

During my first ceremony my awareness took off about ninety minutes after drinking. A higher intelligence began to communicate with me for as much as I would give it my attention and permission to do so. It spoke to me in ways I already had some fluency in, using terms like *pain body* and *chakras,* but the information it gave me was more Yoda-like and profound than my own level of study and the tone it used was "San Pedro" (or maybe my "higher self" with a sense of humor), and not my usual Robyn mind. These effects lasted about fifteen-plus hours, yet I awoke at 7:30 a.m. the next morning and felt quite "normal"—in fact, more grounded and peaceful than usual.

With the second ceremony, I had chosen to drink only half a glass and the effects were more blissful, much less verbal or visual, and I felt the transcendent state fade after nine hours.

I went into each ceremony with a feeling of honor for the incredible opportunity it was, and allowing whatever huachuma and my higher self wanted to heal or teach me. I had little interest in moving around and so would sit like a stone(d) garden gnome communing with the plant spirit in La Gringa's color-saturated nature sanctuary of a garden. Or I'd be listening to the wisdom that a rock, flower, or dragonfly was sharing with me. The San Pedro experiences were absolutely fascinating, and I decided even then that after my second ceremony with Ross's group I would be back to drink again in just a few months.

Every time, soon after drinking, my hearing would become amplified and sounds that were at a distance would seem like they were whispering in my ears. I would be sure that my iPod had been accidentally set at full volume yet would find the next level down was mute. I had brought my mp3 player thinking it would be interesting to listen to brainwave frequencies and sacred mantra chants while in the huachuma state to see what would happen. It was like a deep meditation, but possibly limited the potential of the medicine. I later felt that San Pedro had adjusted my own frequency to suit what I needed to rebalance, and that it seemed to wait until I finished experimenting with technology before it stepped forward. I also found that I didn't want to be near much outside noise, including people who were laughing or even the musicians who had been organized to play such beautiful San Pedro-inspired music for the group (sound healing), because the vibrations felt to my energy field like being jabbed with a stick. However, when I played simple mantra chants (the "Om" type stuff), this was helpful in deepening my state of consciousness and connection to nature.

There was a discernible contrast to the thinking of my own inner voice when huachuma began to speak. The words flowed effortlessly with a greater sureness and clarity. "He" (San Pedro) commenced by telling me why so many of the relationships throughout my life have been disappointing. There were a few reasons. But in particular he was clear that I needed to understand and respect my "feminine" energy, to allow my heart to stay open and to trust it, not to live primarily by way of the male (as in, expression through intellect and physical action) as I had been doing most of my adult life. I had to heal my relationship with my mother first and know her truth behind her "social mask." And then become aware of the masks I wore too and realize that it was also essential that I forgive myself. This would help me to spiritually grow up out of a somewhat extended adolescence so I would "stand in my power," be present and of greater service to others in this stage of life.

By withholding love through judgment and rejection of my primary female role model (of her emotional coldness and distance) unknowingly I was gradually becoming more like her than not. It was the same quality of energy except hidden from my awareness by it being expressed uniquely in my own "right" way. I don't have a family of my own, but other than the fact that my work necessitates contact with living bodies (entirely—I do bodywork), I had become more solitary every year. Sensitive and nurturing with my own inner circle of friends, I was emotionally armored around other people.

Simultaneously during this time of learning I was shown by sensation the effect of my manner of living. I could feel coldness build and grow heavier along my left side and into the center of my chest and heart, making it hard to breathe. I was told that if I continued to live as I had been, like my mother I would also have issues with my heart (my mother had survived a major heart attack fifteen years ago). I also received the impression that when I acted aloof socially, my presence literally felt cool and uncomfortable to others.

This lesson went on for many hours. The revealing of my mother as she is in spirit beyond her personality, surprising me, brought out so much emotion. I cried from a depth I had no idea existed. I felt gentleness and compassion in her heart then and learned the reasons for her choice to be my mother in this life and the lessons we would learn from one another. I saw too that her emotional distancing had influenced me to take care of myself and find my spiritual support within, my character strengths developing out of a negative.

Another gift I discovered after this experience was that I could breathe more fully and it has been that way ever since, even in the high altitude of Cusco. I sense it was from letting go of sadness from my past that previously I hadn't felt able to express and from forgiveness.

Then something like an argument began between—I swear this is the best I can describe it—my feminine side (my emotional side, the heart, perhaps) and my masculine side (my rational mind?). While in San Pedro's mystical world somehow it all made sense. The feminine side had quite a bit more to say, assertively and with love. Something along these lines:

Do not tell me how I should look, move, smell, or sound. Stop controlling me and just let me BE. Your idea of perfection is unknown to me. There is no good or bad, there just is. There are no mistakes, only lessons for soul evolution. My energy must be allowed to flow and change. Tune in to me first before you will the body to work, to feel what I've inspired to you. Then you decide if and how to take action to create what was inspired. The divine masculine protects the space of the divine feminine. The feminine holds the energy of love and nurturing and inspires the masculine to take right action. That way what is created will not do harm.

Nine hours later the effects were still going strong, and I was still absorbed in the insights I was receiving. I was also playing with the window of opportunity where it seemed I'd become superpsychic and I could ask anything and receive an answer. When needing help to walk outside La Gringa's hostel where I was staying, the inner dialogue continued. A sympathetic assistant was asked to walk beside me to ensure I didn't fall down the hundred stairs of San Blas while in my nebulous state of mind, guiding me to where I wanted to go. After this excursion where my spirit body felt as if it was walking a step ahead of my physical one, I said thank you to the beautiful man for his help. However, I was inspired to not mention that the enlightened cactus in my head was also sharing interesting details about the man's personal life and what he was thinking about.

Along the way I had become aware of how I was slurring my words, stumbling, and that my matted hair (from having sat out in the rain) and dilated pupils had given me an extraterrestrial appearance. I thought how I'd probably be embarrassed if I wasn't feeling so much unconditional love for everyone, including myself, and wondered what the women were thinking whose eyes shifted away after showing alarm when I walked by. San Pedro interrupted my thoughts with:

If you had cleaned yourself up out of fear to look "acceptable" before the others could see you, they would have missed a learning opportunity for their spiritual growth. What you see in another and judge as wrong shows you what you want to accept and love in yourself. You are only judging yourself.

This teaching continued with recognizing the sacredness and necessity for the "dark" (as in the yin, opposite of the yang, "light") in all its manifestations, especially in ourselves. It said that the dark has a right to be ("it is as it is") and while being aware of choosing to place attention on what felt better, the negative was not to be judged as unworthy of unconditional love or inferior to what is perceived as that of the "light." Respecting the darkness, not pushing it away and demonizing it, was also critical to the shifting of consciousness that is happening globally now. There was much more to it that I'm still recollecting and beginning to understand. In May the following year I returned to La Gringa's garden in Cusco and I joined in four other ceremonies. Each one went deeper into my consciousness and the "here-now"—that state of existence where I'd be in my hostel dorm afterward and it would be just a room with two beds existing somewhere in space. It was like everything other than the room and the beds was brought into my five senses on a need-to-know basis. I had the impression that the world beyond the door (and the bathroom, fortunately) rematerialized its collectively agreed-upon thoughtforms on cue with my doubtless faith that it would be there.

While en route to Peru a painful childhood memory had been persistently in my thoughts. Brought to mind again during my third day, I was guided to transform it into one where I became the adult I am now, with awareness of the feelings of the players in the drama, to speak my truth that I couldn't then and to heal the memory in a way that included humor. That memory now holds no negative emotional charge when recalled and no longer persists. The healing of it feels complete, and I sense it also affected the ones who were involved as I remembered them.

I then saw and experienced myself as a baby in the year of my birth, looking up at my parents who were in love with life, each other, and with me. From their energy I sensed how I was a beautiful gift to them, that I was unconditionally good enough, and that my existence in their lives was welcomed. In the previous work I had done with ayahuasca two weeks prior, before drinking the tea I had asked for healing by being spiritually "rebirthed." I was thinking that maybe I could, in a sense, skip years of troubleshooting and just delete all defective "Robyn" files and reboot the whole system.

Ayahuasca had powerful wisdom of her own and, as it turned out, I received something different than what I thought I wanted. In my San Pedro healing now, I was told that a renurturing of my child self rather than a rebirthing would help me as an adult to know a greater sense of inner worth and love in my life. It was then that I was shown the infant scene I have mentioned and realized that my parents were in fact me as a more spiritually evolved female and male version. As well, I could feel the healing assistance of the mother energy of the Earth and the father energy of the sun as I lay on my back in the garden.

Later, in the background of what was like my conversation with God, my rational mind began to fret about the welfare of my teeth. I've had years of lectures by dentists to brush my teeth after eating anything, especially candy. My thoughts lethargically obsessed about how I should get up now and find my toothbrush. (I noticed that even thinking of doing this task while on San Pedro made me feel very heavy, yet to walk through the garden was like floating.) I got the message then that

> your physiology is being well looked after [while on the plant medi-
> cine]. The food and drink on the teeth are not the primary causes of
> dental deterioration; there is much that's involved on a subtle energy
> level. Your teeth will decay and bone loss will occur if you consist-
> ently feel powerless to effect change and lose interest in participat-
> ing in life. As well, consumption of chemicals, devitalized food, and
> demineralized sugar weakens the auric field around the body and
> can allow in energies that feed off the body's life force. The mind
> can be influenced by their presence to resonate with lower-vibration
> thought and cravings. Consume foods that have a high natural min-
> eral content as it will strengthen and protect the entire body.

In another ceremony there was instruction about how to deal with a chronic pain around a particular area (uterus):

Excessive thinking brings heat into one's head, creating coldness and contraction in the body. Keep the "pot" stirred and warm by placing your attention there [the lower abdomen] deliberately with love. Do more movement such as dancing and yoga. With pain, breathe from the belly, breathe love and acceptance into the area of pain, breathe it down into the Earth and ask that the energy be received and transmuted.

So far, the healing given during that time has resulted in a significant diminishment of menstrual pain. I was told that it would be a gradual process and that I would need to work on using the knowledge given and avoid using chemical pain-blocking medication to suppress it. Also from my first San Pedro ceremony, I had asked for and held an intention to heal from celiac disease. Since that day my doctor has told me I am about 75 percent healed of this disease that had affected me my entire life.

I was guided to see that a health therapy (a deep-tissue abdominal massage that facilitates emotional detox) that I was planning on studying was something my heart was saying wasn't for me at this time. My mind had been giving good-feeling reasons why it was a fantastic idea, but I couldn't understand why it was hard to visualize myself doing the work at my studio. The pragmatic commentary during the San Pedro session helped. "Do you really want to be digging your elbows into other people's cesspools of emotions, stirring up what you haven't completely healed in yourself? Can you see your clients needing to get off the table to help you feel better?" Following that I was given many insights into how healing works and the therapies that work only on the energy field soon becoming more used than physical treatments.

There was a lot taught about the truth in emotions and about paying attention to what actually feels better in contrast to following what the mind wants. "You had become like a big head dragging your body behind you as if it were an extra appendage whose purpose you had forgotten." I was told that when you live from the heart work is effortless effort.

Use your mind to figure out how to read a map and get you to the airport in time, but not to choose the location without checking with the heart or deciding what will bring you joy. Happiness is not found on the path of struggle. Set your intention for happiness and then go out and play and your greater good will find you there.

In my last communion with the spirit of San Pedro, there was insight given about oneness and how we all come from the same one source, reminding me of a quote from the late comedian Bill Hicks: "We all are one consciousness experiencing itself subjectively."

Meanwhile, during this time whenever one of the members of the group I was sharing the ceremony with came into my line of sight, my mind prepared to put up its deflector shield of aloofness so I could keep to myself and not have to make conversation. Most of my life I held a strong belief that I was socially awkward and didn't quite fit into the mainstream world of how things are done. I preferred to blend into the background. San Pedro commented on this with amusement.

You don't recognize yourself do you? You shrink down in fear around people but they are you wearing another face. You are all gods, all of God. You feel separate and it is real but understand that it's not truth. Your reality is the hallucination. All are playing a role in each other's drama for learning but you are one being playing all the roles. You are waves in the infinite ocean of one pure Spirit.

Later in the journey I felt inspired to create a new reality for my life (since I was a goddess, after all). It was ideal to do this while dwelling in the right-brain world of infinite possibility and with San Pedro's guidance. I was reminded that "it is done unto you as you believe," that I still had to do the work when I got back into my everyday life to hold the vision of my dream and faith in its reality now while the "old" life transitioned into the new. I had fun with that, regardless if the results unfold.

Update, four months later: while not a magic eraser of problems

I have seen undeniable evidence over these months that things have improved for the better and that they're continuing to do so. Situations like my reaction within a drama that previously would have ungrounded me, setting me back into a pattern of depression or an energy-draining verbal retaliation, the negative "hook" to my old programming, is now more often seen by me from an interested but detached point of view. It's much easier to let it be as it is and move on. And insights have flowed into my mind, notably during times when something extraordinarily shocking has occurred (as happened recently), and the sense I get is that connection to huachuma's wisdom never fully leaves.

San Pedro also gave me the gift of seeing the source of the thought patterns that created certain problems for me and where better choices could be made. It was always clear that it would be up to me to put what was learned into action for it to work its miracle of transformation. Otherwise, what was offered from the medicine as tools for healing would just become interesting "food for thought."

My San Pedro journeys turned out to be a return ticket to go out of mind. It took me on an endless trip deep into my heart, connecting with my soul and everything else through the oneness of all, carefully losing some of my heavier emotional baggage along the way. I give thanks, too, that this experience is available to anyone who may decide to simply travel to Peru.

12
The Universal Heart

Daniel Moler

> *Beauty is life when life unveils her holy face.*
> *But you are life and you are the veil.*
> *Beauty is eternity gazing at itself in the mirror.*
> *But you are eternity and you are the mirror*
>
> KAHLIL GIBRAN, *THE PROPHET*

For our anniversary my wife and I attended a *mesada,* a medicine ceremony of the San Pedro cactus (or *huachuma*). I was completely terrified.

A couple of years ago I underwent an entheogenic experience without the proper ceremony or setting, and it ripped me to shreds. I felt torn away from the world in a horrific, isolated way. Instead of making me better it made me worse, resurfacing old haunts within my psyche. I opted never to go back to that space ever again.

But as circumstance would have it, synchronicity aligned us to this juncture. As scared as I was to undergo another "psychedelic" experience, the opportunity seemed to fit just right with the stars. The shaman assured me everything would be fine and he would be there to facilitate my healing. I also have a heart condition that arises during panic, derived from when I was diagnosed with post-traumatic stress disorder. He said San Pedro would take care of that too, calling it what his wife termed "a masterful lover."

The San Pedro cactus (*Trichocereus pachanoi*) is one of the oldest entheogenic substances used in shamanic practice that we know of. Originating from the Chavín culture in northern Peru, San Pedro can be found in carvings dated as far back as 1300 BCE. The name San Pedro was adopted during the early European colonization of Latin America. A legend exists of Saint Peter using the mystifying powers of the cactus to uncover the hidden keys to heaven to share with all humanity. Scholars of shamanic studies Ross Heaven and Howard Charing state, "Considered the 'maestro of maestros' San Pedro enables the shaman to open a portal between the visible and the invisible world for his or her people."[1]

San Pedro is known to be a great healer for all ailments mental, physical, emotional, and spiritual. This may all sound baffling to the average person but the shaman's claim is that nature is minded: "A plant may not talk but there is a spirit in it that is conscious, that sees everything, which is the soul of the plant, its essence, what makes it alive."[2]

As we arrived at the shaman's lodge my fear boiled inside me, causing my heart to throb so hard it affected my vision. There were approximately twenty people attending the ceremony including the two *auxillios* (the shaman's proxies, available to assist with our needs and hold the space as a sacred container). We waited nervously outside the main lodge as we listened to the shaman rattle and sing inside. We were called in one by one.

I was placed in the northeast section of the chamber. The shaman knew who we all were weeks in advance, spending this time preparing the San Pedro brew with our names, our prayers. As well, he had systematically configured the room to align our energies with the four cardinal points. As we were all seated he gently explained the process of the night. Then we opened the ceremony by charging the *mesa*.

A mesa is "a shamanic altar containing ritually empowered objects, which are aesthetically arranged on a sacred textile to reflect the system of medicine work employed by its carrier."[3] The mesa also reflects the four directions, symbolizing the four elements that we paid homage to: Pachamama in the south, representing Mother Earth; Mama Killa in the west, representing water, Grandmother Moon; Wirococha in the north, representing air, the world of Spirit; and Inti in the east, representing fire, the Sun. Finally, K'uychi in the center is charged, the universal hub of all that is, the *axis mundi*.

The shaman facilitated an energetic interaction between us and the mesa, which would be the central anchor of the night's ceremony. All nourishment, even water, would come only from the mesa for the rest of the evening.

The shaman blessed the San Pedro brew and drank it first. He drinks as we drink, enabling him to energetically see, diagnose, and treat our ailments. Then he called us up to drink from the same cup, one by one. When my name was called I almost passed out in anxiety. When I stood I shook with fright, dizzy with heart-pounding anxiety. Maybe I can back out I told myself. I don't have to do this do I? I was constantly rehashing Terence McKenna's statement in my mind: "A touch of terror gives the stamp of validity to the experience because it means, 'This is real.'"[4] I also recalled the shaman's advice to me weeks before: "If you are afraid of it that means it is exactly what you need to do." I have to overcome my fear.

I placed myself on the south side of the mesa, facing the rest of the chamber. I clasped the cup in my trembling hands and whispered my prayers into the brew: "Give me courage San Pedro. Help me overcome my fear, my pain. I want to know how to love. Make me a vessel for Spirit." I held the cup up to the members of the room. "Salud!" Everyone repeated back: "Salud!" And I drank. No way back now, I said to myself, "Best just surrender to the ride."

Your pain is the breaking of the shell that encloses your
understanding. . . .
Much of your pain is self-chosen.
It is the bitter poison by which the physician within you
heals your sick self.
Therefore trust the physician and drink his remedy in
silence and tranquillity.[5]

Everyone finished, and we settled into our positions. The shaman and his auxillios blew out the few remaining candles in the chamber, making it completely dark save for the faint moon glow through the windows. Huachuma ceremonies generally take place at night in utter darkness. Mythologist Joseph Campbell asserts, "Since the yonder world is a place of everlasting night, the ceremonial of the shaman has to take place at night."[6] The sudden darkness was very jarring and I readied myself for the unknowable.

Before beginning his healing work the shaman appointed the first hour to allow San Pedro to work within us. I focused intently on my breathing, trying to calm my heart. In and out, fueling my body with the rhythm of breath.

Before long I began to see and feel the San Pedro in my stomach. It appeared as a luminescent purple globule inside of me, reaching out with octopus-like tentacles. I remembered what McKenna terms the "violet psychofluid," seen by shamans under the influence of the entheogen ayahuasca:

A substance that is described as violet or deep blue and that bubbles like a liquid. . . . This violet liquid comes out of your body; it also forms on the surface of the skin like sweat. The Jivaro do much of their magic with this peculiar stuff. . . . The nature of this fluid is completely outside of ordinary experience: it is made out of space/ time or mind.[7]

This "psychofluid" churned within and around me to discover the ill inside. It was immediately setting itself to work! Of course it was not long until it latched onto my heart, which was racing in panic. As the "psychofluid" enveloped it, my heart began to race even faster. My fears became paramount: Why was I here? Can I still get out of this? What if I die? What if I have a heart attack? What if I come out of this experience with permanent psychosis?

After the first hour the shaman began his work. Each person, again one by one, was called to the mesa, the Altar Mayor, to receive the shaman's diagnosis and be given the opportunity to release whatever it was they needed to release.

Once the shaman makes his diagnosis, guided by his mesa and San Pedro, he begins his treatment. The treatment can take a variety of forms depending on what ails the individual: rattling, soul retrieval, singing, whistling, feather fanning, staffs, sucking, blowing, spitting. Whatever was happening each of us had to sit through each person's healing process, all of this in pure darkness. If an individual was moaning in pain we felt that pain too. If the shaman shook his rattle it reverberated throughout our entire bodies as if it was inside of us. What was so interesting about this process—and, at first, difficult to manage while doing our own inner work with San Pedro—was how communal it was. The message I received from this was: there is no way out, we are all in this together!

My panic at times was daunting. My heart, I felt, was going to give out. But the logistics of the ceremony inspired me. I looked over at the black shape of my wife and could tell somehow that she was dealing with some hard pain. I had such love for her and all I wanted to do, without any sort of return, was comfort her. I stroked her back calmly and I watched the shadowy forms of the shaman and his auxillios in the center of the chamber work on his patients. All of this began to inspire me. As terrified as I was to have my name called, this inspiration guided me to a place of sudden surrender to San Pedro.

Then, the shaman called for me: "Daniel."

That which seems most feeble and bewildered in you is the strongest and most determined.[8]

I stood. I don't know how but I did. Without falling, without a breakdown of panic. In absolute darkness I walked up to the northern side of the mesa, on top of a pallet of deerskin. My shaman sat on the south end watching me, prepping his diagnosis. Surprisingly, despite my fear, courage overwhelmed me. It was my moment to state my intention: "I am Daniel Erin Moler. I call myself to myself. San Pedro help me thus."

My shaman verbally acknowledged my intention. Then one of the auxillios brought me a *singado* (an infusion made from tobacco leaf macerated in alcohol, taken in a shell). I was instructed to inhale/ingest the singado into my left nostril, to release whatever it was I was intending to release. (I was incredibly nervous for this moment; I've never so much as done a neti pot!)

He began to rattle. I ingested the liquid into my nostril, imagining my fear rushing away . . . coughing, choking, spraying bits of the juice onto my face. The rattling stopped and I confirmed the action with a whisking blow from the shell into the mesa. Then the next singado came; I was to inhale this down my right nostril to intention what I want to bring in to my life.

The rattling started again. When I inhaled this time, imagining courage and love, it went down easier. A mighty rush overflowed me as I blew into the mesa. I felt power, such mighty and magnificent power. Not a dominating kind of power . . . the real kind, the medicine kind. A gentle power, what my wife would call "wick."

Next, the shaman approached me. He picked out a staff that resonated with my frequency and began his work. Using the staff, he called on great powers and spirits to assist, to remove any obstacles in my way to achieving my purpose. He used the staff to push out the *hucha* (heavy or dense energy from stress-related attachments) within my body. I noticed he specifically had to push harder around my heart area. After that he placed his mouth on my chest many times and tried to suck out the hucha, coughing from its toxicity and spitting it back into the mesa. This is part of the act of *ayni,* the sacred reciprocity of energetic interchange with the universe.

Then I was showered with *agua de florida* as he spit/sprayed it on the back of my neck, my face, and the rest of my body. Walking back to the mesa the shaman selected one of his *artes* (medicine tools kept on the mesa used to cleanse the energy field of a patient) and returned to place it in my hand. It was a marble heart.

"Take this heart," he said. "Go back to your seat. Draw the energy from it for the rest of the evening. You did good brother." And he embraced me.

> For even as love crowns you so shall he crucify you
> Even as he is for your growth so is he for your pruning.
> Even as he ascends to your height and caresses your
>   tenderest branches that quiver in the sun
> So shall he descend to your roots and shake them in
>   their clinging to the earth[9]

I really felt like his brother at that moment.

I have never been close to my own family. I grew up in a very unhealthy dynamic that made it difficult for me to assimilate relationships, to love people and know how to love in return. Even my friendships have been tainted with this same venom. Now more than ever I need to know how to love . . . for my wife, for my children . . . for everyone in my life. When my shaman embraced me and I held that marble heart in my hand I felt so connected. I felt truly loved, truly grateful to the universe—for the first time ever—for life!

What was truly revealing was the image of the heart. My wife had found a heart-shaped rock on the beach almost a year ago and gave it to me as a gift. It has always been at my bedside, a favorite medicine piece.

The first time I visited my shaman the arte he gave me was a small heart-shaped rock made out of the same substance as the one my wife gave me, as he found it on a beach in Hawaii. This one I got to keep assisting me in controling my fear and anger in tumultuous situations. Then about a week ago my wife found a heart-shaped piece carved out of wood, which has become an integral part of my mesa and (unbeknownst of the shaman) I brought it to the ceremony to assist in my healing. The fact the message was so clear, that I received another heart, chimed in my spirit with a clear and strident sanction.

Now . . . I could spend hours talking about the visions given to me by San Pedro that came after the healing work: the puma face cringing at me, the insectoid patchwork covering my vision, the San Pedro cacti in the windows dancing back and forth, the vibratory resonance of the universe literally (physically) shaking my body, the insight to our sacred ancestry, our connection to the Star People, my being selected by one of these Star People to guide and teach me for the years to come in my shamanic apprenticeship, or watching the "violet psychofluid" seep out of everyone's pores. This is all fine and magical but the point of the entire evening may be missed.

When the healing work was complete we waited until dawn. As the sun slowly eked over the horizon a creeping incandescence emanating brighter and brighter within the chamber, the shaman and his auxillios spent that time in the center of the mesa creating a *refresco,* a citrusy alchemical concoction made to rejuvenate the body after a full night's work with San Pedro. It is loaded with sugar, fruit bits, flower petals, and the playful joy the shaman and his auxillios generate while preparing it. When it was ready the auxillios brought each patient a cup with a kiss to seal the sweetness. It is a drink to be savored as it connected us back to the Earth from our experience.

Finally came the flowering. We each received a white rose and were told to put them by our bedsides at night, to eat one of the petals before sleeping so that San Pedro can continue its work in us.

The shaman put on an almost goofy headband with puffy balls

trailing the back in a sprightly array. We all stood while he playfully danced from person to person spraying aromatic waters on the women's breasts, on the men's tummies, pouring flowery essences down our shirts and spraying us with powder. We all laughed and giggled like children, soaked to the brim in oils and smelling like a pungent, exotic garden. Our connection to each other was unbound and intertwined . . . a great serpent eating its own tail, the infinite *ouroboros*, T'eqsimuyu Amaru. We will always have this experience together. San Pedro will always be in our system, fused into our DNA. It will always be our Great Teacher, our "Masterful Lover."

So, what did I learn? Because it's all about learning, isn't it?

> *Say not "I have found the truth," but rather "I have found a truth"*
> *Say not "I have found the path of the soul." Say rather "I have met the soul walking upon my path"*
> *For the soul walks upon all paths*
> *The soul walks not upon a line, neither does it grow like a reed*
> *The soul unfolds itself, like a lotus of countless petals*[10]

It surprised me to realize how unengaged I was with the visionary appeal of the experience. Given my interest in psychedelic phenomena and art I thought the visionary aspects of San Pedro would be the primary catalyst of my journey. How wrong I was! I was 100 percent focused and engaged on the ceremony of the night not San Pedro's visionary affects.

What San Pedro taught me was how to love.

The shaman is the pure embodiment of Love. Whatever we had to go through that night the shaman went through as well. He drank from the same cup as we. Where we had time to be with our inner work while on San Pedro the shaman spent every waking moment giving of himself. If it was bad enough that we had to inhale singado down our nostrils, the shaman did it twice over. While we were sitting on the floor he was always up and working . . . every minute containing space, every minute extracting hucha, every minute healing our spirits. Tirelessly he gave himself throughout the entire evening: the true embodiment of the llama, of self-sacrifice.

The shaman has become *my* shaman. The embodiment of Christ Consciousness. I understand now why the Peruvian shamans had no issue with adopting the Christ story into the Pachakúti Mesa tradition. The crucifix generally lies in K'uychi, the heart of the mesa, the Universal Heart. Jesus Christ has the same message, lived the same life.

The shamans continue that story with the work they do; giving their lives over selflessly to the healing experience, they embody the Universal Consciousness of self-sacrifice. This is how to love: without fear, without anticipating return. Giving oneself to another endlessly and selflessly is the only true way to heal, to evolve.

San Pedro taught me that no good will come from festering on the hurt and pain. That will only breed more hurt and pain. To give of yourself to others, unbound, without fear, without limitation is how one heals one's heart. How one grows into the man or woman one wants to be. Thus, like the shaman prescribing for each patient to their own individual needs, so must I love the people in my life each to their own individuals needs . . . not—as it once was—to my own.

Am I enlightened? No. Has my life suddenly changed for the better? No. All of that work has to be on my own.

What I did walk away with from San Pedro's teachings was a firm gratitude and confidence for what I must do and how I must do it . . . a deep energetic self-assurance I never could have received from a book or a class or any other external source. San Pedro infused itself within me and I have no doubt it will continue to teach me in mystifying ways for many years to come. As well, it cemented a human and cosmic connection with my shaman, my *curandero,* as teacher, guide, and brother.

"Shamanic mastery is attained not in radical insight of universal truth and order, rather it is discovered over and over again through joyful surrender to the process of accretive growth."[11]

Happy anniversary, my wife, my Love. My commitment to growth remains forever strong.

We are the seeds of the tenacious plant and it is in our ripeness and our fullness of heart that we are given to the wind and are scattered.[12]

NOTES

1. Ross Heaven and Howard G. Charing, *Plant Spirit Shamanism: Traditional Techniques for Healing the Soul* (Rochester, Vt.: Destiny Books, 2006), 92.

2. Jeremy Narby, *The Cosmic Serpent: DNA and the Origins of Knowledge* (New York: Penguin Putnam, 1998), 104.

3. Matthew Magee, *Peruvian Shamanism: The Pachakúti Mesa* (Kearney, Neb.: Morris Publishing, 2005), 39.

4. Terence McKenna, *The Archaic Revival: Speculations on Psychedelic Mushrooms, the Amazon, Virtual Reality, UFOs, Evolution, Shamanism, the Rebirth of the Goddess, and the End of History* (San Francisco: HarperCollins Publishers, 1991), 37.

5. Khalil Gibran, *The Prophet* (New York: Alfred A. Knopf, 1968), 52.

6. Joseph Campbell, *The Hero with a Thousand Faces* (New York: Princeton University Press, 1973), 99.

7. Terence McKenna, *True Hallucinations: Being an Account of the Author's Extraordinary Adventures in the Devil's Paradise* (San Francisco: HarperCollins Publishers, 1993), 69.

8. Gibran, *Prophet*, 92.

9. Ibid., 11.

10. Ibid., 55.

11. Magee, *Peruvian Shamanism*, 18.

12. Gibran, *Prophet*, 82.

13
Deciding to Live Not Die

Sonna-Ra

This morning I woke up to the gentle pattering of rain against my bed-room window. There was a sense of peace in my heart at the memories of my journey with San Pedro in Cusco. I couldn't wait to get out of bed to write this down. Words kept flowing effortlessly, like Mozart's symphonies, waiting to be written.

During spring equinox in 2009 a group of my friends gathered at a retreat somewhere north of Wellington, New Zealand. I was invited to be the weekend's cook in exchange for the cost of the retreat. Finances had been tight since I decided to return to university that year.

One night Judith-Anne related to me her experience at our mutual friend's recent death. She had died of a brain tumor just thirteen weeks after diagnosis. Judith-Anne said that when our friend stopped breath-ing, every family member in the room broke out in a *haka* (a traditional Maori chant or challenge) to celebrate her departure from this world. The noise and energy in the room was explosive and Judith-Anne felt the presence of God. After hearing that I was moved to tears and we both had a good cry in each other's arms.

Following that episode I couldn't stop thinking about my own mortality. I decided to live a bit more daringly and do some things that I had been too chicken to do. One evening shortly after the retreat, I was having a meeting with some friends and mentioned that I would like to go to Peru to attend Ross Heaven's workshops, but I couldn't afford it unless I checked out the money I had been saving for my funeral.

Gwyneth looked at me and said that when I passed on my friends would throw a big healing fair to raise money for my burial, as long as I don't mind what I got. Sandra chirped in that she thought the *kohas* (monetary gifts) from the fair would be more than enough to hold a big party and a decent burial, plus a coffin for all my friends to express their creative art on. It was such a hilarious image that we were laughing till our sides hurt. I was so touched by such sincere generosity from my friends that I confidently went and booked my flights and workshops the next day before my mental Scrooge returned.

For someone like me who had never taken recreational drugs nor smoked a joint in my life (being a natural health therapist) many of my close friends thought it was quite an unbelievable thing to go all the way to Peru for ayahuasca and San Pedro ceremonies. But there I was, getting off the plane at Cusco after twelve days in the Amazon jungle getting to know ayahausca.

Outside the airport I was immediately immersed in the high vibration of the place. I saw gold light around people and all over myself. The next day I had a mild headache, which was intensified by drinking coca tea. Everyone recommended this tea for altitude sickness but the more I drank the worse I felt. After breakfast I had a huge headache and when I moved I felt nauseous. I could only walk five steps and my heart was pounding and I was short of breath. I finally got up the steps to the *casa* where Ross's group was meeting and met up with Ross's assistant, Donna. Donna told me that San Pedro would fix my altitude sickness; it did for Ross! I couldn't wait to try it. At that point, out of desperation I was willing to drink snake venom just to feel better.

We went to the Temple of the Moon for our first ceremony. The wind was cold and I had a thick blanket with me. Our shaman, La

Gringa, gave us a talk about San Pedro. She said that we were drinking Light and that San Pedro would open a doorway to experiencing oneness with nature. Then we received our glass full of this interesting-looking liquid, which was thick and tasted a bit bitter. We had to hold the medicine down for forty minutes for it to take effect. Ten minutes after drinking it, however, I was puking in the flowerbeds and started to feel heavy. I grabbed a branch of a plant beside me just for a solid connection to the world in case I lost my mind somewhere, I thought.

From then on my whole body relaxed and I could feel San Pedro's energy moving through me. I started to cry from some sad feeling of abandonment and aloneness. Then I felt my son holding me and giving me so much love that it moved my soul. Without words I knew that we both had a strong bond and our love will always be there. San Pedro brought it to my conscious mind to know it like an etching on a wall, so solid that I will always remember. Then I experienced love from my close friends from New Zealand.

The journey continued with San Pedro circulating in my body, and I felt my temperature fluctuate and pain surface at different places. La Gringa's three dogs were present in the garden where we drank, and all were great healers. One of them kept turning up whenever I was in pain. He would park his body along my back and within a few minutes the pain would diminish and he would trot off to minister to another person.

Later, I lay on the mattress with a thick blanket over me, staring at the sky and feeling the wind on my face. The San Pedro songs playing in the garden were like nothing I had ever heard in my life. My whole body received the lyrics and the sounds with joy. I felt I was in oneness with the songwriter's creation and surfed in a frequency of ecstasy. Man, this body is so cool. San Pedro removed my miserable thoughts and tuned me into ecstasy!

My next San Pedro ceremony was amazing in itself. On this occasion we had two Peruvian musician-healers with us. I held down the drink quite well this time and trusted its power more. The music and chanting took me through ancient landscapes on the wings of a condor.

The voices from the healers were sweetly haunting and soulful. I could feel my heart spinning in my chest and a voice in my head said, "You are the essence of love and everyone mirrors back to you." It was so deeply profound and I realized that all that is in my world is a reflection of me. I am the one who gives meaning and purpose to my existence. I am the one responsible for my thoughts and feelings. There was a sense of gratitude inside me for this connection with Pachamama.

At the end of the day the sky opened up and poured with rain. We huddled beneath the canopy of the veranda with a cup of hot tea. It was the happiest day of my life. If there is an opportunity in the future I would love to share a San Pedro experience with my son who is eighteen.

At the end of the workshop five of us traveled to Machu Picchu. It was another amazing adventure, as if Pachamama continued to present us with her generous gifts of love.

When I was on the plane leaving Cusco I looked out the window and saw another plane with Machu Picchu painted on its tail. Tears rolled down my face. I cried not from sadness at leaving this place but from gratitude. I had thought that this place was a hellhole when I arrived and had experienced such altitude sickness but now I felt utter gratitude for all it had given me: a precious deep sense of love for myself and my world. I also felt that my journey to Peru and with San Pedro wasn't just for me. I had drunk it for those at home too who couldn't come personally. To my surprise many of my loved ones felt a strong heart connection to me during my absence, they told me later.

Peru is such a gentle, heart-centered place, and those who ran the San Pedro ceremonies were so kind and caring, making it a safe haven for us to journey into ourselves. A special magic came home with me and it is still working beautifully in my life.

PART FOUR
San Pedro and Creativity

There is no poetry among water drinkers.

Ovid

IF THERE IS PRECIOUS LITTLE WRITTEN about the influence of San Pedro on healing, there is nothing at all about its influence on creativity and the creative process, although anyone who has drunk the cactus remarks that new solutions have been presented to them and new insights received, insights that are creative and remarkable in themselves and have led to new approaches in their lives. This is the essence of creativity.

This section is a first step, therefore, to forming a link between San Pedro and creativity, and consists of an examination of the role of this teacher plant in artistic and musical processes.

PSYCHEDELIC RESEARCH

In fact, there is limited research per se on the uses and effects of psychedelics in the creative process, and most of what does exist was conducted in the 1960s and 1970s, at a time when the world was more fascinated by the "psychedelic movement." Some of this historic work may, however, be helpful to us as a starting point.

Rick Strassman reviews this research in his essay, "Creativity and Psychedelics."[1] "Many of us think of creativity in psychological and practical terms which are relatively familiar and not especially controversial" he says, "for example: The quality of being able to produce original work or ideas in any field" [or] "An act of construction: the combining or organizing of existing materials into a new form." Another definition of creation taps more abstract areas and is of a grander scale.

The act of creation; especially in a theological sense, the original act of God in bringing the world or universe into existence. This introduces religious and spiritual elements. Indeed, the creative process is often compared to a state of grace or deep meditative contemplation. Creating also may be the most obvious way in which we are made in God's image: producing something from nothing. In all cases, creativity manifests through its results, some of which are visible. But what drives the creative process is interior, subjective and invisible. The ability to contact and use these inner resources is necessary for creation.

The 1960s was an explosion of creativity—in fashion, music, art, literature, values, and lifestyle—much of it fueled by a willingness to explore these inner resources through a new awareness of and experimentation with psychedelics such as "magic" mushrooms and LSD. Unfortunately, however, as Strassman points out, while the world was turning differently and undeniable evidence of this new creativity and its origins in the psychedelic experience was pretty much self-evident, there have only been a handful of research efforts that have tried to understand the process.

In 1960 a Hungarian experiment using DET (a synthetic relative of DMT) found that five out of thirty-eight volunteers (just 13 percent), who were already a creative group, became "inspired" for some weeks after their psychedelic experience. The study itself did not involve acts of creativity, but examined DET's effects on brain waves. The researchers described their subjects only as experiencing "the rather passive state of accumulating impressions prior to creative work."

In 1967 an American group conducted an LSD-based creativity study. Strassman remarks that the setting for the experiment was not exactly conducive to "optimising the aesthetic or creative experience" as it took place in "a sterile clinical research ward." The researchers did not tell their subjects what drug they were getting until the morning of the study and provided little information about what to expect. They did find, however, that lower doses of LSD were successful in raising scores on tests that reflected "psychoanalytical views of creativity."

Results from "the most well-executed and designed study to date" (in Strassman's view) appeared in 1966. Volunteers received extensive preparation and screening for explicitly stated research on how psychedelics affect creativity. The results showed that low to moderate doses of LSD and mescaline (the "active ingredient" of San Pedro and peyote) enhanced creative problem solving, as assessed by subjective reports and the practical applicability of the solutions they came to. There also seemed to be a carryover of enhanced creativity for some weeks afterward.

"Unfortunately for scientists of any persuasion, human research with psychedelics ended abruptly in the early 1970's," says Strassman, "due to public health concerns of widespread illicit use combined with the political climate of the time, especially the civil unrest resulting from opposition to the war in Vietnam." And that is more or less it. Not a great deal of further research exists.

NINETY-ONE ARTISTS

There is one other study that is of interest, however. In 1967, in an attempt to discover which psychedelics were being used by artists as well as the views of the users, Stanley Krippner studied ninety-one artists who had had one or more psychedelic experiences.[2] Among them were an award-winning filmmaker, a Guggenheim Fellow in poetry, and a recipient of Ford, Fulbright, and Rockefeller study grants in painting.

Eight-one percent of those surveyed felt that the term *psychedelic artist* could be applied to them and agreed with the definition of a psychedelic artist as someone whose work shows the effects of the psychedelic experience. Of the substances mentioned to achieve these effects, LSD was the most popular, followed by marijuana and DMT, but peyote and mescaline were also significant (the others included morning glory seeds, psilocybin, hashish, DET, and ayahuasca, and a few had also tried kava-kava, ibogaine, bufotenin, Ditran, *Amanita muscaria* mushrooms, or Hawaiian wood rose).

The artists were asked if their psychedelic experiences had been pleasant. Ninety-one percent said yes while 5 percent gave a qualified yes, stating that their initial trips were difficult but later ones were more pleasurable. This might generally be consistent with the processes of San Pedro and ayahuasca, at least sometimes. Shamans say that the first time you drink either brew it may be that the spirit of the plant needs to perform a clearing or bring you face-to-face with your issues so these can be explored and healed during subsequent ceremonies. Having done so, later ceremonies tend to be easier.

When the artists were asked, "Have your psychedelic experiences influenced your art?" Ninety-one percent said yes. Only 3 percent believed that they had not been influenced, and none of the group felt that their work had suffered as a result of their experience. Those who said that they had been influenced by psychedelics mentioned a number of effects, which fell into three main categories: content, technique, and approach (although most felt that they had been affected in more than one category).

Seventy percent said that the psychedelic experience had affected the content of their work, the most frequent example being a new use of eidetic imagery as subject matter.* Fifty-four percent said there had been a noticeable improvement in their artistic technique (a greater use of color was mentioned most frequently). And 52 percent mentioned a change in their approach, such as the elimination of "superficiality," and the discovery of a new depth in themselves as "people and creators."

Some referred to their first psychedelic encounter as a "peak experience" and a turning point in their lives. "My dormant interest in music became an active one after a few sessions with peyote and DMT," said one musician. Another reported that his experience "caused me to enjoy the art of drawing for the first time in my life."

The impact of psychedelics on one individual is illustrated in the

---

*Eidetic imagery: "The ability to retain an accurate, detailed visual image of a complex scene or pattern (sometimes popularly known as photographic memory) or the ability, possessed by a minority of people, to 'see' an image that is the exact copy of the original sensory experience" (Gray and Gummerman). —R.H.

case of the artist Isaac Abrams who was amongst Krippner's subjects. In an interview he stated:

> [The] psychedelic experience has deeply influenced all aspects of my life. It was an experience of self-recognition . . . which opened my eyes to drawing and painting as the means of self-expression which I had always been seeking. During subsequent experiences many difficulties, personal and artistic, were resolved. When the personal difficulties were solved energy was released for the benefit of my art.

Abrams became a part of the "psychedelic fellowship" when he was offered psilocybin by a friend. Under its influence, he realized for the first time in his life that he had been acting for years "like a person who had no mind," driven as if by a mission but with no idea of what that mission might be.

A few months later he took mescaline. "It was beautiful," he said. His inner life having been opened by these episodes, Abrams thought that he might discover his "life's mission," a new sense of meaning, but in fact that did not come until three years later when he took LSD for the first time. During that session he began to draw. "I experienced a process of self-realization concerning the drawing," he said. "When the drug wore off I kept on drawing. I did at least one ink drawing every few weeks." He began to attend art classes and to learn about technique and materials. His skills developed and he began to paint.

Abrams concluded:

> For me, the psychedelic experience . . . has been one of turning on to the life process, to the dance of life with all of its motion and change. Before . . . my behavior was based on logical, rational and linear experience. Due to psychedelics I became influenced by experiences that were illogical, irrational and non-linear. But this too is a part of life. This aspect is needed if life is to become interrelated and harmonious. Psychedelic drugs give me a sense of harmony and beauty. For

the first time in my life I can take pleasure in the beauty of a leaf; I can find meaning in the processes of nature. For me to paint an ugly picture would be a lie. It would be a violation of what I have learned through psychedelic experience.

I have found that I can flow through my pen and brush; everything I do becomes a part of myself—an exchange of energy. The canvas becomes a part of my brain. With the psychedelics you learn to think outside of your head. My art attempts to express or reproduce my inner state. . . . Psychedelic experience emphasizes the unity of things, the infinite dance. You are the wave but you are also the ocean.[3]

Krippner noted that he rarely found artists among the casualties of psychedelic usage and suggested that an artist must stand apart from his culture in order to create. "To invent something new" he said, "one cannot be completely conditioned or imprinted. Perhaps it is this type of an individual—the person who will not be alarmed at what he perceives or conceptualizes during a psychedelic session—who can most benefit from these altered states of consciousness."

Despite studies like Krippner's and examples like Abrams, the research data on creativity and psychedelics (at least as far as it relates to LSD) were finally summarized with the rather noncommittal statement, "Whether LSD does or does not increase creativity remains an open question. . . . All that can be said at this time about the effect of LSD on the creative process is that a strong subjective feeling of creativeness accompanies many of the experiences."

MORE RECENT RESEARCH

Strassman's more recent experiments with the psychedelic experience (some of them reported in his book *DMT: The Spirit Molecule*) were driven by a desire, he says, "to understand the biological basis of mystical experience, although the experiments themselves partook, and stayed within the bounds, of traditional clinical research models. The drug that drew my interest the most was DMT, or dimethyltryptamine."[4]

As stated elsewhere, Strassman eventually became disillusioned by the lack of long-term effects that DMT had on the subjects he studied. Although many of them experienced deeply mystical and highly creative states, not many did much with the new awareness they had been given. They did not apply it to their lives.

Doing something with it is important for achieving full healing from the plants. We must use what we have learned in the business of living, otherwise it becomes merely a concept or a flight of fancy and nothing much in our lives can change.

In this section we hear from two artists—a painter and a musician—who *are* doing something with it. In their essays they talk about the healings they have received from San Pedro and how they have put their insights to work. As we hear, not only their art but their lives have been improved and enriched by doing so.

David Hewson. David ("Slocum" to his friends) is an internationally known artist trained in Italy, Switzerland, and New York who now lives in the Amazon rain forest near Iquitos, Peru. As well as portraits, which he sells worldwide, he has produced altar pieces and frescos for churches in America and elsewhere that illustrate his interest in religious iconography and themes—but with a twist. His style could be described as "modern Renaissance." Inspired by the old masters and often including gold and water gilding in his highly studied portraits, murals, and frescos, the twist comes from his incorporation of jungle scenes, visionary experiences, and his knowledge of plant medicines into his work. In the article that follows he writes about his interest in plants and shamanism, and how San Pedro has helped shape his views on life as well as his work.

Peter Sterling is a musician who is also inspired by his work with San Pedro and other teacher plants. His first album, *Harp Magic,* was nominated for the NAIRD* Indie Award, and in 2004 his CD *Harp Dreams* went to number one on the N.A.R. top-100 radio playlist, remaining there for eight weeks and making it the most played new age music CD in the United States, Canada, and Europe. It was then nominated for Album of the Year. As a result, Peter signed with the prestigious Real Music record label for the worldwide release of his CD *Shadow, Mist, and Light*. He performs worldwide and has a website at www.harp-magic.com. In this article he writes about a healing he underwent with San Pedro and the inspiration he has drawn from it, which he now uses to guide his music and his life journey.

Before we hear from these artists, however, I present a short essay on the interrelationship between San Pedro and the use of music and art by shamans to draw closer to the spirits and as a channel for healing their patients.

NOTES

1. Available in full at www.maps.org/media/strassman-spring03.html. Accessed June 27, 2012.
2. Stanley Krippner, "Mescaline, Psilocybin, and Creative Artists," available at www.psychedelic-library.org/artist.htm. Accessed June 27, 2012. The article is an excerpt from "The Psychedelic State, The Hypnotic Trance, and the Creative Act," a paper published in *Altered States of Consciousness*, edited by Charles T. Tart (New York: John Wiley and Sons, 1962).
3. See www.isaacabrams.com/altindex.html for details of the artist and examples of his work. Accessed June 27 2012.
4. Strassman Rick, *DMT: The Spirit Molecule; A Doctor's Revolutionary Research into the Biology of Near-Death and Mystical Experiences* (Rochester: Vt.: Park Street Press, 2000).

---

*NAIRD stands for National Association of Independent Record Distributors.

14
San Pedro in Art and Music

~~~~~~~~

Ross Heaven

There has always been an affinity between art, music, and teacher plants, and the number of shamans who are also artists is remarkable in itself. In ayahuasca healing the best example of this is Pablo Amaringo.

Amaringo, one of the world's greatest visionary artists, trained first as a shaman in the Amazon, healing himself and others with ayahuasca from the age of ten, but gave this up in 1977 to become a full-time painter and art teacher at his Usko-Ayar school. His book, *Ayahuasca Visions: The Religious Iconography of a Peruvian Shaman,* coauthored with Luis Eduardo Luna, was published in 1993 and has become a classic of visionary art.

In my own book, *Plant Spirit Shamanism,* Amaringo had this to say about the connection between art and plant medicines:

My visions helped me understand the value of human beings, animals, the plants themselves and many other things. Plants—the great living book of nature—have shown me how to study life as an artist and shaman. They help us to know the art of healing and to discover our own creativity because the beauty of nature moves

282

people to show reverence, fascination and respect for the extent to which the forests give our souls shelter. The consciousness of plants is a constant source of information in medicine, alimentation and art and an example of nature's intelligence and creative imagination. Much of my education I owe to these great teachers. Thus [in my art] I consider myself to be the "representative" of plants. . . . Any painting, or book or piece of art that spreads this message is to be respected.[1]

In San Pedro shamanism, probably the best known *curandero* was Eduardo Calderon, and he too was an artist. Douglas Sharon, an anthropologist who apprenticed with Calderon, writes in *Wizard of the Four Winds* about Calderon's initiation into shamanism.[2] "During my youth from more or less the age of seven or eight years I had some rare dreams," Calderon is quoted as saying.

I flew . . . and I went to strange places in the form of a spiral. . . . I tried to restrain myself and I could not. . . . I have seen things as if someone opens a door and the door is closed. I have had nightmares but not ordinary ones. I have seen myself introduced through a hole in the air and I went through an immense, immense world. I have felt numbness in all my body as if my hands were huge but I could not grasp. I could not hold up my hand.

Those familiar with shamanism (for example from Mircea Eliade's classic study, *Shamanism: Archaic Techniques of Ecstasy*) will recognize here the onset of what has come to be called the initiatory crisis of the shaman: the call of the spirits in dreams and life experiences that are sometimes unsettling and can lead to physical or emotional illness until the shaman-elect heeds the call and agrees to shamanize.[3]

Sharon continues: "Medicine seemed to be the best avenue of expression for Eduardo's idealism but it was not economically feasible. His frustration, however, was temporarily mitigated by his growth as an artist . . . art provided the best medium of expression."

And so for Calderon as for Amaringo, his means for both making sense of and translating the messages of the spirits was art, a creative process he continued to work with for the rest of his life, even when he became one of Peru's most famous healers.

This is not surprising, as there is an obvious connection between visionary worlds and visionary expression. It is a yearning within human beings to understand the world of the spirits through engagement with them beyond the experience itself and to honor these worlds through art. Shamans are known as walkers between worlds, and art is one way by which the intangible is brought into the tangible and the unseen realms become seen.

It is fitting, too, that this process takes place through art. The information given to us by teacher plants tends to be revealed in a visual way (not exclusively so; information may also be passed to us in an auditory or kinesthetic fashion or, especially with San Pedro, as a mood or feeling) so it is logical that we would wish to represent the worlds we have been shown in the way that they have been shown to us.

Many depictions of the shamanic experience also arise from a time before the written word (such as cave paintings, some of which have been dated to forty thousand years ago) so perhaps the alternatives then were limited.

But there may be more to it than this. Grant Eckert in his essay, "Art and How it Benefits the Brain," writes:

Art is very important in helping the brain reach its full potential. . . . It introduces the brain to diverse cognitive skills that help us unravel intricate problems. Art activates the creative part of our brain—the part that works without words and can only express itself nonverbally. Art, in thought and through the creative processes, activates the imaginative and creative side, the spatial and intuitive side of our brain. Art jumps over the process of linear and logical thinking. It trains the brain to shift into thinking differently, broaching old problems in new ways.[4]

This, too, is the nature of the entheogenic experience: it is non-rational and nonverbal, the insights coming at an almost cellular level through a remodeling of the self. Trying to capture this experience in words is often too limiting for those who have undergone it. By splashing paint on paper, however, we put ourselves back into connection with the experience itself and reengage with the creative processes that took place then. Because we are no longer completely "in" the experience, however, we can also glean more information from it as we record our sensations in art. We become, in a sense, walkers between worlds ourselves, not quite of this world or fully of the psychedelic one that we have explored and reemerged from.

Eckert continues:

There have been copious studies on the relationship between art and its benefits to the brain. Semir Zeki, a former professor of neurobiology at University College London and co-head of the Wellcome Department of Cognitive Neurology published an article, "Artistic Creativity and the Brain," in *Science* magazine in July 2001 [where he] detailed the relationship between the development of cognitive abilities and the creative process. He stated that artistic expression is the key to comprehending ourselves. He also considered art and its expression as an expansion of brain function. In other words, art helps the brain in its search for knowledge.

Art therapy is now a common means of helping individuals to improve and enhance their physical, mental and emotional well-being. It bases its approach on the belief that the creative process involved in artistic self-expression helps people in a number of positive ways. It facilitates them in ending or finding a solution to various conflicts and problems. Art also aids them to manage their behavior, develop interpersonal skills, increase self-esteem and self-awareness, lessen stress and attain insight.

So what are the benefits of art on the brain? When individuals create art and reflect on it, the processes increase self-awareness, initiate awareness of others and help people cope with stress and traumatic experiences. Art enhances cognitive abilities and provides individuals with the ability to enjoy [life].[5]

In many ways then, artistic expression is the perfect adjunct to work with a plant such as San Pedro, which itself helps those who drink it to gain insight and overcome stress-related health issues and traumas.

Research on brain function supports many of Eckert's conclusions. Neurologist António Damásio, in his book *Descartes' Error: Emotion, Reason, and the Human Brain* (Penguin 2005) points out that in any new situation human beings first experience the world emotionally (a response typical of the San Pedro experience, too). This is true even though we have been taught to believe that the brain is our most important organ and that rational thought is our most vital attribute. In fact, the rational part of our experience arises after an emotionally based decision has already been made from the information that the world has presented to us and that we have absorbed in a nonlinear way.

"The departing point of science and philosophy should be anti-Cartesian" says Damásio: "I am (and I feel) therefore I think."

We have been trained by society to use more of the left (rational) hemisphere of the brain, and like any muscle this has grown in power and dominance while the "muscle" of the right hemisphere—associated with the creative imagination, serenity, synthesis, and selflessness—has atrophied.

Music, silence, art, and other reflective techniques that lead us into a calm and meditative state begin to correct this imbalance and bring us into more fullness of ourselves. We move from an everyday beta brain wave pattern (where we are consciously alert or agitated, tense or afraid, with frequencies from thirteen to sixty pulses per second in the hertz scale) to an alpha pattern of physical and mental relaxation, with frequencies of around seven to thirteen pulses per second. By doing so we put ourselves in the ideal condition to process, learn, and retain new information.

Relaxation is the state we are in when we drink San Pedro and when we create art, hence artistic expression is more than just a representation of the entheogenic encounter; it *is* that encounter relived, even if the work on the canvas bears no "actual" similarity to what we have seen or experienced when we drank the cactus.

According to neuroscientists, relaxed states like these also produce significant increases in the levels of beta-endorphin, norepinephrine, and dopamine, all of which are linked to greater mental clarity and the formation of new memories, and this effect can last for days. It is an ideal state for synthetic thought, creativity, and learning. Hence artistic expression fully supports the processing of information and insights delivered by San Pedro.

"It does not seem to be accidental that Eduardo the visionary shaman is also an artist," writes Sharon Lommel (in *Shamanism: The Beginnings of Art* [New York: McGraw-Hill, 1967], 148), who sees shamanism as intimately related to man's earliest artistic works and who contends that "without artistic creation in some form or another there is no shaman."

Calderon himself put it this way:

The power of artistic sensibility in curanderismo is . . . according to my evaluation, essential. In general the artist is sensitive, extremely sensitive in this field.

All that the artist effuses toward the outside world in his expression is of a character which is not intellectual but spiritual. For this reason it goes without saying that within curanderismo artistic appreciations are essential . . . because the symbols are perceptible only to persons who really note a line, a trajectory of appreciation in order to be able to dominate the distinct phases of a curing scene. . . . Those individuals always related art with mysticism, with the esoteric, with the mysteries.

The earliest artistic depiction of San Pedro so far discovered is a carving on a block of stone, dating from around 1300 BCE, which was excavated from the sunken plaza of the Old Temple at Chavin de Huantar in the northern highlands of Peru. It shows a mythological being, believed to be the central Chavin deity, with serpentine hair, fangs, a serpent belt, and eagle claws holding a four-ribbed cactus in his outstretched right hand.

Textiles discovered on the south coast of Peru dating from roughly the same period show a spineless cactus along with hummingbirds and feline figures. Both animals are associated with shamanism and healing: the former representing the shaman's ability to suck magical pathogens from victims of sorcery, and the latter believed to be the alter ego or ally of the shaman.

Ceramics made by Chavin artists, dating to 1000 BCE, show the cactus with another animal: the deer that, according to Sharon, symbolizes swiftness and is associated with the shaman's ability to exorcise evil spirits from his patients. ("Hunting the deer" or "the blue deer hunt" is also the name given to the ceremonial collection of peyote in Mexico, another sacred mescaline cactus).

In the art of the Moche period (north coast, from around 100 BCE), San Pedro is often depicted with a shawl-clad female figure who has the features of an owl (the alter ego of the curandera). In these images the healer holds a slice of San Pedro or, in later cases, a four-ribbed cactus of approximately the same length as would be used to prepare the healing brew.

Even where the cactus is not explicitly shown, such as in modern Andean art—like the paintings sold on market stalls or peddled to tourists by street sellers—the influence of San Pedro can still be felt, perhaps not in the themes but in the colors chosen by the artists.

In the Amazon the majority of locally produced art follows typical medicine themes, the plant medicine of this region being ayahuasca. Hence forest scenes are often depicted, where trees reveal their spirits, the "lady of the forest" is shown naked and sensual, giant serpents wind their way through the land or cross a moon-filled sky, or the *chullachaqui* (the mystical jungle dwarf who leads the unwary into the bosque and more deeply into an awareness of the otherworld) is shown ready to entice, confuse, and initiate. These works are typically produced in and on natural jungle-derived materials—black or sepia *huitol* ink (from the juice of the huitol fruit) on a canvas of bark—or else in muted tones that are themselves reminiscent of the jungle: shades of green and brown.

This reflects in many ways the nature of the ayahuasca experience. Ceremonies take place in *molokas* (ceremonial temples) open to the forest, at night when the colors around are themselves muted, and the visions produced reveal magical scenes of a living forest teeming with life and spirit. In this sense at least Amazonian art, although often fantastical, is also representational.

With San Pedro healing by contrast (particularly in its more modern form where ceremonies are held in daylight) color saturation is often a feature of the process. In *The Hummingbird's Journey to God,* I wrote of how during one San Pedro journey a simple marigold became so brilliantly bright that I couldn't look at it and had to close my eyes.[6] This brilliance is referred to by several other participants in that book, and for some it is evidence of intelligence, sentience, and a living God-like quality to nature.

The author Aldous Huxley wrote similarly of his mescaline experiences in his book *The Doors of Perception:*

> I was seeing what Adam had seen on the morning of his creation—the miracle, moment by moment, of naked existence . . . flowers shining with their own inner light and all but quivering under the pressure of the significance with which they were charged . . . a transience that was yet eternal life . . . the divine source of all existence. . . .
>
> I continued to look at the flowers, and in their living light I seemed to detect the qualitative equivalent of breathing—but of a breathing without returns to a starting point, with no recurrent ebbs but only a repeated flow from beauty to heightened beauty, from deeper to ever deeper meaning.[7]

It is this vibrancy and life that Andean artists seek to capture in their work, using bright and contrasting colors to create a sense of this beautiful "naked existence."

Simple everyday scenes often form the themes for their works—family gatherings, trips to the market—the essence of "transience" that is yet "eternal life," for it is the simple things that San Pedro reminds us of: the beauty of love and friendship, the living nature of everything we see and are a part of, the wonder of life, and the sacred in the mundane. The remembrance of these qualities in fact may be where the healing arises from with San Pedro, bringing us a reconnection to the Earth, to ourselves, and to a God who is not distant from us and judgmental of our actions but ever present and loving.

MUSIC AND SONG

In Amazonian shamanism *ayahuasceros* find power songs for themselves, called *icaros,* which are more than just tunes to be whistled, hummed, or sung in ceremony—they are carriers of energy and magical intent. It is their vibrational frequency that counts. This vibration can be used to charge or change the energy patterns within the body of a patient, remove illnesses and blockages, and restore a person to luminosity and balance.

Some icaros are learned from others (usually the shaman's maestro or teacher), some are copied and do the rounds, as it were, from healing center to healing center and moloka to moloka, but the most powerful are personal gifts from nature that the shaman has found for himself while dieting particular plants or searching for healing skills during ayahuasca ceremonies.

So it is too with San Pedro shamanism. While some *huachumeros* believe that there are not and cannot ever be icaros for San Pedro—not in the same sense as Amazonian songs—music and ritual chants form a part of most cactus ceremonies and, like icaros, they are personal to each shaman and carry his healing intent.

Sharon, writing about the San Pedro shaman's *tarjos,* or chants, reported that Calderon "learns the traditional rhythms but as with the various power objects [on his mesa]—positive and negative—he elaborates on the basic complex with his own particular talents and according to the inspiration he receives from a variety of extrapersonal and supernatural sources."

Calderon had tarjos for many purposes. To "open an account" (begin a ceremony) for example, "The invocation consists of chanting and whistling a special sacred tune (composed by the healer) to the accompaniment of his rattle." To know whether a deceased person is in "Heaven, Purgatory or Hell" another song is used. "This is a special task, it is a special account and chant with which one looks in rarely encountered cases."

Even the ceremonial structure of Calderon's nighttime rituals was divided by song. From 10:00 p.m. to midnight there were prayers, rituals, and tarjos interspersed with whistling while San Pedro was drunk and its guardian spirits were called. From midnight to 6:00 a.m.—the curing part of the ceremony—each person present took a turn before the mesa while the curandero chanted a special healing song in his or her name. Other tarjos were sung as particular power objects (swords and staffs for example) were used to heal the patient, the shaman using song to summon the spirit of each. A final song closed the ceremony.

Sharon described Calderon's practice as a "modern" interpretation of traditional shamanism. His fieldwork, however, was carried out between 1970 and 1974, and things have moved on in the intervening years. There are now even more modern interpretations to be found in the towns of the Sacred Valley and shamans who work with song and sound in a different way again.

Chaska Lu, for example, is a healer from the town of Aguas Calientes in the foothills of Machu Picchu whom I have worked with many times in ceremony. With her partner, Carlos, she uses a variety of traditional instruments as well as songs and chants to heal during San Pedro rituals. She calls her work "sound healing" and offers a simple explanation for what she is doing.

Sound breaks up energies. You have all seen opera singers who are able to shatter a glass with their voices and you know that ultrasound can be used in the treatment of cancer. This is similar to how we work with sound: to shatter and disrupt accumulations of negative energy which we see in the body of the patient or in his magnetic field [energy body].

If there is a light energy [which I see as] like smoke or cobwebs in the patient I may use a horn to move it since a blast of air will usually disperse it. If it is denser and thicker, then a shrill whistle may be needed as a high-pitched sound will break it into a thousand pieces, like a pane of glass shattering. Throughout the day I also sing prayers for the patient since God is a musician and prefers the sound of beautiful song to dull requests, or I may chant or intone my healing into the patient. This is a form of prayer which finds its mark through song.

Just as with the icaros of the Amazonian shaman (and perhaps influenced by their practice in fact since improved transportation has resulted in a greater blending of the Amazonian and Andean cultures in recent years), the tarjos of the San Pedro shaman are no longer used just to mark points in the ceremony or call on the spirits, but as healing tools in their own right.

Shamanism is the archaic predecessor to many modern therapies and again, as with art and its documented positive effects on the psyche, perhaps it is no accident that music and song have long been incorporated into teacher plant ceremonies, not just as a means of guiding the journey and delivering healing, but because it brings benefits in its own right. Psychologists who have made a study of the effect of music on the brain, on mood, and on healing have demonstrated some of these. Research by Sangeetha Nayak, for example, showed that music therapy is associated with a decrease in depression, improved mood, and a reduction in anxiety. It also has a positive effect on social and behavioral outcomes.[8]

In depressed adults, another psychologist, Suzanne Hanser, was able to show an improvement in quality of life, a new sense of involvement with the environment, increased ability to express feelings, raised awareness and responsiveness, and new positive associations as a result of music therapy.[9]

Other research suggests that music can increase motivation and positive emotions even among those suffering from serious illness (stroke victims),[10] and that when music therapy is used in conjunction with traditional treatments it improves success rates significantly, enabling patients to recover faster and better by increasing their positive emotions and motivation.[11]

A 2009 review of twenty-three clinical trials also found that music may reduce heart rate, respiratory rate, and blood pressure in patients with coronary heart disease. Benefits also included a decrease in levels of anxiety.[12]

Similarly, research suggests that listening to some music (in this experiment, Mozart's piano sonata K448) can reduce the number of seizures in people with epilepsy. This has come to be called the "Mozart Effect."[13]

San Pedro has the ability to amplify beauty—in the quality of music as it is heard as much as in art and nature—and a poignant or perfectly timed song can shift the mood of a participant or steer a ceremony in a new direction or provide new insights and inspiration. It may well be that the first San Pedro shamans understood the more physically beneficial effects of music on their patients, which studies like these are now confirming in a modern clinical setting.

NOTES

1. Ross Heaven and Howard G. Charing, *Plant Spirit Shamanism: Traditional Techniques for Healing the Soul* (Rochester, Vt.: Inner Traditions, 2006).

2. Douglas G. Sharon, *Wizard of the Four Winds: A Shaman's Story* (New York: The Free Press, 1978).

3. Mircea Eliade, *Shamanism: Archaic Techniques of Ecstasy,* Willard R. Trask, trans. (Princeton, N.J.: Bollingen Foundation, 1974).

4. Grant Eckert, www.self-help-healing-arts-journal.com/art-benefits-brain.html. Accessed July 19, 2011.

5. Ibid.

6. Ross Heaven, *The Hummingbird's Journey to God: Perspectives on San Pedro, the Cactus of Vision* (Brooklyn: O Books, 2009).

7. Aldous Huxley, *The Doors of Perception: Heaven and Hell* (London: HarperCollins, 1977).

8. Sangeetha Nayak, Barbara L. Wheeler, Samuel C. Shiflett, and Sandra Agostinelli, "Effect of Music Therapy on Mood and Social Interaction among Individuals with Acute Traumatic Brain Injury and Stroke," *Rehabilitation Psychology* 45 (3), August 2000, 274–83.

9. Suzanne B. Hanser and Larry W. Thompson, "Effects of a Music Therapy Strategy on Depressed Older Adults," *Journal of Gerontology* 49 (6), November 1994, 265–69.

10. Barbara L. Wheeler, Samuel C. Shiflett, and Sangeetha Nayak, "Effects of a Number of Sessions and Group or Individual Music Therapy on the Mood and Behavior of People Who Have Had Strokes or Traumatic Brain Injuries" *Nordic Journal of Music Therapy* 12 (2), 2003, 139–51.

11. Soo Ji Kim and Ilojoo Koh, "The Effects of Music on Pain Perception of Stroke Patients during Upper Extremity Joint Exercises," *Journal of Music Therapy* 42 (1) 2005, 81–92.

12. http://onlinelibrary.wiley.com/o/cochrane/clsysrev/articles/CD006577/frame.html. Current as of July 20, 2011.

13. John Hughes, Yaman Daaboul, John J. Fino, and Gordon L. Shaw, "The Mozart Effect on Epileptiform Activity," *Clinical Electroencephalography* 29 (3), 1998, 109–19.

15
San Pedro
Inspiration and Art

David "Slocum" Hewson

I live in the upper Amazon, in the jungle of Peru. When you are in the jungle anything is possible all the time. It embodies limitless potential made manifest through the constant cycles of light and dark, life and death. It also has an uncanny way of grounding one's nervous system in the biorhythms of the Earth, allowing you to connect more with your surroundings. For me it expresses itself through an unfolding of consciousness.

Ross asked me to write about art and inspiration through my work with San Pedro, but to do that I have to first go back to an ayahuasca experience ten years ago. I initially drank twice with a shaman in the States, and the experiences were so powerful that I later hosted him and organized groups for two subsequent visits. I did perhaps twenty ceremonies during this period, and those experiences successfully rewired me and allowed me to make fundamental changes in my life. I stopped complaining about the outside world so much and went inside and started maintaining my inner world instead, which is after all the only place where true peace exists. This was the beginning of a path that unfolded further when I decided to visit the shamans in Peru in 2006.

I had done a lot of traveling by that point in my life. I spent seven years studying and working in Italy and lived for a year in London and a year in India. I was always looking for some kind of artist's paradise in which to settle—an inexpensive place that offered beautiful models, the company of other artists, and the chance to live a fruitful life. It was a bit of a bohemian dream but it kept a fire within. Italy fulfilled that dream for a while, and India had many attractions, but even there, something was holding me back. By the time I got to Peru I had given up looking for that imaginary place.

On my first visit to Iquitos I had just finished a religious commission. In fact, the last six years of my life had been dedicated to religious works that provided steady work and also gave me time to create pieces of my own inspiration. After six years though, I found myself wondering if I wanted to do religious commissions anymore.

I went to the jungle to experience ayahuasca in its place of origin. The idea of a hot, sticky place with lots of insects did not interest me, but the longer I stayed I began to feel a growing sense of connection. I was staying with my shaman friend about ten kilometers outside of Iquitos. We were drinking ayahuasca two nights a week, sometimes with others, sometimes just the two of us. About a month into my stay, however, I realized that he was not the one I wanted to work with, and perhaps that realization opened me to the vision that came next.

In my vision a native woman came to me as if she was floating on the heads of a group of Shipibo Indian women, set against a golden Shipibo-patterned perspective. I had never seen such brilliant colors before, not even in reality. The woman had humility and seemed to be a healer yet she had a powerful presence. She looked into me eyes and said, "Use your talents, depict the beauty and destruction of the Amazon and show your people." My previous experiences with ayahuasca had given me beautiful visions, personal and cosmic insights, and transformations, but this incident was very special. It cast light on every cell in my body and it was clear to me that I should not take this vision lightly.

My first reaction was a bit egocentric. I said out loud, "Why did I not think of that?" Working with ayahuasca, as with any of the master teacher plants, you have to transcend your normal, rational state of mind. The rational approach, in my experience, tends to minimize what it does not understand, and it takes courage to listen to the heart. After receiving that powerful vision there was no doubt that I was going to carry it out, prepared to embrace both failure and success.

I returned to the States after a few months in the jungle with a new sense of purpose. I sold most of my belongings, gifted the rest, and soon enough found myself back in Iquitos ready to start a new life there. I had no idea how long it would take or how everything would be organized, but I was committed to carrying out the work ordained from the vision. I would take trips into the deeper parts of the jungle and see the beauty and destruction up close. The beauty was clear to me. It was there in the people, in their living mythology, and in the integrative work of ayahuasca.

I did not want to paint the destruction, however, so I extended into new mediums: film, photos, and maps. From my previous trip I had already begun a dialogue with groups working directly with indigenous causes, championing their struggle for humanitarian rights in relation to the oil companies, which was a great place to start. The idea was to organize trips with a guide to areas where there were native communities, stay with them, drink their plant medicine if possible, and also see areas where the oil companies were working so I could make my own assessments of the contamination problems.

In the Amazon there is a living mythology and though little is written, all things are known through oral history. Many people have their own personal accounts and I drew inspiration from hearing them. In each community I visited I found the most interesting faces and drew sketches of them. I also asked about their experiences with various figures from their mythology, such as tricksters and spirits of the water. These stories alone led to rough sketches out of my head, which I completed later with live models.

Drinking ayahuasca with natives was always insightful and often led to creative leaps in my work. I remember drinking raw aya with the Orejone natives, no cooking at all, just *chakruna* and the vine pulverized for hours and squeezed with our hands in water. I had never heard of raw aya before and was surprised by the effects. After drinking the medicine, the chief of the community, Liberado, put two large tablespoons of granulated tobacco mixed with cacao in my mouth between my cheek and gum. It had an aged ammonia flavor. I kept it in for about five minutes and then was told to spit it out.

I became very lightheaded and had to lie down. I was out on the floor for thirty minutes, shooting off into space. I was signaled to go to my mosquito net and after lying there for some time I had visions of traversing the jungle ground and water as if looking through the eyes of a serpent. I was at the jungle surface among all the rot and decay of the forest floor where all life begins anew. I saw sprouting plants and flowers coming from the dead and mushrooms gracing the landscape. I thought of my time in India and how the lotus flower emerges from a murky swamp. It is an allegory of the slow awakening of consciousness, the jewel in the lotus.

As my visions took me under the water there were all sorts of zoomorphic beings: fish heads with human bodies, alligators with wings, mermaids, human serpents, even an octopus. A whole life existed that I had never seen before. Perhaps that's what happens when drinking in the deep jungle, far from so-called civilization. I realized my visions had an interesting movement about them and became aware that I was seeing through the eyes of a snake. This went on for a while, and later I surfaced into a Westernized bourgeois house setting filled with plastic and air conditioning and people bickering about what they didn't have and using all their energy to protect what they did have.

It made me nauseous and I wanted it to stop, but I remained patient as it continued. I was dumbfounded by the vision. Later the shaman told me that seeing through the eyes of a serpent allows one to bridge the material and spiritual worlds. It made sense and gave me relief from the nausea. The next morning I roughly sketched some images that I reworked in the studio a year and a half later. I completed the piece, *Water Spirits,* which was directly inspired by my experience with the Orejones.

That trip led me closer to the Ecuadorian border where I stayed with a community of Huitoto natives. They were a larger community than the Orejones. I stayed with them for a week and enjoyed numerous indigenous delights including coca powder with burnt *setico* leaf, a mixture of pineapple and yucca flower called *cahuana,* and a tasty yucca flower bread called *casaba.*

The community had an abundance of great faces and I stayed busy doing head drawings and sketches. As I worked, hearing their stories of interactions with spirits was a creative whirlwind. A man told me he saw Chullachaqui, a forest dwarf and the trickster-protector of the jungle. If someone hears the voice of a friend or family member in the jungle and gets lost, it is attributed to this trickster. This man had a rum still and he claimed to see Chullachaqui steal a bottle and proceed to get drunk as he stumbled into the green density. I was told Chullachaqui also gets upset when there is deforestation and when animals are killed for sport and not eaten. In that I saw a great symbol of resistance against the massive influx of international corporations to the Amazon, companies that are plundering natural resources to maintain the status quo of the West and support "progress" in the East. These stories were so inspiring it led to numerous drawings and paintings of Chullachaqui alone.

During my stay there, we prepared ayahuasca cooked with a lot of tóe (a plant in the nightshade family also known as brugmansia or datura). I questioned the amount of the datura admixture they put into the brew. They said it was normal but it seemed like a lethal dose. The experience that night was more like datura than aya, so I can only bring back bits and pieces. I was mainly in a confused, drunken state. Of the fifteen people there, only half drank the brew while the others observed. The shaman was so out of it, vomiting and moaning, that it was difficult to know who was running the show! I tried to enjoy the open air and moonlit night but my knees were trembling and I knew something was making me uncomfortable in the ceremony. Many times when that happens I leave the circle. My guide came to help me back to the *maloka*. As he showed me the door I could see it clearly but my datura-drunk motor skills led me to walk right into the wall.

The next day I was offered a sixteen-year-old virgin. I talked my way out of it with a little comic relief, stating that I already had a harem and I was not doing a good job of taking care of them. I explained the experience to my guide and he concluded that they were doing witchcraft on me because they wanted me to stay and be part of the community. Not all medicine work with isolated natives is what we project it to be . . .

Near the Ecuadorian border I was shocked by what I saw. Perhaps I was more sensitive because of a connection with the spirit world through ayahuasca that had brought me to realize that everything is connected, without the intellect getting in the way, rather knowing the truth of things in my heart. So when I saw the pipelines put in by Occidental over thirty years ago, from a technology already long outdated, it was disturbing. In some areas the pipelines seemed to be haphazardly laid on the jungle floor. There were areas of previous spills where nothing grew. I felt a sense of the rape of innocence swell inside me. I photographed and filmed the site, installed by an embarrassment of a corporation that made billions of dollars treating the Earth as a brothel. The recently signed U.S.-Peruvian Trade Agreement (TLC) had opened pristine parts of the Amazon to unprecedented levels of development by mining and oil companies.

A representative from Environmental Defense had told me that the impact from this development is shaping up to be the largest human-created environmental travesty ever. And nobody is talking about it. I could not be a bystander anymore. The best way for me to be proactive was through my artwork, just as the native woman from my vision had said. I felt profoundly connected with her again; in fact I think she is partially present in every woman I meet.

Back in Iquitos I began to put it all together. Various trips and meetings were arranged with groups working to tell the truth about oil contamination. I contacted a few environmental groups in the States as well. Since this was a new area for me I turned to ayahuasca for guidance. Much of the inspiration came from my experience with natives and ceremonies, but now it was back to the studio to give it form. At the time I did not have a method to the madness, but in hindsight it seemed to form certain cycles. It took me two years from the powerful vision to finally assemble a traveling exhibit.

When I was in full working mode, I would have periods of 90 percent raw fruits, nuts, and vegetables supplemented with *maca* and *chlorella*. I was drinking aya two days a week by myself and would work for a month to six weeks—then have a little fish and some cooked food in between the dieting periods. I was getting confirmations from aya that this was best to maintain stable energy and good health. There were some weeks I never went more than a block or two from my studio/apartment, leaving only to get food in the market in Belen. Some evenings there would be a temptation to reward myself by going out to dinner or drinking beer. In those moments of desiring a distraction I would sit and meditate, in most cases I would look over the day's work and end up refining and adjusting oversights.

In some cases, if I got blocked on how to complete a piece I would drink aya and "ask" for guidance on one of the various steps in the process. My work is a combination of initial drawings and live models. The drawings are transferred to a prepared wood panel onto which symbols and patterns are carved. The panel is gilded with real gold leaf and the last part is the painting. It is important to have a precise drawing because once carved and gilded the painted parts cannot be moved around much. I found aya very helpful with making decisions about complicated pieces. In other moments of the ceremony I would get inspired to do a completely different piece. The key for me was to surrender my little self, my "ego," and allow my higher self to communicate to the plant, stepping out of the way enough to be a medium for creativity.

However, this does not always happen smoothly. The ego has clever ways of slipping back in. Aya has a mysterious way, however, of keeping the ego in check, but of course she can also trick you into thinking it is your higher self acting when it is actually the ego. With aya there is no easy way of discerning what is real and what is illusion.

Not all the ceremonies were pleasant and not all guided me as I wished. I remember at one point having to look at something from my past that was emotionally painful. I was on the receiving end of what I had done to someone else, reviewing my actions from the perspective of the very person I had done it to. The message aya gave me to help heal myself of this energy was to contact that person and to explain that I understood the pain they had gone through, as a form of atonement.

I had an old contact for that person but it was a dead end. I searched the Internet off and on for about two weeks to find an e-mail address, but to no avail. I gave up searching, feeling that maybe I should not have to do this, perhaps I was not understanding the message aya was conveying. I left it alone, feeling a bit bewildered by my "clear" mission. Within a month, however, I got an e-mail from the very person I was searching for, a nonchalant note asking me how I was. I felt it was a confirmation to express my truth. Even though it was painful, the humility of coming clean with my behavior healed something profound in me and in the process helped the other person heal as well.

It can be a very bumpy road to comprehend what exactly aya is communicating with you. Sometimes it can be very explicit and others times caution and careful discernment should be used. I had a dear friend who lived in Iquitos for a time. He had great intentions but he believed everything aya said was the truth, that "ayahuasca does not lie." This lack of discernment between a direct, unalloyed vision or revelation and the projections of one's own imagination is a tricky thing to navigate, and not everyone can make a clear distinction. Not doing so led my friend eventually to a series of follies, and ultimately he had to leave Iquitos due to poor financial health. Aya can play tricks on the ego: you have to filter how attached you are to this ego or be fooled by it.

In the course of organizing my traveling exhibit I had contacted a number of galleries, but most did not find the "destructive element" appealing or sellable to their clients. In fact, there was no money involved with this aspect of the show; it was just a sharing of information. I relied on art centers, a private college, a gallery willing to take a "risk," and connections of friends. An agent got me into a group show at the United Nations in New York City. Ultimately, I organized six exhibits in eight months in the United States and one in Canada. After the body of work returned with me to Peru, there were exhibits in Lima, Cusco, and Iquitos.

I was not alone in this process; I had a lot of help. I compiled information graciously given to me by native communities, civil organizations, NGOs, and environmental groups. With this information at hand I did a series of presentations at every exhibit, showing documentaries on the Amazon, a history of the oil industry, and a presentation of shamanism. I also did demonstrations to show the process of water gilding. The whole thing was the greatest creative and personal transformation of my life, and it all stemmed from an ayahuasca ceremony that gave me the vision to carry it out.

The transition from ayahuasca to San Pedro (or *huachuma* as it is also known) was natural for me, although the plants are totally different. Ayahuasca is taken in darkness and there is a journey into the internal world. My huachuma ceremonies, in contrast, were done in daylight and involved going out with an open heart to interact with the natural world. Both plants, however, are masters at teaching you to be in the present.

By the fall of 2009 my traveling exhibit had completed its North American tour and was on display in Cusco. I found myself in a relaxed, fulfilled state of mind. My host was a shaman who does weekly ceremonies from her home in the mountains just above the city. It is a stunning location and ideally suited for huachuma ceremonies. You open the front door and fifty meters away is an ancient Incan fertility temple known as the Temple of the Moon.

I had previously tried huachuma four different ways: powder, chips, cooked, and raw. Eating it raw was the most challenging but the most powerful, while cooked huachuma was a close second. The shaman I was working with cooked her huachuma down for many hours, which made it more concentrated and easier to drink. My first ceremony gave me an overwhelming love of Mother Earth—I could see her breathing, a living being. An abundance flowed out, everything that nurtured me came from her. I deeply felt the connection with her, which was a splash of grace in comparison to what I had seen externally in my travels.

In the late afternoon I went atop the Temple of the Moon to watch the sunset. I had recently started the practice of sun gazing and coming down from huachuma was the perfect time for it. I stared into the sun for the final five minutes before it reached the horizon, and as I watched it I went into trance.

In this state I began to see very specific geometry emanating from the sun: a sacred geometry. With my bare feet planted on the Earth and the sun entering my eyes, I felt I was a plant myself, between Mother Earth and Father Sun, there was nothing separate; all existed together along with the planets, stars, moon, galaxies all being one. A difficult moment to put into words, but I felt totally present. Every cell in my body was connected to it all, no past, no future, just present. I was in rapture with the beauty. I thought it would be a lovely thing to paint even though I am not a landscape painter.

Just before arriving in Cusco I'd been contacted by a hospital in the States inquiring about a possible commission. They wanted an artwork for the entrance of the hospital's heart center wing. They sent me a handful of words and phrases for the subject matter of the piece, but none of them except "nature" resonated with me.

Having visions such as those in San Pedro or ayahuasca helps tremendously for translating images into visual art and so does a strong sentiment, but without the visuals it can be more challenging to execute. In this case I got a strong feeling of a woman emerging from the Earth who was the Earth or a part of it anyway. In the background she was framed by the thing that gives me most peace: sunsets. That image eventually became the basis for the hospital commission.

While in Cusco I got into the practice of *despachos*. This is a ritual that is done to show gratitude to the Earth and involves burying totemic objects in the ground. If the despacho also involves your personal wishes and intentions, it is burned instead. I had done this kind of offering before, but never really knew about the fine workings of it. While I was staying in Cusco I did a despacho with a friend of a friend who taught me about the process. He was a Q'ero Indian, one of a small Quechua-speaking community who live at high altitudes in an extremely remote corner of the Peruvian Andes. An isolated people for five hundred years until the mid-1990s, the Q'ero traditionally worship Pachamama (Mother Earth) as well as other spirits of the mountains. My friend was a sweet man with an angelic demeanor and he shared everything with me. He even gave me the confidence to do the despacho ritual solo.

Later, four friends and I decided to take a trip to Tiahuanaco to see some sacred sites and do a huachuma ceremony. We got to the Bolivian border after an overnight bus to Puno and a combi ("rough bus") to Desaguaderos. There were complications with the paperwork for my British friend and me. My residency was in transit and I could have lost it by crossing the border. We thought about sneaking across, a suggestion of my Peruvian artist friend who had done it before, but five people was a bit more complicated than one and so we came up with another plan. We stayed in Peru and went north to Amaru Muru (in Quechua, "Willka Uta") outside of Juli on Lake Titicaca.

Amaru Muru is an ancient portal carved into a massive rock that resembles a dragon's back surfacing from the Earth. There was no one else there except for the local farmers who look after the place. We decided to stay and do a ceremony. It is said that if you leave all worldly attachments behind you can pass through the door to other dimensions.

Since I had a good handle on the intent of doing a despacho from the Q'ero, I figured this would be the best place for it. The energy of the site was already high vibration and with huachuma I imagined the intensity would be off the charts. We spoke with some of the local caretakers for permission to stay, and then asked for some wood for a fire later in the night as it was quite cold. They came back with dried cow dung that we could burn and we set up camp. Afterward we all went off on our own to clarify our intentions for the night. We went in different directions. I scaled the top of the rock almost directly above the door itself. It was near sunset so I did sun gazing and saw the same exact sacred geometry swirls emanating from the sun. I thought perhaps they are always there and I just never noticed them in daily life. Perhaps huachuma helps you to see the beauty that is always there.

My intent was clear: I was going to ask for guidance in making the commissioned hospital piece to create something that spoke of showing gratitude to Mother Earth, exactly what I experienced at the Temple of the Moon. It was clear to me that I was not going to be confined to the parameters given.

As I finished sun gazing I looked down to my left and there was a flat piece of rock and in the middle of it there was a little pool of water. I could see a star and a few clouds reflecting in it. The more I looked the less natural it seemed, and sure enough it had been put there by someone. I set my intentions again and put three coca seeds into the water as a trinity of Mother Earth, Father Cosmos, and connection with the Holy Spirit.

Later my friends and I met up at the campsite, lacking tents and sleeping bags, with just layers of ponchos and small backpacks, a casual and spontaneous camp. It was my first nighttime ceremony. We drank huachuma at nine o'clock and soon my friend Sampi was in full conversation, channeling all sorts of fascinating themes and theories. Normally I would jump right in with Sampi, but this time I was not drawn to conversation and kept to myself waiting for the proper moment to proceed with my despacho. A few tourists attempted to pass through the doorway but none succeeded.

After about two hours I got up and went to the door myself. My friend Alex and I spoke for a while and then I asked if I could do my despacho there. I had gathered the proper materials for the offering in Cusco—coca seeds, coca leaves, scallop shell, incense, and a beautiful hand-made alpaca cloth. I laid out the cloth on the inside base of the door and slowly began the process of infusing intent into every object as I had learned to do from the Q'ero, comprising every aspect of my making the artwork including envisioning it complete and the feeling of what it would be like. I spent about an hour and a half blowing my intentions on every symbol, including a crystal I had carried in my pocket for years. I find this very powerful: to give away something you are very attached to and do it with love.

I wrapped up the offering and tied it with string then sat there in silence listening to Sampi ranting in full trance, ridding himself of demons in the near distance. It was the twenty-first of December and a full moon night and the light was fantastic, but well after midnight the clouds started to come in. I went over to the burning dung to warm my body, taking my despacho with me. I sat by the fire for a while and when the moment felt right I set the offering on fire and allowed the air to carry my wishes.

I dozed by the fire, opening my eyes occasionally to look across Lake Titicaca and watch the lightning way off in the distance. I opened them later on and it seemed that the storm was closer. I dozed off again and the next time I looked the storm seemed right on top of us. I felt a few drops of rain and, though wanting to sleep and stay next to the heat, we were all compelled to grab our belongings and run to a small stone shed nearby. By the time we got there, hail and rain had engulfed the area, and we couldn't hear each other over the noise of the rain and hail on the tin roof. There was no floor, just a pile of stones, as if it were a stone shed to store stones.

We eventually went to sleep and awoke as the light came, without getting much sleep, although I felt an unusual fullness within me. I would not be aware of the full impact and power of the ceremony until a year later, however, when I was back in the States putting the final touches to the painting.

I returned to the Amazon to begin my studies for the piece. I did a sketch out of my head of the ceremony in Cusco and used that as a base. I had a few months to send a more refined sketch of the composition for the approval of the hospital officials who had commissioned it. From the huachuma it was evident what to paint, but it was still a commission and the hospital had given me parameters. I scrapped the parameters, however, and went with the inspiration of the ceremony.

I e-mailed them an image of the 2 x 4–foot drawing along with a breakdown of the meanings of the symbolism it contained. They approved the idea, were very pleased with it, and said it was exactly what they wanted. They even sent me a poem that one of the donors wrote from being inspired by seeing the drawing. They told me, "Just do it, we love it," and I was amazed at just how easy it was.

I started on a 4 x 8–foot version of the image next, using numerous studies of landscapes, figures, serpents, gilded symbols, and hummingbirds. I researched the sacred geometry I had seen around the sun as well, and found that it actually exists and has a name: twelve golden ratio spirals with radials.

There is inspiration, and there is another thing maintaining it throughout the making of art. From my experience with ayahuasca I believe that dieting is crucial for showing devotion toward what you are doing, representing the power that comes from giving up something you are attached to. The first couple of days may be uncomfortable, but in the long term it is much more rewarding. It had been almost two years since I had been back to the States, and after I arrived there I went out drinking for a few nights in the beginning. But I began to see the escapism and sadness that is inherent with alcohol. There were some people I had known since grade school and I don't think they ever took a break from it.

I saw in them a lot of negative emotional stuff, which came up more and more as the drinks continued, and for a few it was the same stuff they were talking about twenty years ago. I thought of Ganesh Baba who warned against the "beefy alcoholics" who ate and drank themselves to death, and observed that "a nonpsychedelic can never enlighten a psychedelic." That is to say, meat-eating drunks have little to teach a person who has taken psychedelics and (by extension) a person who lives a healthy life.

It was evident that I would have to adjust my lifestyle and stick with the 90 percent raw fruits and vegetables I had worked with back in Peru. Maintaining the inspiration for the art I was working on required devotion, and true devotion comes from within. The actual practice might seem to delve into the mundane, but I was ripe for the mundane. This was contrary to all those years in Italy where drinking wine and celebrating Bacchus was almost a daily ritual, but that energy did not work any more.

The raw food approach has been a lifestyle for me for about ten years now, and I find it works wonderfully with plant medicine. Two blocks from my rented studio were friends who have a healing center and a full-time raw food chef, and they offered me open doors. They introduced me to phytoplankton and the mineral indium and a few other nutritional delights. I brought back kilos of freeze-dried acai and aguaje powder from the jungle, two outstanding superfoods.

I gave myself three months to complete the hospital piece. I set up my temporary studio and got to work. I purchased the materials, prepared the wood panel, gessoed it, and while waiting for curing for the panel I would make subtle changes and refinements to the cartoon. By the first month I had the panel etched and gilded and was ready to begin the painting. Normally I work in natural daylight and the studio was big but not ideal for this, an old house with little light, so I got natural daylight bulbs to compensate.

I got into a rhythm taking care of odds and ends during the day, and then painting in the evening and through the night, finishing between 3:00 a.m. and dawn depending on my energy. Then I would sleep until noon and have a superfood smoothie and do it all again. As long as my nutrition was sufficient I did not lose inspiration, but there is a fine balance between inspiration and burning yourself out. I have forty-five years of experience of going to extremes, but what I practiced here was a constant, steady stream of inspiration and I was always open to take breaks when necessary. I motored through the first nine weeks of work, and then as the painting got more complex I began to slow down. (When starting a painting I usually paint 80 percent of the time and observe for 20 percent, blocking in the bigger images, but near the end that gets reversed.)

It was not until the twenty-first of December rolled around again that I thought back to the despacho I had made at Amaru Muru exactly a year before. Over the last three weeks of work until the painting was finished I had been gobsmacked at where all my energy had come from, almost looking at the work and wondering how it had got there. There had been some challenging moments in it but on the whole it turned out to be the most fluid, joyful piece I had ever created, and there is no doubt that the spirit of huachuma was with me as I made it.

16
San Pedro and the Healing of the Divine Mother

Peter Sterling

Since I was a small child, I have been mystified by the standing stones and pyramids of the ancient sacred sites of the world. Their enigmatic presence has captivated my imagination along with millions of other people around the world.

It seems as though I have been on a quest in one form or another to travel to these mystic places in search of ancient knowledge and spiritual insight, and I have been lucky enough to experience firsthand some of the most famous of these mysterious wonders of the world. From the Mayan jungle lands of the Yucatán to the desert lands of the pharaohs and the stone circles of the British Isles, I have quested to discover their hidden meanings and the sacred knowledge they have held for millennia. Out of all the sacred sites I have visited, however, there is one that has inspired me most: Machu Picchu.

Rising from the veiled rain clouds that surround its lofty peaks, this mountain kept its presence hidden to the world for centuries until its discovery in 1911. Now a symbol of the mystery and magic of the

311

ancient world of the Inca, its terraced ruins and magnificent stonework have stood for centuries and still inspire modern seekers to marvel at its architectural uniqueness and rarefied spiritual atmosphere.

In the winter of 2009 I found myself part of a small, intimate group of people being led on a shamanic journey through the sacred lands of the Inca in Peru. This was to be a transformational journey. Not only would we explore the ancient cities of the Inca and all the wonder and mystery that they hold, but participate in shamanic ceremonies where we would ingest the powerful plant medicines used by indigenous shamans to cross over into the realm of spirit and soul.

Although I had been familiar with the plant teacher ayahuasca before coming on this trip, my primary interest now was to experience its companion medicine, *wachuma,* or as it is more commonly known, San Pedro. I had felt a connection with this plant for many years as we share the same name—Peter—and I have been referred to at times by the name Saint Peter because I play the heavenly instrument of the harp and create transformational musical experiences inspired by the angels and heavenly realms.

So for many years I felt an intuitive connection to this powerful medicine plant of Peru. I sensed that when the time was right I would have an experience with it and through it would no doubt be transformed in one way or another. I'd heard from people familiar with this medicine that it is psychedelically similar to peyote, which is used by Native Americans and also part of the cactus family. Apparently both San Pedro and peyote share the main active ingredient of mescaline, which is a highly light-infused psychedelic that tends to bring a shimmering brightness to all the eye beholds. Whether one is looking within or outward to external reality, mescaline brings a halo of light to all the eye perceives.

I had tried peyote many years before while living in Arizona and had very powerful and unusual experiences with it. In the books by Carlos Castaneda, who speaks of his apprenticeship under the shaman don Juan, there are many references to the use of peyote and connecting with the deva of the plant, Mescalito. In my experiences with peyote I recall very clearly having the experience of meeting with the spirit of the plant, which seemed to communicate with me in an inner dialogue that brought me to various realizations of my spiritual process and personal relationships. It was healing and illuminating in many ways. Now it was time for me to connect with peyote's cousin, the great San Pedro.

We arrived in Cusco and made our way to our accommodation for the next few days, a little hostel called Casa de La Gringa, a quaint and funky international hostel owned and run by a beautiful South African woman called Lesley or, as she is known in the area, La Gringa. It is at this casa that people come to connect with the powerful plant medicine and teacher San Pedro. La Gringa came to the area thirteen years ago on her personal journey to explore the lands of the Inca. It was on her trip to Peru that she was first introduced to San Pedro. Her experience was life changing and inspired her to learn more about the medicine and share it with others, so that they could transform their lives as she had. She ended up buying a hostel in Cusco and creating a place where people can connect with the sacred medicine.

I remember walking in the front door and down the hall into the main gathering area. Immediately my attention was drawn to a hand-painted sign with an image of a beautiful flowering cactus that said "San Pedro journeys." At first I was a bit surprised by this openness, but subsequently discovered that San Pedro and ayahuasca are both legal in Peru and ceremonies are advertised around many of the cities and towns of Peru. As I walked around and looked in the various rooms of the casa, to my surprise I saw a Paraguayan harp in the corner of the TV room! I took this as a very good sign and immediately felt at ease, as if angels were guiding my journey.

After a couple of days exploring Cusco and acclimatizing to its altitude of eleven thousand feet, it was time for our first medicine experience at another retreat owned by La Gringa in the hills above Cusco. This special hacienda is called the Mountain House and sits adjacent to the ancient Incan Temple of the Moon, an enigmatic ancient structure carved out of solid rock by ancient shamans, where elaborate ceremonies would be performed at the time of the full moon. As the moon would rise in the night sky, its light shone down into an inner sanctum of the cave and illuminated an altar carved by hand many centuries ago, where sacrifices would be performed to honor the lunar goddess.

We were visiting the area during December, the rainy season of the Southern Hemisphere, and the hills and mountainsides were green and lush. It was the perfect place for us to discover the secret truths of our souls.

We arrived at the Mountain House at approximately 11:00 a.m., and after settling in we commenced our ceremony with San Pedro. La Gringa had prepared a beautiful spot for us in her garden, a protected, walled sanctuary with many plants and colorful flowers to delight the eyes and senses. There were areas on the periphery where the San Pedro cactus grew in patches and clusters. San Pedro is a single-stalk cactus that grows tall in a beautiful star-formation pattern. Some grow in six-, seven-, eight-, and nine-pointed stars along its central axis of growth, and La Gringa told us that the different numbers of stars have an effect on its potency and visionary properties. Today we would be drinking a seven-star cactus, which according to La Gringa is her favorite to work with.

We gathered around an altar space in the garden where several colorful blankets had been laid out for us to sit on. Then, after a brief talk and a few short prayers to the spirit of San Pedro, we drank our glasses of the unusual light-green liquid, thick and similar to the juice of aloe vera. It had a slightly bitter taste and was somewhat pungent, but it went down relatively easy for me, although for some it was more difficult.

In our group that day there were four of us including La Gringa. There was Isabella, our group leader and tour guide from Southern California, an attractive blond woman in her midforties; Mary, a devoted wife and healer also from Southern California; and Ken, a fortyish unmarried architect also from Southern California. Ken was new to shamanic work and was at first a bit hesitant about using medicine plants, as he had no previous experience with them. Yet after hearing everyone's amazing stories he became eager and ready to try them. He was a good-natured fellow who spoke very good Spanish and had become our unofficial interpreter for most of our journey.

After about thirty or forty minutes the medicine began to take effect, and I noticed that the colors around me began to look more vibrant and intense as I gazed at the flowers and plants in the garden. I could also feel subtle changes in my perceptions as I looked at the plants and the blue sky above me with its wispy clouds that began to resemble animals, people, and angelic beings. Quite naturally we all found our own little place to sit and come in to this new energy that was quickly becoming more and more evident with each passing moment. I could feel its pulsations as the medicine began to become stronger.

I had heard that San Pedro comes in waves that rise up in great swells that overtake you and carry you deeper and further with each passing set. A wave will come, rise to a crest of intensity, and then subside gently into a period of relative calm and ease. This is what was happening to me. With each wave I would get more energized and activated. I felt the need to move some of this energy by walking, and so I ventured out into the open landscape to explore the Temple of the Moon and its surrounding valleys.

The day was cool and rain was threatening, so I bundled up in my fleece jacket and waterproof and as I walked and took in the view of my surroundings, I found it difficult to hold back a grin. I was definitely getting very altered. Visually I was overcome by the beauty of what my eyes were seeing. There seemed to be light emanating from all the plants and emerald hillsides that surrounded me. Before coming on this trip I had lost my expensive Ray-Ban sunglasses. I took this as a sign that perhaps I was not to have sunglasses on this journey so that I might be able to fully absorb and receive the light and color of the Andean countryside. And now as I stood there looking out on this gorgeous view with its vibrant waves of energy that seemed to permeate my whole body, I realized why I was not wearing sunglasses: to me, it was because they would have blocked out the ultraviolet spectrum of light, which corresponds to the third eye and the crown chakra. It seemed to me that the vibrancy of the color was very rich in the ultraviolet spectrum of light frequencies, which were coming into my retina to the optic nerve and stimulating and awakening parts of my neocortex. I could feel my pupils dilating in order to take in more light, as if my eyes were feasting on a rich banquet of luminescence and iridescent Technicolor pulsations from the rocks, plants, grass, and hillsides as well as the cobalt blue sky overhead. It truly was like being in a psychedelic dreamscape.

At one point I began to have visions of past times as I looked at the Temple of the Moon, intricately carved with stairways and altar places. I had a remembrance or imagination of ancient times when there would be large celebrations where all the people would take San Pedro during the various seasonal festivals. I imagined colorfully adorned people standing on all the rocks across the valley and dancing to the music of drums and flutes that reverberated throughout the valley and highlands. This must have been the original "rainbow gathering!" I could feel the joy and festive atmosphere of this ancient celebration.

As this beautiful vision intensified I was overcome with a feeling of being embraced by the Earth Spirit or Pachamama as she is known in the Incan cosmology. It felt like the feminine spirit of the Earth embracing me with beauty and healing energy. I could feel her and almost hear her voice as she spoke to me like a mother to a child. I felt her desire to nurture and take care of me and provide me with the sustenance of her harvest. I also felt her pain because humanity had forgotten her conscious spirit and could no longer hear her voice. After decades of environmental degradation and destruction, Pachamama felt almost at the end of her capacity to deal with this destruction, yet she continued to embrace and love me unconditionally. The knowledge of this was very healing to me on many levels, and I felt a renewed connection to the planet and her spirit.

I then climbed a high rock outcrop that overlooked the valley. From there I had a commanding view of the Temple of the Moon with the twenty-thousand-feet Andean peaks in the distance. It was breathtaking! I sat there in contemplation and experienced intensifying waves of hallucinogenic euphoria, but I also began to struggle to catch my breath. Two days before I left for Peru I had contracted a respiratory infection with the symptoms of a raspy cough and runny nose, and I had been struggling with my breathing ever since I arrived in Cusco. Now as I sat on my eagle's perch my symptoms began to intensify and my breathing became more rapid and difficult.

Instinctively, I reached for the small bag of coca leaves in my back-pack, which supposedly counteract altitude sickness. Chewing the leaves up quickly I sucked their bitter green juices in the hope that they would bring me relief. Unfortunately it did not work quickly enough, and I became concerned that I was having an asthma attack like I used to as a little boy. To compound this I started to feel my heart race as I became overcome with anxiety from my shortness of breath. Over the years I have had various episodes with my heart and I wondered now if perhaps I would have a heart attack. I decided at that point that it might be wise for me to make my way back to the Mountain House. I did not want to be alone in case I went into some sort of critical situation.

Focusing on deep breathing and staying relaxed I did my best to remain calm as I made my way back to the sanctuary of the garden. As I entered through the heavy wooden gate I could see the others from the group sitting and laying in various places around the garden, all deep in their own experience. I immediately went to La Gringa and told her my predicament and she fetched some cans of oxygen that she kept for emergencies like this. As I inhaled I immediately felt a relief and my breathing began to stabilize.

As I sat there trying to regain composure I started to have memories of childhood. I remembered how when I was a small child, maybe five or six all the way up to my teenage years, my mother, who was a heavy smoker, would light up in the car with all the windows closed forcing me to breathe her smoke. I developed asthma when I was seven or eight due to this unfortunate situation. For years I struggled with my breath-ing, especially when I would exercise. My parents sent me to doctors who prescribed various inhalers that I would have to carry with me and use from time to time. Not once did my doctors or my parents consider that perhaps my symptoms were caused from breathing the exhaust from my mother's smoking. As these memories resurfaced now, I experienced an emotional release and I began to get angry and cry from the memory of my childhood struggle. I went with it realizing that perhaps it was just "old stuff" being cleared out of my emotional body.

After a few moments I got up and moved inside the house and found a comfortable place to sit. I told La Gringa that I felt like I was dying, as I was overcome with more waves of anxiety and fear due to my problems in breathing and the potential I felt for a heart episode. She looked at me and smiled and said, "Yes, perhaps you are dying!" I understood in that moment that this is the teaching of San Pedro. Perhaps I was meant to have just this transformational death experience. I surrendered to the increasing waves of anxiety and stress and asked La Gringa to put on some music that might help calm my nerves. Instinctively I requested the music of Deva Premal, who is a beautiful channel for the divine feminine through sacred mantra and Sanskrit chant music. As her angelic voice began to sing to my soul, I brought my hands to my heart in prayer and embraced the feeling of dying that continued to overtake me. Once again I felt the spirit of Pachamama holding me and I began to connect more deeply with the spirit of the Earth, with my own mother, and with all the past loves of my life.

I'd recently ended a three-year relationship and my heart was still tender from the end of our affair. I could feel an upwelling of emotion at this, connected to feelings of remorse for this ended love and every other ending over the years. I began to cry healing tears of deep release as I lay on the floor in fetal position. La Gringa watched over me and Isabella stood by as well as my crying intensified and I began to wail and sob uncontrollably. Even though it was painful to access this type of emotion it also felt incredibly healing. I realized I had not cried like this in many years and I embraced the opportunity to access the pain that was obviously stored within me.

After perhaps fifteen or twenty minutes of this I looked up and saw La Gringa looking down at me with a gentle smile and eyes full of compassion and understanding. Sitting up, I asked if she would hold me. She said yes and I moved to the couch where I laid my head in her lap and began to sob more deeply than before, releasing the greatest pain that I have ever felt. This went on for perhaps an hour. Occasionally I would look up at La Gringa and Isabella with snot running down my face and my eyes red with tears. I was a wreck! Yet also I was grateful for what was to be one of the deepest emotional healing experiences of my life. As I lay in La Gringa's lap and she stroked my head I felt the comfort and nurturing of a Divine Mother like I had never had before. I had no conscious memory of ever being held like this by my own mother or any other woman. It was wonderful and liberating and healing at the deepest levels.

After a while my tears subsided and a feeling of deep peace overcame me. Thank God it was over. I felt cleansed, healed, and renewed. It was like being reborn. I looked up with a feeling of gratitude for what had just transpired and happily said, "Yay!" I told La Gringa that I thought the pain I had just released I would take to my grave, but that the alchemical combination of the wachuma, the garden healing sanctuary, and the spiritual presence of Pachamama had all combined to facilitate one of the deepest healing experiences I'd ever had. I had waited many years for this moment but now I knew that I was forever changed.

After a short period of time I collected myself and decided to take another walk out into the beautiful green countryside. I strolled through tranquil valleys with trickling streams where the birds sang as the sun broke through the dancing clouds to shine warm golden rays on my face. My senses were enlivened to where it seemed I was seeing, smelling, and hearing everything in a way I never had before. There was a vividness and aliveness to things, and I felt filled with peace, joy, and love like the radiance of a divine and holy light.

As I walked, each step had the feeling of sacred presence, and my soul seemed present in my body like never before. I felt extraordinarily and deeply connected to the Earth and sky and to all of God's creation. It radiated from my heart in all directions simultaneously. It was like I had been awakened and rewoven into the very fabric of God through my newly enlivened senses. How thankful I am for that healing and for the grace of God, the Divine Mother, and San Pedro.

As the sun began to set over the horizon and the stars began to twinkle in the sky, our group gathered again while hot soup and fresh bread were served to us after a long day of fasting. One by one we shared our beautiful stories of the healing brought by the sacred medicine. Everyone was radiant with the spirit of love and transformation.

Looking at one another we realized how lucky we were to be able to share such a potent moment in our lives. Looking at La Gringa I felt tremendous appreciation for her medicine work and wondered how many others had sat at this table feeling the same as I did now. I also sensed the unbroken lineage of shamanic teachers and guides that have used this medicine through the centuries to heal the hearts, minds, and souls of men and women who have found their way to San Pedro.

I knew in that moment that some day I would share this story with others and hopefully inspire them to journey to their own healing San Pedro experience. As I share this story with you now perhaps you may hear the call of the ancient ones and the spirit of wachuma. May you, too, be guided by the angels and great beings of light and love who encourage us now more than ever to surrender all that does not serve us so that we might make room in our hearts for the illumination of divine love. This is my prayer and my wish for you.

17
The Songs of San Pedro

Ross Heaven

The shamans of Peru insist that plants are alive, sentient, aware, and that their intention is to assist the growth of human consciousness. They are not only able but desirous of helping human beings, easing the flow of energy in certain situations, and providing us with more evolutionary potential. Plants are the conduits for spirit, healing, and "good luck."

This is exciting news if we choose to believe it—but they are also extraordinary claims. To compound the problem, if you were to ask the shamans (as I have done many times) how they know that plants behave in this way or have these qualities, "personalities," and intentions, it is likely that they will say simply that "their spirits told us." For the Western mind this can be rather deflating. We'd like proof before we place our trust in a statement like that.

The more that you work with plants and drink the great teachers like San Pedro, the more you come to understand and appreciate that the shaman's view is fundamentally, absolutely, directly, and very obviously true. It can be frustrating for those starting out in this work, however, since it seems to make no sense and is in opposition to the Western rational model and to the way our minds have been taught to explore the world and receive information from it. It would help us if there were scientific evidence to support the assertions of the shamans that plants have personalities of their own or can communicate with us and act purposefully. Luckily there is.

RESEARCH INTO PLANT COMMUNICATION

Cleve Backster was a scientist working in the field of lie detection and interrogation techniques, specializing in polygraph testing, who decided more or less out of curiosity one day to attach the electrodes of a lie detector to the leaf of a plant to see if the device was sensitive enough to pick up reactions from a nonhuman subject. Further, he wondered if he might elicit some reaction from the plant if he burned the leaf to which the electrodes were attached.[1]

As soon as he thought this, before he had even picked up a match, there was a dramatic peak in the tracing pattern on the polygraph chart (a signature that he would come to recognize as fear). Intrigued by this he continued his research, testing almost thirty different plants in the same way: attaching electrodes to them and thinking of some action he might take toward them. The results were always the same.

It was significant that the plants reacted before any action was taken, leading Backster to conclude that not only are plants as sensitive (or more so) as human beings but are capable of precognition and able to read emotions and intentions because there is a form of psychic connection or affinity between plants and people. This might be interesting for further study in terms of the current research into San Pedro and precognition by David Luke and others. What if plants are naturally capable of precognition as Backster's results suggest and by drinking certain plants like San Pedro that quality passes at least temporarily into us. . . ?

As his work progressed, Backster realized that plants react not just to threats but to presences or movements in their environment. He demonstrated to a group of Yale University students, for example, that the movement of a spider in the same room as a plant caused changes in the trace patterns of a polygraph to which that plant was attached. The plant had a sense of the impending results and was attuned to intention before the movement itself. "The spider's decision . . . was being picked up by the plant," said Backster.

Backster's other results show that plants have memory, emotions, and very humanlike reactions as well as "psychic" abilities. In one of his experiments, six students randomly drew lots to see which of them would destroy one of two plants in a room. The person chosen would commit the killing in secret so not even Backster and the other students knew his identity. The only witness would be a second plant in the room. When the destruction was done, Backster attached a polygraph to the second plant and paraded his students in front of it. The needle went off the scale when the murderer appeared.

In a kinder experiment, Backster demonstrated the love and empathy between a plant and its owner. One day he accidentally cut his finger and noticed that a plant being monitored demonstrated a stress reaction, as if it was experiencing his own pain and shock at the sight of his blood. Using this perceived affinity as the basis for his research, Backster then walked to a different building some blocks away and directed loving thoughts toward the plant. The polygraph recording when he returned showed a heightened trace as the plant picked up his intentions.

Even when the plants were locked in a lead container the results were the same. Whatever created empathy between plant and human came from something outside the electromagnetic spectrum.

Another lucky accident led Backster to explore this further. One evening he was about to feed a raw egg to his dog and noticed that as he broke the shell one of his plants reacted strongly. Curious to see what the plant might be experiencing or what feelings the egg was transmitting, he attached another egg to a galvanometer and monitored it for nine hours.

What he got was a trace corresponding to the normal heartbeat of a chicken embryo even though the egg was unfertilized. His conclusion could only be that there is a life force or energy within all things, which exists first in a nonmaterial plane before a physical being even comes into existence—for want of a better word, a soul.

This, of course, is redolent of the shaman's notion that all things derive from spirit, that thoughtforms exist as a potential in their true state before they are ever made manifest, or more simply, that "the world is as you dream it." The world (and all things seen and unseen) has soul and we can connect with this and draw from it to create our own reality by giving birth on the material plane to the forces of the universe, shaped as we will.

THE IMPORTANCE OF LOVE

Another researcher, Alfred Vogel, brings us closer to an understanding of the nature of this soul through the work of one of his students.[2] As an experiment, his student picked two leaves from a plant and took them into her house. Each day she projected love toward one and the intention that it would live, despite giving it no water and leaving it on her bedside table; the other leaf she completely ignored.

A month later Vogel went to her home to photograph the results. The leaf that was ignored was dry and decaying, as you would expect from any leaf that had been out of water that long, but the second was as fresh as the day it was picked, even though its circumstances were no better. The essence of the soul of the universe, then—the energetic force that Backster discovered—is love. This is what sustains life.

"Plants . . . may be blind, deaf and dumb in the human sense," said Vogel, "but there is no doubt in my mind that they are extremely sensitive. . . . They radiate forces that are beneficial to man. One can feel those forces! They feed into one's own force field, which in turn feeds energy back to the plant."

Vogel, like all of the shamans I have ever met, believed that respect for plants is also vital for effective communication between our species. He remarked of scientists conducting experiments with plants that:

> If they approach the experimentation in a mechanistic way and don't enter into mutual communication with their plants and treat them as friends, they will fail. Hundreds of laboratory workers around the world are going to be . . . frustrated and disappointed . . . until they appreciate that empathy between plant and human is the key and learn how to establish it. . . . The experimenters must become part of their experiments.

SACRED SONGS

If you can allow from this evidence that plants can and do communicate with us and have our best interests at heart, it becomes easier to understand the shaman's contention that they can also transmit their wisdom and healing to us. One of the ways in which they do so, which is consistent across all shamanic cultures that work with plants, is via song.

Icaros, for example, are magical chants or melodies that are whistled, sung, or whispered during an ayahuasca ceremony to control and balance the energies in the room, or they may be sung directly into the energy field of a person who is to be healed, to provoke new insights, healing, and a new alignment of energies.

Tarjos perform the same function in San Pedro ceremonies, where the *huachumero* will use them to call helpful spirits, to ensure that energy flows correctly through the ceremonial space, or as the patient stands before the mesa, as a healing tool to realign and smooth the lines of energy within the patient's luminous body.

Many *curanderos* begin their ceremonies with a tarjo that they sing (or have sung for them by their assistants) in order to purify themselves and create a connection between them and God before they start their healing work or approach the *artes* of the *mesa.* This is "The Chant

of Eduardo," which was used by Eduardo Calderon specifically for this
purpose:

> *I go along giving a good enchantment*
> *A good remedy from my bench [the mesa]*
> *Saint Cyprian*
> *Who from the first years*
> *With the three wise men*
> *Cabbalist and surgeon*
> *With my good San Pedro*
> *All the potions*
> *Of dead man's bones, ancients*
> *Snake powder, antimony and minerals*
> *Are all accounted*
> *All the ailments of the entire body*
> *All spiritual shocks, hypnotism, suggestions*
> *Are all accounted*
> *Saint Cyprian with rattle in hand*
> *And his glass with the remedy*
> *Well purified*
> *He accounted in his great times*
> *From the Huaringana I go playing [Las Huaringas are*
> *   the sacred lakes from where many curanderos take*
> *   their power]*
> *Curer, justifier*
> *And at my game*
> *Where beautiful Shimbe are accounted [Shimbe are*
> *   the sacred lagoons of the north, home to some of the*
> *   most famous sorcerers in Peru]*
> *Play!*[3]

Calderon's tarjo is more complicated than many and certainly more
complex than most Amazonian icaros, which are often just a simple list

of plants. He calls on the powers of Saint Cyprian (lines 3–6), a primary ally and guardian, for example, and refers to him as a "cabbalist and surgeon." According to history, Cyprian was born in Carthage to pagan parents who dedicated his childhood to service of the Greek god Apollo. At the age of seven he was sent to apprentice with healers and magicians, and at age fifteen he began his studies with the seven great sorcerers of his age, eventually becoming a magus himself. His practices included calling the spirits of the dead and bewitching individuals through the use of incantations and potions. In his writings he tells of calling demons and commanding them. His conversion to Christianity came in middle age, but he was always a controversial figure within the church, and even today is regarded as the (unofficial) patron of sorcerers.

What Calderon is invoking here, therefore, is not just the saint but his powers to summon helpful spirits and to control and banish demons in cases of spirit possession and exorcism that the shaman may be faced with.

In lines 7–11 Calderon lists (and so "brings to life") the healing tools of the mesa, beginning with San Pedro, of course, then "all the potions . . . dead man's bones . . . minerals," and so on. The potions referred to are plant medicines, *aguas,* and other magical formulas available to him for curing, the spirits of which he knows; the dead man's bones refer to sacred *huacas* (power objects) that may indeed be bones or cemetery dust, or some relic taken from a holy site. The bones of the ancestors (especially if they were shamans or holy men themselves) contain great power, and because they are taken from graveyards this power extends to interventions in matters of life and death. All of these, says Calderon, are "accounted"— that is, awakened by his chant and brought into play.

He next accounts for the body and its ailments, in effect claiming mastery over them. Finally (in lines 19–23), Calderon talks of "playing," a simple word that contains a number of meanings and nuances. Firstly, to play means to cure, but it also recognition of the fact that life itself is play, a "game," and that illness, in a sense, is a role we have chosen for ourselves. This corresponds to the Andean concept of life as a flow and exchange of energies, and the idea that as individuals we must take at least some responsibility for everything that happens to us, as we are the ones who attract and connect to these flows of energy. As we saw earlier in reference to illnesses, for example, even in the case of a magical attack such as *envidia* where a rival is jealous of us and sends bad energies our way in order to harm us, we must ask ourselves why. What have we done to deserve this? Perhaps we were not humble enough about our good fortune and so invited the jealousy that now affects us?

Finally, the word *play* is recognition that, no matter what may befall us, life is beautiful, an adventure, a game, and even in our direst moments we must be aware of this, because to take life seriously is to invite ill health, depression, and a diminution of the soul by becoming too attached to particular outcomes instead of allowing the energy of life to flow.

A lot of information and power is, therefore, contained in Calderon's opening purification. Contrast this with the following icaro from an Amazonian ayahuascero[4] (Javier Arevelo).

> *No me dejes no me dejes*
> *Madre mia naturaleza*
> *No me dejes no me dejes*
> *Madre mia naturaleza*
> *Por que vas i ti me dejares*
> *Moriria o de las penas*
> *Llantos y desesperaciones*
> *Madre mia naturaleza*
> *Si tu tienes el don de la*
> *Santa purificacion en ti manos*
> *Benditas madre naturaleza*

The English translation:

Don't leave me, don't leave me
My Mother Nature
Don't leave me, don't leave me
My Mother Nature
For if you will leave me
I would die of the pain
Tears of desperation
My Mother Nature
Yes, you have the gift of
Sacred purification in your hands
Blessed mother nature

It is a simple prayer to Mother Nature and calls for her support during ceremony, but there is no complexity to it and no invocations or appeals beyond a general one to nature as a whole. Most icaros (and many tarjos) are in fact like this, so Calderon's can in many ways be regarded as the exception instead of the rule.

HOW THE SONGS COME TO BE

The songs of the shaman are energetic forces charged with positive healing intent that the curandero stores inside his body and is able to transmit to another person or into the medicine he is preparing so that this energy is ingested when the mixture is drunk.

The most powerful are taught by the spirit of plant allies or artes that the shaman works with, and the longer his relationship with a particular plant continues, the more songs he may learn from it and the more potent they will be. Typically, the relationship with the plant ally is created through the process of dieting it.

For example, in 2010 I spent several months in Peru with the intention of beginning a more formal San Pedro apprenticeship. During an early ceremony I asked the cactus what other plants I should get to know in order to become a more effective shaman.

A whole range were presented to me but it is never a good idea to diet more than one at a time. You need to spend time with a single plant, just as you would if you were getting to know a new human friend. This can be frustrating when you want to develop your skills with a number of allies, but there simply is no shortcut (shamans say that you must have the patience of a saint to do plant medicine work). So I began the process of dieting one of these plants: Chanca Piedra.

All plants have an essence—a spiritual healing intent—that underlies and is deeper than their purely medicinal properties. Chanca Piedra (also known as Stone Breaker or Shatterstone) can be used for—and is highly effective in—breaking up stones in the body, such as gallstones or kidney stones. In keeping with the Doctrine of Signatures its leaves also look like small round stones.* This in fact is one way in which shamans come to understand the purpose of different plants: according to the doctrine they will tell you by their appearance. The spiritual intention of Chanca Piedra is to crush and break through, and it will do this energetically too: freeing patients from blockages caused by an accumulation of negative energies, which might over time become denser, leading to physical problems such as kidney stones. As important to me in my choice of plant was that Saint Peter (San Pedro) is known as "the Rock," the foundation on which the Christian Church (or more fundamentally, our connection to God) is built.

During the diet you are forbidden certain foodstuffs and activities that might interfere with your ingestion and integration of the spirit of the healing plant, which you take each day in the form of a tea or infusion. Food is especially bland and there can be no sex or alcohol. The diet continues for a minimum of seven days, and because

---

*The Doctrine of Signatures was first postulated by Paracelus, a sixteenth-century alchemist, plant doctor, and revolutionary philosopher, and has been confirmed over centuries of herbal practice. There is more on the subject in my book *Plant Spirit Shamanism* (Destiny Books, 2006). —R.H.

the food offered is unappealing I usually prefer to fast throughout it. For seven days following that there is an after-diet where slightly more flavorsome foods can be eaten but some (alcohol, strong spices, etc.) are still off the menu.

The diet is a commitment, therefore: a promise to the plant and a contract you make between you and it that if you keep your part of the bargain the plant will keep its and offer its power to you so that in ceremony by calling on it and directing its energy toward another, you will be able, in this case, to break through the blockages within a patient that are causing misfortune or ill health.

The direction of these energies is through song, and what you therefore hope for during a diet is that at some point a song will be given to you by the plant. My song for Chanca Piedra arrived on day four of the diet, but like many it is still a work in progress, my connection to it (and through it to the power of the plant) deepening over time.

> *Shatterstone*
> *Chanca Piedra*
> *Encantos! Encantos! [Encantos are magical stones*
> *   with the power to cure disease]*
> *I am your gravity*
> *I hold you*
> *So they [or she or he] in front of me shall be free*
> *Shatterstone*
> *Chanca Piedra*
> *Encantos! Encantos!*
> *I am your gravity*
> *I crush you*
> *So they in front of me shall be free*
> *O medicina medicina*
> *Medicina for the soul*
> *O medicina medicina*
> *Medicina for the heart*

O medicina medicina
Medicina for the mind
O medicina medicina
Medicina for the self
Shatterstone
Chanca Piedra
Encantos! Encantos!
I am your gravity
I hold you
So they in front of me shall be free

In this way shamans have precise and specific songs for many different plants and purposes—to cure snake bites (Jergon Sacha), or to clarify visions during ceremonies (Piri Piri, perhaps), to communicate with the spirit world (Ahlbaca might be one plant option), or even to win the love of a woman. *Huarmi* songs—from the Quechua word *huarmi* (which, loosely, means "woman") are of this type. There are also songs (*canciones de la piedra*) that are taught to the shaman by *encantos* (special healing stones that offer spiritual protection) and songs to the spirits of the elements, such as *canciones del viento,* that call on the spirit of the wind. Others, such as the *ayaruna*—from the Quechua words *aya* (spirit or dead) and *runa* (people)—are sung to invoke the "spirit people," the souls of dead shamans, so they may help with healings during a ceremony.

To connect with the power of the artes on his mesa and call them to assist during ceremony, Michael Simonato (featured in chapter 4) has another approach, which is similar to that of Calderon and other Peruvian healers.

Artes (arts) are power objects that have a specific meaning and intention for the shaman. As described in earlier chapters, they may be mundane things in themselves (stones, bones, etc.) but their symbolic and spiritual content is impressive to the shaman and enables him to connect with power in order to do his work. Or they may be huacas from sacred sites or other specific locations that are generally accepted to have spiritual power (such as water from Las Huaringas, the sacred lakes, or the relics of wise men).

A shaman collects these objects, sometimes intentionally, sometimes because he is called to do so when the items simply present themselves and suggest their powers and applications to him as he is going about his normal business. While walking in the countryside, for example, with no intention of seeking power, he may be inexplicably drawn to a rock or a feather and, acting on impulse or the whispers of spirit, he will take it and explore later the reasons for its calling.

For Simonato, this exploration takes the form of a shamanic journey to the spirit of the arte. On a trip to Peru in 2010, he advised me to do the same with my own mesa. "I drink San Pedro first," he said:

> Then I focus on each of the objects in turn, blending with them so I hear their particular spirit—like hearing from a friend—and that tells me their personality. Then I focus on the mesa as a whole so I understand the connections between these things and how they work together. After that [in ceremony] I know exactly what arte to use for any need that arises because I understand what these objects intend to do.

Following from this, Simonato has developed a divinatory practice for the start of a ceremony (which I have also now adopted). He lays out his mesa and then throws coca leaves into the air above it. Where they land (in which quadrant of the mesa, that is, whether the East, for me representing the body, the South for the emotions, the West for mental healing, or the North for the spirit) and which artes they touch gives him a focus for the day, telling him how the healing will proceed with San Pedro and the type of energy he needs to hold.

THE CREATIVE NATURE OF THE SHAMAN AND HIS SONGS

We began this chapter with a look at some of the research that offers credibility to the idea that plants are sentient and able to communicate with us and through this to teach us certain things about ourselves or pass on information that we might use in healing.

Findings like this can be reassuring to the Western mind, offering scientific support for the idea that such things are possible. But to Peruvian shamans such studies and their results are at best blindingly obvious and therefore unnecessary or, more likely, so limited in their discoveries that they are mostly irrelevant.

Plant shamans were, after all, the first technologists and scientists of plant consciousness; they have learned across millennia through their experience, experiments, trial and error, by testing hypotheses and taking note of healing results, that plants are conscious and willing to help us. They have moved on from self-evident truth and are now examining the specific ways in which particular plants are able to assist. Modern science, by contrast, since it is only a few hundred years old, is playing catch-up and has a long way to go. It has become the predominant worldview of our age and everything we do or "know" must now be "proven" in its terms, but it is at best reinventing the wheel when it comes to plant knowledge, because this wisdom already exists in our shamans.

The real point of difference for science and shamanism is that, for the shaman, making contact with his allies—whether they are plants or artes or some other spirit such as Saint Cyprian who can guide him in his work—connection is first an act of creativity and an application of the creative imagination.

The first step in his process is to clear the mind and enter a state of dreaming. The diet is one way to facilitate this. By depriving ourselves of food and breaking the routines and habits of our normal lives we are catapulted (gently or not so gently) into an Otherwordly state where our focus is on the spirit we are attempting to meet and we are open to suggestions from it. Simonato's idea of journeying to the spirit of the artes is the same approach. In both cases intention is key. A commitment is made and an act of faith put into practice that the spirits will communicate with us and we will learn from this contact.

The question arises of course (especially for Westerners): But is it real—are the spirits really talking to us?—or is it just our imagination?

For the shaman there is no difference. Since we are all aspects of God and God is *the* Creator—the great creative pool of awareness that suffuses the entire universe (including us since we are part of that universe too)—all acts of creation stem from one source. We are That and the inner and outer worlds are, therefore, the same. There is no distinction between them.

Furthermore, there is never any "just" when it comes to the imagination. Everything that has ever been created in this world relies on it. No great building was ever made, no social policy introduced, no love affair started or ended without someone first having an idea that it should be so and the conviction to follow through and make it real. As Einstein remarked, "Imagination is more important than knowledge." For "knowledge" is received wisdom, often bogged down in dogma and, almost by definition, outdated since the world is in motion and things are always in the process of change. "Knowledge" keeps us chained to the past whereas imagination is fresh, new, vibrant, revolutionary, and evolutionary.

The shaman operates in the field of imagination and this is at the core of his creativity. In ceremony, this becomes a unique response moment by moment to the needs of his patient; a ritual, a drama, a "play." His songs are a part of that too, summoning energies that have a beneficial impact on the patient. But it is the engagement, the act of faith on the part of both patient and shaman that these songs will work that creates the change. Through this the shaman awakens the patient's own creative imagination and, as we know from studies that have been conducted into visualization, the effect of prayer and intention, and even the "placebo effect," that such an awakening is the most powerful healing possible.[6]

San Pedro ceremonies are a creative flow of energy between the universe, the mind of God, the spirits, the shaman, and the patient, all with the intention of healing and captured most effectively in the songs of the shaman.

NOTES

1. In Peter Tompkins and Christopher Bird, *The Secret Life of Plants* (New York: Harper Paperbacks, 1970).
2. See Ross Heaven and Howard G. Charing, *Plant Spirit Shamanism: Traditional Techniques for Healing the Soul* (Rochester, Vt.: Inner Traditions, 2006).
3. Eduardo Calderon, Richard Cowan, Douglas Sharon, and Kaye F. Sharon, *Eduardo El Curandero: The Words of a Peruvian Healer* (Berkeley: North Atlantic Books, 1982).
4. For more on Arevelo see Heaven and Charing, *Plant Spirit Shamanism*.
5. For more on the Doctrine of Signatures see Heaven and Charing, *Plant Spirit Shamanism*.
6. For evidence of this see the research summarized in Ross Heaven, *The Journey to You: A Shaman's Path to Empowerment* (New York: Bantam, 2001), and Ross Heaven, *Spirit in the City: The Search for the Sacred in Everyday Life* (Bantam, 2003).

CONCLUSIONS
The Gifts of San Pedro

~~~~~~~~
Ross Heaven

> *The creative process is often compared to a state of Grace.*
> RICK STRASSMAN

What are the gifts of San Pedro? In this book we have heard from people who have drunk it and found healing for a number of conditions—emotional, physical, mental, and spiritual—and who now have a new direction in life. Others have been inspired to create art, song, and music from their work with the plant. And it is also possible that San Pedro may offer us access to the entire vast hidden potential of the mind, giving us the powers of wisdom, knowledge, insight, and precognition. Is there one word that summarizes these qualities? Perhaps there is. Perhaps that word is *Grace*.

Grace (grās)[1] n.

1. Seemingly effortless beauty or charm of movement, form, or proportion
2. A characteristic or quality pleasing for its charm or refinement

337

3. A sense of fitness or propriety

4. a. A disposition to be generous or helpful; goodwill

   b. Mercy; clemency

5. A favor rendered by one who need not do so; indulgence

6. A temporary immunity or exemption; a reprieve

7. Graces, Greek and Roman mythology: Three sister goddesses, known in Greek mythology as Aglaia, Euphrosyne, and Thalia, who dispense charm and beauty

8. a. Divine love and protection bestowed freely on people

   b. The state of being protected or sanctified by the favor of God

   c. An excellence or power granted by God

tr. v. graced, grac·ing, grac·es

1. To honor or favor

2. To give beauty, elegance, or charm to

It is Grace, however, in which we are not absolved from our responsibilities; an "adult" Grace that holds us accountable for the decisions we have made and the consequences of our actions. San Pedro offers us the opportunity to learn from these choices by revisiting them and correcting them where they have not served us or our fellow beings, its intention being to drive the evolution of the planet—through us and our spiritual journey—toward the "Godhead": that place where we finally return to the infinite and become part of the mind and love of God.[2]

If we can learn from our mistakes or let go of and forgive the mistakes of others then we can indeed experience Grace: a restoration of balance to the soul, a clean slate from which to start again, the "peace which passes all understanding."

I'd like to explore this concept of Grace in the following new accounts from San Pedro drinkers. In them we hear of healings received, new strengths found, and new powers given, all of them gifts—graces— that San Pedro has freely bestowed.

The first of these comes from La Gringa herself and describes one of her early experiences with the plant. It hints at precognition (an awareness of things yet to come), connection with all-that-is, and, finally, peace: an understanding that infuses and informs the soul in a kind and gentle way.

"To see the light and the life in all"

Felicia and I went cactus cutting in the mountains of Vilcabamba. We got back to her house and spent three days preparing it with ceremony, incense, and prayers. Once it was ready we hiked up into the mountains near a river and a cave and drank the San Pedro. It's a very bitter medicine to swallow.

I vomited a lot and the visions came on very powerfully as soon as I vomited. I started by sitting on rocks by the river watching the light and color in the water and the colors in the stones; it was as if I could see gold threads running through them. I then went into the cave, I spread my arms across one of the walls, and suddenly I could feel the rock breathing. It was breathing so hard I could feel my body sway with it. At one point I panicked and thought that the cave was going to collapse on me. I calmed myself and told myself to trust. It is the most incredible feeling, to actually feel, hear, and see the Earth breathe, to see the light and the life in all.

After drinking this medicine your whole outlook on life changes. Never again will you think that only certain things are alive. Everything is alive, breathing. I eventually went outside the cave and Mother Earth, Pacha Mama, started to speak to me. She told me, "I want you to experience every bit of love that you have ever had in your life." Immediately I saw faces of people flash in front of me from the time I was born, faces that I never knew, faces that I had long forgotten, and in that instant I experienced the most intense love that one could imagine, like God was there as well, and I knew that they and me and God were all one. I cried profusely. To have all that love in one instant was totally overwhelming. I saw and felt every bit of love that anyone has every given me in my life, every kindness, every look, every feeling.

Then she said that I had to experience every bit of pain that I ever had in my life. In an instant I saw people, also forgotten or thought never seen before and, of course, many remembered, that had ever been nasty to me or caused me pain. The pain was enormous. I saw, felt, every bad thought, intention, and action that was aimed at me since my birth up until that day and beyond.

Then she showed me a cord, an umbilical cord, between my navel and my husband's and suddenly it was cut. My whole body went through excruciating pain. I was crying with the pain. I wondered what this meant. Did it mean that I was going to die—or my husband? Without knowing it then, I went through the future pain of my divorce, which when it happened was "relatively" pain free. (When I got back from Peru upon arrival at the airport with one look at my husband I knew that our marriage had ended).

Mother Earth then told me that I had to bleed for her. I never thought this was possible as my period was over two weeks ago, but in that instant I did bleed. Pacha Mama explained to me that men are young and women are ancient, it was time now for men to mature and the time was coming soon when the young man whose name is Luz, which means light, is going to inseminate the old woman and she would give birth to a brand new world that is only light. All things that women experience so does Pacha Mama experience because women are a part of Pacha Mama, so every time that a woman feels pain the Earth feels that pain, and every time that women feel love Pacha Mama feels that too. If men understood the emotions of women they would understand how the Earth feels and then they would treat the Earth with love and respect. Maybe this is how we heal ourselves, heal the Earth, and reach enlightenment.

By the time we left to go back to Felicia's house it was dark, 9:30 p.m. We had no torches or candles and the sky was full of clouds and dark. I panicked a bit and said, "Hey, Felicia what are we going to do, there is no light, no moon?" Felicia just said, "Let's go."

As we started walking we noticed that all of the plants alongside

us lit up very brightly as if there were electric lights under them, and all
we needed to do was keep walking between the path lit by the plants
and we would be safe. We crossed rivers, cliffs, over mountains, and
we did not stumble. Earlier in the day we stumbled often going there.
The plants led us home.

I looked at Felicia in front of me and saw a huge light at the back
of her head and called to tell her. She looked back at me and said,
"My God, you are covered with hundreds of little lights." And I looked
around me and I was, there were hundreds of these tiny little lights
around me, it was beautiful, I felt like a fairy with glowing dust.

Seeing the light in plants, it is there all the time for all of us to see
but because of the veils and the way we hide ourselves we don't see
properly. If we allowed ourselves to be the light that we are then we
would see the lights in all. And we are meant to see.

Grace: "The state of being protected or sanctified by the favor of God. . . .
Divine love and protection bestowed freely."

"Freeing my soul at last"
The following is from Samantha and illustrates some of the same themes
and qualities.

My soul is pissed off with my current path, my inner self was really
angry and sad. Tears came, message came, why are you doing this job?
It is causing you so much pain and is making you have illness.

I have taken months to unstick myself from my job but now have
done it as I quit at Easter. I have been a primary teacher for eleven
years. . . . Full on. . . . Missed out on my daughter's years of being ten
upward because my energies were being plowed into this crazy job of
endless tasks and ongoing multitasking to make you spin. . . . I have
had to work a three-month notice as that is how it is in teaching but
ever since . . . I have felt ill and wonderful. . . . Noticing how ill this
makes me has made me feel wonderful as I know I am now on the right

path. . . . Freeing my soul at last. (My first thought when I got my first teaching position wasn't happiness but that I had sold my soul. Now I am being given the chance to reclaim it!)

My own insecurities were mentioned: loss of Paul, him running off with someone. Saw in him a need to play, asked why he felt he needed to look after me, he said it was his job.

An event occurred, leading my belief that perhaps Paul needs to learn to receive love. . . . I get the rejected feeling from him but I needed to realize this comes from ME! San Pedro was telling me to keep communicating, listening attentively, learn from each misunderstanding and not go round in circles again and again. . . . Change something, realize the truth not what you perceive it to be.

Said to Paul that I felt like I had transcended . . . seeing connections between trees, connecting with each other, saw our breath and how our breath affects everything around it, moves the air around which journeys away affecting everything. I saw everything as energy. And how everything affects everything with its energy. Drums, fire, from a distance . . . it all dances to the music. I saw how everything is the same thing.

I also saw fairies and tree folk this night. . . . Some of the fairies were shy to come out with Paul and only wanted feminine energy. . . . We watched the stars dance in the sky, felt close to everything.

Messages, which came a few days/weeks later, were . . .

Fill up the self with love so you can share your best energies with others, the most important things in life.

Do not give your energies to things that simply don't matter, don't mean anything.

Since now quitting and much talking to Paul (we have shared so much more) I am following this path with no resistance from the universe. . . . It is just flowing beautifully. I have also apologized and acknowledged to Nicole (my twenty-one-year-old daughter) how much sorrow I have and regret for putting my energies into our financial security and not her emotional well-being of that time. . . . But not with a guilty load, she understood, we both let it go.

I feel so brilliant about the huge life change, my huge change in how I am able to give love, knowing how full of love I am and knowing I am going to channel it to the things and ones that really matter.

Of course this is only since amazing transformations happened in Peru with my first ceremonies where I grew a new core to my very being when San Pedro made me let go of a lot of shit! Wow! How wonderful that people all over the world can share healing with this wonderful medicine. . . . I send much love to you and although I have tried I cannot express with words . . . But you will see it in my eyes when I see you again.

Grace: "Seemingly effortless beauty or charm of movement."

"This healing started from that journey"

For others, such as Helen, the healing is direct, straightforward, and simple.

Just wanted to let you know that after that session where I struggled so much to get rid of that energy around my midriff and I threw up so much, I went for a checkup and x-rays of my pelvis, hips, and lumbar spine because I had lots of osteoarthritis damage and scoliosis, only to find out that I now have the perfect bones of a twenty-year-old. I know this healing started from that journey.

Grace: "Mercy; clemency . . . immunity or exemption; a reprieve."

"I see myself totally differently"

Others, like Kay, have found new freedoms, powers, and skills from drinking San Pedro. They may be small things in themselves but their impact has been huge, in this case life changing.

My first experience with San Pedro was June 5, 2010. The spirit of the plant had been calling me for six months prior to this. I began to dream about San Pedro in January of 2010 and really wanted to experience this medicine. The opportunity arrived when a friend invited me to a San Pedro ceremony at her home.

The first piece of healing I received on this journey had to do with a lifelong fear of water. Ever since I was a little girl, I had been afraid of water. It was such a problem that I would lose my breath whenever water hit my face, including in the shower, and reverted to washing my hair in a sink to avoid showers.

San Pedro helped me to see the event that created the fear. I was four years old and my stepfather had thrown me into the ocean when we were on vacation. I saw myself kicking and screaming as he picked me up and threw me in. I also saw that his intentions were not ill as he was trying to get me over my fear but it instead served to deepen it.

Ironically, the home in which I was doing San Pedro had a pool for which my friend reminded me (often) to bring my bathing suit, much to my distress. After I saw the event that made me fear the water I decided to get into the pool. This was SO healing for me! I must have spent hours in this pool and had many insights about how I view myself.

One major insight while in the water was in relation to a poor self-image. Once again, I was taken back to my childhood where I observed myself sitting at the dinner table with my family. My stepfather was making fun of how I looked. I did remember this event once the vision was given to me, but what I hadn't known before was how that little girl felt when this happened. I actually was able to "feel" how I felt when he said these things to me. There were several times in which my appearance was made fun of by my "parents," and I then was able to see how hurt the child in me was and how I formed a negative self-concept at that time that carried me forward into adulthood.

Since this piece of healing, I see myself totally differently. I am able to practice self-love and hold a view of myself very different than I used to, and as a result the world around me is holding me in a different way. This has had a far-reaching impact on several areas of my life, and is even shifting the way my daughters are holding their own self-image. Truly amazing impacts are being delivered with this shift in myself that San Pedro gifted me.

After this part of the healing was completed I ventured out onto solid ground. While on the Earth the journey took another turn. As I lay on the Earth I felt a surge of emotions rising to my throat, but I could not identify what they were attached to.

Without needing to "know" I allowed the emotions to come to the surface. I wanted to scream but I couldn't as others were all around me and I was concerned about interrupting another's journey, so I asked spirit if I could release whatever this was by blowing it out and off of me. I had been working on some issues surrounding me being able to speak my truth so it wasn't too surprising that I did not want to let the scream out. So I began blowing the emotion outward. But I felt the energy lying over me and I asked the spirit of San Pedro to help me release this emotional toxin. Out of nowhere, a huge gust of wind came and blew over me for about ten to fifteen minutes. I was amazed and felt so appreciative of nature's help.

Then as I continued lying there I felt a sudden burst of joy coming from my heart. I lay there seeing the auras of the trees and plants, a kite bird flew over me as did two eagles. I saw a figure of a peacock within the wood of a tree in front of me. There seemed to be a lot of bird energy around me and it was beautiful.

Then, from a sun shining day came rain. It poured onto my face and I didn't flinch, wind blew over me and I felt cleansed. This was truly a day of working with the elements through the gift of San Pedro, and I healed many aspects of myself for which I am truly grateful. I am not the same as I was before I did this journey. I am healed on many levels and walk differently in the world today. And my daughters are shifting as a result.

At the end of the day my friend came over to me and said that she needed me to do something with her. She took me over to where I

*was lying and doing my work during the day and asked me to scream
into the Earth. Being that I had been working with finding my voice
I immediately said no, no way, I can't do it. But she held her ground
(thank God) and told me that Mother Earth wanted me to find my
voice again. She did not know that I had been working on speaking my
truth for years and was still unable to "scream." So with her help I
screamed into the Earth. I am a changed woman since that day.*

*She then gave me a song to sing to help me find my voice and to
continue practicing using it. Little did I know then that I would be not
only singing this song but leading others to sing it, as well. Five days
later I left for Peru.*

Grace: "The state of being . . . sanctified. . . . An excellence or power
granted by God."

THE NATURE OF GRACE

The Catholic Church, which has had, historically, such an impact
on Andean culture and San Pedro shamanism, defines Grace (*gratia,
Charis*) as "a supernatural gift of God to intellectual creatures for their
eternal salvation, whether the latter be furthered and attained through
salutary acts or a state of holiness."

> Actual grace derives its name, *actual*, from the Latin *actualis* (*ad
> actum*) for it is granted by God for the performance of salutary acts
> and is present and disappears with the action itself. Its opposite
> . . . [is] habitual grace, which causes a state of holiness, so that the
> mutual relations between these two kinds of grace are the relation
> between action and state.[3]

Habitual Grace, also known as "sanctifying or justifying grace,"
refers, therefore, to a new and enduring way of being. It is this, I
believe, that San Pedro—the keeper of the keys to heaven—can give us.

We saw, for example, in the section on healing (and in some of the accounts above), that unlike other entheogenic experiences (such as DMT—see Strassman[4]) there is something about San Pedro that lasts beyond the encounter itself.

As I remarked in that section, a number of people who have drunk the plant with me and through it seen the truths of their lives have gone on to make significant, positive, and lasting—even life-defining—changes and new commitments. Some have ceased procrastination and put desire into action by fulfilling a long-held ambition to write a book, others have opened healing centers, recovered from addictions and stayed clean, some have left relationships or started new ones, and many have repaired the damage done to old or existing ones. Theirs is a new state of being, a new presence in the world, and this is the essence of habitual Grace.

"Once you have drunk San Pedro it remains in you forever and it will always be there to guide you," says La Gringa, and I have certainly found that to be true for myself. It is as if I have a new maturity now and a new moral scale within me: I know when I have done wrong and I am willing to make amends for it. It is a quality that I have somewhat lacked before. Wrapped up as I was (like most of us are, I suppose) in my own needs, fantasies, illusions, and the busyness I created for myself, I did not know before drinking San Pedro that I have hurt others often without meaning to, without even knowing I was. But San Pedro is a constant reminder now, and I try to choose my words and actions more carefully and to think about their consequences for myself and others before I use them. I try also to empathize more and to see other people's points of view. I am far from perfect but that is something I am also aware of and I am trying to be better.

At the same time, this new sense of what I have called "maturity" means that I try to set proper boundaries, owning my actions and taking responsibility for them, but not taking on those of others. In any conflict, for example, there are two sides and two combatants. Ideally there would be no conflict at all, but that is not the real world. Yet all disagreements have the potential to be resolved well so that something better may flow from them. Life presents us with these opportunities and when they arise now, rather than withdraw from them or try to control them, I own my part and I hope (without seeking to blame or judge) that the other side will own theirs.

Such qualities suggest what Castaneda from his own work with mescaline cactus (peyote) called "the Ally."[5] It is as if you have a new force within you, a discrete and new personality or power, an inner guide that you can refer to in times of uncertainty or need. To me, the Ally of San Pedro is Dignity: a strong, self-aware gentleman who is older and more experienced than me, fatherly and wise. It is to his judgment that I try to defer in situations where I am unclear or unsure.

I don't always need to drink San Pedro to do this; I simply breathe, tune in, and refer to the spirit I have inside me. Sometimes his advice is counterintuitive or seems detrimental to my own desires or agenda (which is how I know that it's real), but I am growing up now and I realize (at least philosophically sometimes!) that there is a greater force in the universe than me and a greater need to be served, and so I listen to what San Pedro has to say. His vantage point is better than mine because he is not me. He is both within and outside me, and while my agenda is often caught up in personal needs and dramas, I know and trust that his is pure.

LIVING WITH GRACE

The church says of sanctifying or habitual Grace that

> since the end and aim of all efficacious grace is directed to the production of sanctifying grace where it does not already exist, or to retain and increase it where it is already present, its excellence, dignity and importance become immediately apparent; for holiness and the sonship of God depend solely upon the possession of sanctifying grace.[6]

According to the church the first step in receiving habitual Grace is to prepare for it.

> In the process . . . we must distinguish two periods: first, the preparatory acts or dispositions (faith, fear, hope, etc.); then the last decisive moment of the transformation of the sinner from the state of sin to that of justification or sanctifying grace, which may be called the active justification (*actus justificationis*). With this the real process comes to an end and the state of habitual holiness and sonship of God begins.

We come to San Pedro in the same way. Perhaps we are fully aware of an issue in our lives that needs to be healed or an illness or dis-ease that we have, or perhaps we have only an inkling that something is not right in us, that things are not going well or could be better. Perhaps we cannot name it but there is something—some "faith, fear, hope"—that draws us to the ceremony so we can explore and perfect ourselves. This, then, is our stage of preparation.

If we are honest, open, and earnest in our prayers for change, experience suggests that San Pedro will hear us and provide us with the tools and insights to take the next step. La Gringa's account is just one example of how this Grace may come to us: "I experienced the most intense love that one could imagine, like God was there as well, and I knew that they and me and God were all one. I cried profusely. To have all that love in one instant was totally overwhelming."

Having seen ourselves and received the gifts of San Pedro, the church tells us that to remain in a state of Grace we must then make it our habit to do so; in our case, we must refer to our Ally, our new inner guide, and take counsel about how we should live in order to be "the true human."

"Sanctifying grace may be philosophically termed a 'permanent, supernatural quality of the soul,'" says the church, which becomes "a supernatural infused habit (*habitus infusus*)." For there can be no change in the world or in our lives without us making that change.

And again we have seen from the accounts of those healed by San Pedro that the cactus does offer us this power to create new "habits" and new ways of life so we can live in "holiness" and make lasting changes that better serve us and our fellow beings. Samantha tells us of the guidance she continues to receive from San Pedro, months after the experience itself.

> *San Pedro was telling me to keep communicating, listening attentively, learn from each misunderstanding and not go round in circles again and again. . . . Change something, realize the truth not what you perceive it to be. . . . Fill up the self with love so you can share your best energies with others, the most important things in life. Do not give your energies to things that simply don't matter, don't mean anything.*

She is acting on this advice, making it her "habit," and finding that life is better for her as a consequence. "I am following this path with no resistance from the universe. . . . It is just flowing beautifully."

La Gringa says of San Pedro that it

> *teaches us to live in balance and harmony, it teaches us compassion and understanding, and it shows us how to love, respect, and honor all things. It shows us too that we are children of light—precious and special—and to see that light within us. . . . Drinking San Pedro is a personal journey of discovery of the self and the universe . . . The day that you meet San Pedro is one you will never forget—a day filled with light and love, which can change your life forever . . . always for the better.*

I believe that is true, and through the Grace of San Pedro so do many others who have shared its wisdom and healing.

NOTES

1. www.thefreedictionary.com/grace. Accessed June 27, 2012.
2. Pierre Teilhard de Chardin, *The Phenomenon of Man* (New York: Harper Perennial Modern Classics, 2008).

3. www.newadvent.org/cathen/06689x.htm. Accessed June 27, 2012.

4. Rick Strassman, *DMT: The Spirit Molecule; A Doctor's Revolutionary Research into the Biology of Near-Death and Mystical Experiences* (Rochester, Vt.: Park Street Press, 2000).

5. Carlos Castaneda, *The Teachings of Don Juan: A Yaqui Way of Knowledge* (Berkeley: University of California Press, 2008).

6. www.newadvent.org/cathen/06701a.htm. Accessed June 27, 2012.

San Pedro Testimonials

These comments were recently received from others who have drunk San Pedro with La Gringa and I. Too short to be journey accounts in themselves, they are more like testimonials for the process. I include them here just as they were written with no editing or analysis of their contents as simply an overview of how San Pedro can heal.

> Our recent trip to the Andes in Cuzco took us to great spiritual heights and physical healing. Our journey was sometimes difficult but your strong support and loving care made it possible for us. We appreciate the dynamic program you put together that has definitely changed our bodies and lives forever. We may be sixty-six and seventy-two but we now feel and look like forty. San Pedro healed me in ways I never dreamed possible.
>
> PATRICIA AND JOY, RETIRED,
> IRELAND AND UNITED STATES

> This trip was exactly what I needed—and what I imagine many, many people need! In Cusco so much of my life, so much of everything I've ever known was given the space and brilliance to be brought together. The results were deep!
>
> KYLE, MUSICIAN,
> UNITED STATES

The most powerful, profound experience of my life. I had intellectually understood about us coming from and one day returning to energy; I had even glimpsed this in the past but on this occasion I became energy. I completely dissolved—no room for ego! I breathed with the sky. I became the Breath of Life, Infinite and Eternal Love. I now dedicate my life to honor and integrity and to accepting life's path rather than trying to dictate it. If everyone experienced this the world would be very different. It has become better for me already! I strongly recommend the experience!

DONNA, TEACHER,
UNITED KINGDOM

San Pedro showed me just how beautiful life is. I had a sense of completion, like I had healed everything that was meant to be healed. I am so grateful to San Pedro for these insights and for the revelations it shared with me.

SIMON, AUTHOR,
UNITED KINGDOM

I have been home a week and I still feel changed; not coming down from the high of our trip and its mind- and heart-opening experiences. It was a wonderful highlight to my life and the lessons are becoming ever-clearer as I share them with friends. I was stretched way beyond where I thought I could go—and enjoyed it!

KATHRYN, DRUG AND ADDICTIONS COUNSELOR,
NORFOLK ISLAND

San Pedro was life changing. I felt such peace and acceptance. I had an overwhelming sense of belonging to the Earth and of the importance of every curve of the mountain range, every boulder, rock, stone, and blade of grass; all part of the same incredible tableau and all of equal importance. I could have a normal conversation and was in full control of my words and thoughts but I found that I was choosing words carefully, realizing their power—and that I didn't have enough vocabulary to express how I felt anyway. Through the eyes of San Pedro the world is an exceptionally beautiful place. Every living thing has its place. I have come home with new eyes and can bring the beauty of the world to mind—and into reality—by just remembering the experience.

Tracie, counselor and teacher,

Australia

This experience will never leave me! San Pedro answers your questions clearly and without confusion or the need for interpretation. I got the healing I was after. I understood and let go.

Kane, writer,

United States

I became the sky, the clouds, the flowers and I saw the beauty in all things, including myself and my relationships. I realized at some deeper level than we are ever usually aware of that everything is exactly as it was meant to be. It changed something in me and within two weeks I had met the man who would become my husband. There's no bigger way to say that it healed my relationship problems because that would not have been possible without it. San Pedro gave me my daughter.

Cara, journalist,

United States

I was overcome with tears of sheer joy and gratitude . . . for all my ancestors for bringing me into this world, for giving me this beautiful opportunity to be here under this sky with these birds and those gently swaying trees, for making my life so beautiful and for delivering me to this place where I arrived in full knowledge and love of myself.

Jamie, caregiver,

United States

The message of San Pedro was clear: I create the reality I want. I felt like a new person—so alive, so full of courage and energy, energized, aware, and calm. Over the next few weeks I was transformed. Anything seemed possible. I was ready to create what I most desired.

Michael, sports coach,

Canada

I decided not to book a flight back to the States. I am staying on here in the mountains instead, loving life, for another month . . . or two . . . or three. The lessons keep coming and life gets better and better!

Alec, skydiving instructor,

United States

San Pedro was the best day of my life—it was so surprising and so hard to explain. I feel I have been waiting for this for so long. I just looked in the mirror and I did not recognize myself.

Julie, teacher,

United Kingdom

Thank you for this powerful introduction to a new world. May I be worthy of what I was given, may I benefit the world in some way! Ayahuasca and San Pedro are the shortcut: why waste time sitting in a circle for years being lost and feeling like you are not on the right road when a couple of weeks here will get you there! The Cusco trip was amazing. San Pedro definitely sorted me out to a place of clarity and clearness. I came with trepidation about taking healing and visionary plants having never taken any drugs, never believing I needed anything to journey, but that was my first block.

As I watched myself empty I could not believe what I held inside—the scars, the pain, the memories I had long forgotten all screwing me up and blocking my progress. I am now cleared clean, I feel new and invigorated. I am firmly on my path with new confidence and a brighter light within. I just sent an e-mail to a person I know and all I did was describe how I feel and his reply was, "This is the best e-mail you have ever sent." I am a changed person! My life has been transformed in many ways. I would recommend the San Pedro experience to one and all. It honestly has shown me another way to see my life and the world we live in. I can now identify with love, give it—and most importantly receive!

LES, BUSINESS OWNER,
UNITED KINGDOM

I met San Pedro with trepidation but we quickly made friends which resulted in wonderful insights and understandings. The words that spring to mind when I think of San Pedro are *gentle, kind,* and *empowering.*

ALEXIA, THERAPIST,
UNITED KINGDOM

It took me a year to process everything. I had no words for it. I guess you hang on to your defenses until you can't hold on anymore but something inside you knows everything and the healing never leaves. Inside me now there is a happy two-year-old and I am going to find her and bring her home. I guess I will need to see San Pedro again! See you there!

ANGELA, NURSE,
AUSTRALIA

San Pedro was so amazing . . . a lot of love and a lot of understanding. It was like seeing for the first time in my life, not with my eyes but with my heart and soul.

LAURA, STUDENT,
SOUTH AFRICA

The most life-changing and healing experience I have ever had, including having a week of ayahuasca ceremonies seven years ago. There was much that was taught and at least one chronic health condition was healed. It was not only the San Pedro journeys but the entire events that were full of magic, learning, and healing. I am grateful that this program exists and for the work that all involved have done to make it so powerful and accessible to as many as possible.

ROBYN, MASSAGE THERAPIST,
CANADA

The energy I brought back is magical. I am still basking in the love of San Pedro and this happiness is staying in my heart.

SONNA-RA, HEALER,
NEW ZEALAND

Thank you is not adequate. The whole experience was magical and sacred! It brought me home within myself. I wish that every person could experience San Pedro. The world's heart would beat freer and more fiercely than ever before!

ERIN, ADMINISTRATOR,
UNITED STATES

A big thank you for everything. I really appreciate it. I have noticed changes in my life already.

FERNY, MODEL,
SOUTH AFRICA

I would like to thank you for the two best weeks of my life. I had such a positive experience I long to return and never leave. With San Pedro now with me I know I have a powerful ally. I know that I'll someday soon be hanging out with you again. Til that day comes keep spreading positivity to all that you meet and stay safe, my friend.

JASON, PH.D. STUDENT AND LECTURER,
UNITED STATES

The San Pedro ceremonies were excellent and I am very happy with the guidance and help from all the shamans who attended us. It was top class. I received greater healing than I expected and feel it still to this day. Something was given back to me and my life is richer from it. I thank everyone concerned who helped to make the two weeks in Cusco an experience I will never forget. A must-do once in your life that I recommend to everyone.

DARRYL, SELF-EMPLOYED,
SWEDEN

About the Author

Ross Heaven, the author of several books on shamanism and healing, runs workshops on these themes in the United Kingdom, Spain, and Peru, including plant medicine retreats with San Pedro, ayahuasca, and other plant teachers and healers, and journeys to Peru to work with indigenous ayahuasca and San Pedro shamans.

He has a website at **www.thefourgates.org**, where you can read more about these as well as forthcoming books and other items of interest. He also provides a monthly newsletter update by e-mail, which you can receive free of charge via e-mail at **ross@thefourgates.org**.

Index

BOOKS OF RELATED INTEREST

Plant Spirit Shamanism
Traditional Techniques for Heing the Soul
by Ross Heaven and Howard G. Charing

Shamanic Quest for the Spirit of Salvia
The Divinatory, Visionary, and Healing Powers of the Sage of the Seers
by Ross Heaven

Plants of the Gods
Their Sacred, Healing, and Hallucinogenic Powers
by Richard Evans Schultes, Albert Hofmann, and Christian Rätsch

The Encyclopedia of Psychoactive Plants
Ethnopharmacology and Its Applications
by Christian Rätsch

DMT: The Spirit Molecule
A Doctor's Revolutionary Research into the Biology
of Near-Death and Mystical Experiences
by Rick Strassman, M.D.

The Psychedelic Explorer's Guide
Safe, Therapeutic, and Sacred Journeys
by James Fadiman, Ph.D.

The Secret Teachings of Plants
The Intelligence of the Heart in the Direct Perception of Nature
by Stephen Harrod Buhner

The Shamanic Wisdom of the Huichol
Medicine Teachings for Modern Times
by Tom Soloway Pinkson, Ph.D.

INNER TRADITIONS • BEAR & COMPANY
P.O. Box 388
Rochester, VT 05767
1-800-246-8648
www.InnerTraditions.com

Or contact your local bookseller